THE PANIC OF 1819: REACTIONS AND POLICIES

NUMBER 605

COLUMBIA STUDIES IN THE SOCIAL SCIENCES

EDITED BY

THE FACULTY OF POLITICAL SCIENCE

OF COLUMBIA UNIVERSITY

THE PANIC OF 1819

REACTIONS AND POLICIES

BY MURRAY N. ROTHBARD

COLUMBIA UNIVERSITY PRESS

NEW YORK AND LONDON: 1962

The Columbia Studies in the Social Sciences
(formerly the Studies in History, Economics,
and Public Law) is a series edited by the
Faculty of Political Science of Columbia University
and published by Columbia University Press
for the purpose of making available
scholarly studies produced within the Faculty.

Library of Congress Catalog Card Number: 62-9975

Manufactured in the United States of America

PREFACE

The Panic of 1819 was America's first great economic crisis and depression. For the first time in American history, there was a crisis of nationwide scope that could not simply and directly be attributed to specific dislocations and restrictions—such as a famine or wartime blockades. Neither could it be simply attributed to the machinations or blunders of one man or to one upsetting act of government, which could be cured by removing the offending cause. In such a way had the economic dislocations from 1808–15 been blamed on "Mr. Jefferson's Embargo" or "Mr. Madison's War." [1] In short, here was a crisis marked with strong hints of modern depressions; it appeared to come mysteriously from within the economic system itself. Without obvious reasons, processes of production and exchange went awry.

Confronted with a new, vital phenomenon, Americans looked for remedies and for understanding of the causes, the better to apply the remedies. This epoch of American history is a relatively neglected one, and a study of the search for remedies presents an instructive picture of a people coming to grips with the problems of a business depression, problems which, in modified forms, were to plague Americans until the present day.

The 1819–21 period in America generated internal controversies and furnished a rich economic literature. The newspapers in particular provide a relatively untapped vein for study. The leading editors were sophisticated and influential men, many of them learned in economics. The caliber of their editorials was high and their reasoning keen. The newspaper editors constituted, in fact, some of the leading economists of the day.

The depression galvanized the press; even those papers that had been wholly devoted to commercial advertisements or to partisan political squabbles turned to writing and arguing about the "hard times."

In order to provide the setting for the discussion of remedial proposals, Chapter I presents a sketch of the economy and of the events of the postwar period. The postwar boom and its culmination in the crisis and depression are also set forth. In addition to its major function of indicating the economic environment to which the people were reacting, this chapter permits us to decide to what extent the depression of 1819–21 may be considered a modern business-cycle depression.

The bulk of the work deals with the remedial proposals themselves, and the speculations, controversies, and policies arising from them. Arguments were especially prevalent over monetary proposals, debtors' relief—often tied in with monetary schemes—and a protective tariff. At the start of the depression each of these problems was unsettled: the tariff question was not resolved; the monetary system was new and troublesome. But the depression greatly intensified these problems, and added new aspects, and made solutions more pressing.[2]

This book would never have come into being without the inspiration, encouragement, and guidance of Professor Joseph Dorfman. I am also indebted to Professors Robert D. Cross, Arthur F. Burns, and Albert G. Hart for many valuable suggestions.

CONTENTS

I

THE PANIC AND ITS GENESIS: FLUCTUATIONS IN AMERICAN BUSINESS 1815-21

The War of 1812 and its aftermath brought many rapid dislocations to the young American economy. Before the war, America had been a large, thinly populated country of seven million, devoted almost exclusively to agriculture. Much cotton, wheat, and tobacco were exported abroad, while the remainder of the agricultural produce was largely consumed by self-sufficient rural households. Barter was extensive in the vast regions of the frontier. Commerce was largely devoted to the exporting of agricultural produce, which was generally grown close to river transportation. The proceeds were used to import desired manufactured products and other consumer goods from abroad. Major export products were cotton and tobacco from the South, and grain from the West.[1] The cities, which contained only 7 percent of the country's population, were chiefly trading depots channeling exports to and from abroad.[2] New York City was becoming the nation's great foreign trade center, with Philadelphia and Boston following closely behind.

The monetary system of the country was not highly developed. The banks, outside of New England at least, were confined almost exclusively to the cities. Their methods tended to be lax; government control was negligible; and the fact that most banks, like other corporations of the period, had to gain their status by special legislative charter, invited speculative abuses through pressure on the legislature. The result was a lack of uniformity in dealing with banks within and between states.[3] Until 1811, the existence of the First Bank of the United States had influenced the banks toward uniformity. The currency of the United States was on a bimetallic standard, but at the legal ratio of fifteen-to-one gold was undervalued, and the bulk of the specie in circulation was silver. Silver coins were largely foreign, particularly Spanish, augmented by coins minted in Great Britain, Portugal, and France.[4]

Before the war, the American economy lacked large, or even moderate-scale, manufactures. "Manufacturing" consisted of small-scale, often one-man, operations. The manufacturers were artisans and craftsmen, men who combined the function of laborer and entrepreneur: blacksmiths, tailors, hatters, and cobblers. A very large amount of manufacturing, especially textiles, was done in the home and was consumed at home. Transportation, too, was in a primitive state. Most followed the time-honored course of the rivers and the ocean, while costly land transport generally moved over local dirt roads.

The War of 1812 and postwar developments forced the American economy to make many rapid and sudden adjustments. The Anglo-French Wars had long fostered the prosperity of American shipping and foreign trade. As the leading neutral we found our exports in great demand on both sides, and American ships took over trade denied to ships of belligerent nations. With the advent of the Embargo and the Non-Intercourse Acts, and then the war itself, however, our foreign trade was drastically curtailed. Foreign trade had reached a peak of $138 million in imports and $108 million in exports in 1807, and by 1814 had sunk to $13 million imports and $7 million exports.[5] On the other hand, war conditions spurred the growth of domestic manufactures. Cotton and woolen textiles, those bellwethers of the Industrial Revolution, were the leaders in this development. These goods were formerly supplied by Great Britain, but the government now required them for war purposes. Domestic manufactures grew rapidly to fill this demand as well as to meet consumer needs no longer met by imports. Households expanded their production of textiles. Of far more lasting significance was the growth of textile factories, especially in New England, New York, and Pennsylvania. Thus, while only four new cotton factories were established during 1807, forty-three were established during 1814, and fifteen in 1815.[6] Leading merchants, finding their capital idle in foreign trade, turned to invest in the newly profitable field of domestic manufactures. Some of these factories adopted the corporate form, hitherto largely confined to banks, insurance and bridge companies. The total number of new factories incorporated in the leading manufacturing states of Massachusetts, Connecticut, New York, New Jersey, and Maryland, averaged sixty-five a year from 1812 to 1815, compared with eight per annum before the war.[7]

The war wrought great changes in the monetary system as well. It brought heavy pressure for federal government borrowing. New England, where the banks were more conservative, was opposed to the war and loaned only negligible amounts to the government, and the federal government came to rely on the mushrooming banks in the other states. These banks were primarily note-issuing institutions, generally run on loose principles.[8] Little specie was paid in as capital, and it was quite common for the stockholders to pay for their bank stock with their own promissory notes, using the stock itself as the only collateral. Usually, the officers and stockholders of the banks were the most favored borrowers in their own institutions. Contributing to the expansion of the note issue was the practice of printing notes in denominations as low as six cents. With the restraint of the Bank of the United States removed, and the needs of government finance heavy, the number of new banks and the quantity of note issue multiplied rapidly. The great expansion of bank notes outside of New England contrasted with the conservative policy of the New England banks, and led to a drain of specie from other states to New England. The relative conservatism of New England banks is revealed by the fact that Massachusetts bank notes outstanding increased but slowly—from $2.4 million to $2.7 million from 1811 to 1815. Furthermore, specie in the bank vaults increased from $1.5 million to $3.5 million in the same period.[9]

There was no uniform currency except specie that could be used in all areas of the country. Furthermore, the government, borrowing Middle Atlantic, Southern, and Western bank notes, had to make heavy expenditures in the New England area for imported supplies and for newly burgeoning textile goods manufactured in that region. The resulting specie drain and the continuing bank note expansion led inevitably to a suspension of specie payments outside the New England area in August, 1814. The government agreed to this suspension, and the banks continued in operation—the exchange rate of each bank's notes varying widely. The notes of the suspended banks depreciated at varying rates with respect to the New England bank notes and to specie. The suspension of the obligation to redeem greatly spurred the establishment of new banks and the expansion of bank note issues. The number of banks in the United States rose from 88 in 1811 to 208 in 1815, while bank notes outstanding rose from $2.3 million to $4.6 million in the same period.[10] Expansion was particularly large in the Middle Atlantic states, notably Pennsylvania. The number of banks in the Middle Atlantic states increased from 25 to 111 in this period, while banks in the southern and western states increased from 16 to 34. Pennsylvania incorporated 41 banks in the month of March, 1814.[11]

The war also saw a great rise in prices. Prices of domestic goods rose under the impact of the rapid expansion of the money supply; prices of imported goods rose further as a result of the blocking of foreign trade. Domestic commodity prices rose by about 20–30 percent; cotton, the leading export staple, doubled in price. Imported commodity prices rose by about 70 percent.[12]

The first war of the new nation, therefore, wrought many unsettling changes in the American economy. Trade was blocked from its former channels, the monetary system became disordered, expansion of money and a shortage of imported goods drove prices upward, and domestic manufactures—particularly textiles—developed under the spur of government demand and the closing of foreign supply sources. The advent of peace brought its own set of problems. After the wartime shortages, the scramble for foreign trade was pursued in earnest. Americans were eager to buy foreign goods, particularly British textiles, and the British exporters were anxious to unload their accumulated stocks. Total imports rose from $5.3 million in the last prewar year to $113 million in 1815, and to $147 million in 1816.[13] British exports to the United States alone totaled $59 million in 1815, and $43 million in 1816.[14] The renewal of the supply of imported goods drastically lowered the prices of imports in the United States and spurred American demand. Imported commodity prices at Philadelphia, for example, fell in one month (March, 1815) from an index of 231 to 178. Import prices continued to sag afterwards, reaching 125 by early 1817.[15]

The ability and eagerness to import was increased by the continued inflation and credit expansion of the banks, which still were not obliged to redeem in specie. Furthermore, the federal government aided imports by allowing several months to more than a year for payment of import duties. British and other foreign exporters were willing to grant short-term credits on a large scale to American importers, and these credits played a major role in meeting the large balance of trade deficit in the postwar years. A further spur to imports, again particularly in British textiles, was the emergence of a system of selling these goods at auction sales instead of through regular import channels. British manufacturers found that auction sales through agents yielded quicker returns; the lower prices were compensated by the lower costs of operation. The auction system flourished particularly in New York City. Total auction sales in the United States during 1818 were $30 million. In New York City they totaled $14 million, in contrast to $5 million before the war. Half of these sales consisted of European dry goods, in contrast to a sale of $1 million of American-made dry goods.[16]

The influx of imports spelled trouble for war-grown manufactures, especially textiles, which suddenly had to face the onrush of foreign competition. The manufacturers did not share in the general postwar prosperity. Bezanson's index of prices of industrial commodities at Philadelphia (including such products as dyes, chemicals, metals, textiles, sugar, soap, glass), which had increased from 141 to 214 during the war period, fell abruptly to 177 in March, 1815, and continued to fall, reaching 127 in March, 1817.[17] This drop indicates the difficulties confronting the fledgling manufacturers. The households which had increased textile manufacturing during the war could easily suspend their work as imports resumed, but the new factories had invested capital at stake. A few of the up-to-date factories, such as the famous cotton textile firm of Waltham, Massachusetts—a pioneer in American mass production, using the new power loom to make plain white sheeting for lower income customers—could easily withstand the competition, but most factories were hard-pressed.[18] The decline continued for several years; new factories incorporated in five leading manufacturing states averaged nine per annum from 1817–19, in contrast to sixty-four per annum in the war years.[19]

American exports continued to expand greatly, however, although by far less than imports. Europe's hunger for agricultural staples was stimulated by poor postwar crops abroad, and the prices and values of American staples exported, notably cotton and tobacco, increased greatly. Such leading customers as Britain and France led the surge in European demand. In spite of this, exports never reached the peak prewar totals. Re-exports of foreign goods fared badly, never attaining more than one-third of their prewar level, when neutral ships of the United States had a virtual monopoly of the European carrying trade. Domestic exports totaled $46 million in the fiscal year 1815, and $65 million in 1816, compared to a prewar peak of $49 million. Re-exports, on the other hand, totaled $7 million in 1816, and $17 million the next year, compared to the prewar peak of $60 million.[20] The net balance of foreign trade, in sum, was a deficit of $60 million for the fiscal year of 1815, and of $65 million for the fiscal year 1816. Agricultural produce accounted for $14 million of the $19 million increase in domestic exports from 1815 to 1816. Agricultural produce exported rose from $38 million in the fiscal year 1815 to $52 million in 1816. Cotton furnished about half of the agricultural exports, and tobacco, wheat, and flour formed the bulk of the remainder. Of the exports in 1815, cotton was $17.5 million, tobacco was $8 million, and wheat and flour exports totaled $7 million. In 1816, cotton increased to $24 million, and tobacco to $13 million.[21]

Prices of American exports increased as a result of increased European demand and monetary expansion at home. The boom in export values was largely a price not a physical production phenomenon. Cole's index of export prices at Charleston rose from 93 in March, 1815 to 138 in March, 1817, and cotton prices rose even more in the same period. The physical quantity of cotton produced and exported, on the other hand, increased slowly in these years.[22]

The rise in export values and the monetary and credit expansion led to a boom in urban and rural real estate prices, speculation in the purchase of public lands, and rapidly growing indebtedness by farmers for projected improvements. The prosperity of the farmers led to prosperity in the cities and towns—so largely devoted were they to import and export trade with the farm population.

The postwar monetary situation was generally considered intolerable. Banks continued to expand in number and note issue, without the obligation of redeeming in specie, and their notes continued to depreciate and fluctuate from bank to bank, and from place to place.[23] The number of banks increased from 208 to 246 during 1815 alone, while the estimated total of bank notes in circulation increased from $46 million to $68 million.[24] There was a great desire for nationwide uniformity in the currency, and the Treasury chafed under the necessity of receiving depreciated bank notes from its sale of public lands in the West, while it had to spend the bulk of its funds in the East in far less depreciated money. It was clear, however, that the inflated banks could not return immediately to specie convertibility without an enormous contraction of credit and deflation of the money supply. As an attempted solution, a Second Bank of the United States was authorized by Congress. It was required to redeem its notes in specie, and was expected to provide a sound and uniform currency. It began operations in January, 1817, but the state banks agreed to resume specie payments by February 20, under the proviso that the new Bank discount by that date a minimum of $2 million in New York, $2 million in Philadelphia, $1.5 million in Baltimore, and $500 thousand in Virginia—a minimum of $6 million.[25] The banks also extracted a pledge of support in emergencies. The Bank, indeed, was not averse to a credit expansion of its own. Its main office and southern and western branches soon overfulfilled their promises. It was run as a strictly profit-making enterprise, under very liberal rules. Like many of the state banks, the Second Bank of the United States accepted its second and later installments of capital in the form of IOUs instead of specie. Eventually, such stock loans totaled $10 million, and the loans were particularly heavy to the important Philadelphia and Baltimore officers and directors of the Bank.[26] Control over the branches of the Bank was negligible, and the southern and western branches greatly expanded their credits and note issues. The officers of the Baltimore branch, indeed, engaged in outright embezzlement. By the beginning of 1818, the Bank had loaned over $41 million. Its note issue outstanding reached $10 million, and its demand deposits $13 million, for a total money issue of $23 million, contrasted to a specie reserve of about $2.5 million.[27]

The boom therefore continued in 1818, with the Bank of the United States acting as an expansionary, rather than as a limiting, force. The expansionist attitude of the Bank was encouraged by the Treasury, which wanted the Bank to accept and use the various state bank notes in which the Treasury received its revenue, particularly its receipts from public land sales.[28] The expansion of its note issue encouraged the state banks throughout the country, especially outside New England, to multiply and continue their credit expansion. The number of banks had increased from 246 in 1816 to 392 in 1818. Kentucky alone chartered 40 new banks in the 1817–18 session.[29] Bank expansion was spurred by the decision of the Bank of the United States and the Treasury to treat the notes of nominally resuming banks as actually equivalent to specie. The Bank thereby accumulated balances and notes against the private banks without presenting them for redemption. Many of these notes were original Treasury balances which had been deposited with the Bank but not claimed from the state banks. In New England, on the other hand, both the private banks and the branches of the Bank of the United States pursued a conservative policy. Indeed, they were forced to contract, as the New England branches of the Bank were continually forced to pay out specie on the expanded note issue of the western and southern branches, since by prevailing Bank rule, all branches were liable for the notes of all other branches. As a result, the notes of the Massachusetts banks declined from a total of $1 million in June, 1815 to $850 thousand by June, 1818.[30]

A generally uniform currency prevailed throughout the country, most bank notes circulating at par.[31] There were exceptions, however; during 1818, for example, notes of some banks in Pennsylvania were depreciated by as much as 30 percent, and in Virginia, Kentucky, and Tennessee by as much as 12 percent.[32]

Investment in real estate, turnpikes, and farm improvement projects spurted, and prices in these fields rose. Furthermore, the federal government facilitated large-scale speculation in public lands by opening up for sale large tracts in the Southwest and Northwest, and granting liberal credit terms to purchasers.[33] Public land sales, which had averaged $2 million to $4 million per annum in 1815 and 1816, rose to a peak of $13.6 million in 1818.[34] Speculation in urban and rural lands and real estate, using bank credit, was a common phenomenon which sharply raised property values.[35] Furthermore, this speculation increased Treasury balances in western banks, and added to the flow of the Bank's notes from west to east. Federal construction expenditures also helped to further the boom: they rose from $700 thousand in 1816 to over $14 million in 1818.[36] Beginning in 1816, there was a construction boom in turnpikes, especially in New York, Maryland, and western Pennsylvania.[37] Turnpikes were built by corporations, each of which received special charters from the states, and corporations in turnpike construction rivaled new banks in number. The share of transportation in the boom is also demonstrated by high and rising freight rates on steamboats, which were just beginning operation.[38] Shipbuilders also shared in the boom prosperity.[39]

It does not seem accidental that the boom period saw the establishment of the first formal indoor stock exchange in the country: the New York Stock Exchange opened in March, 1817. Traders had been buying and selling stocks on the curbs in Wall Street since the eighteenth century, but now they found it necessary to form a definite association and rent indoor quarters. The period also marked the beginning of investment banking: commercial banks and individual bankers bought blocks of stock and sold them in small lots on the market or sold the stocks as agents of the issuer. Prominent in this new business were former merchants in foreign trade who had accumulated capital, such as Alexander Brown and Sons, and persons with fortunes amassed elsewhere, such as Astor and Son.[40]

As a result of the monetary and credit expansion, imports continued at a high rate, exceeding the rising exports, and financed by specie outflow and by credits from foreign merchants. After the rush for imports in 1815 and 1816, import values, though remaining at a relatively high level, declined in 1817. This temporary decline from peak levels was spurred by the uncertainties surrounding the return of the banking system to specie payment in 1817, and the consequent relative slackening in monetary expansion during that period. However, imports increased sharply again in 1818 to $122 million. Imports of foreign goods into Cincinnati—the major western depot—doubled in 1817–18 over the 1815–16 totals.[41] In contrast, prices of imported goods, determined largely by conditions outside America, remained almost constant during these years.

Exports, helped by European prosperity and poor crops abroad, continued to rise in price and value. They rose to $88 million in 1817 and reached a peak of $93 million in 1818. Exports of domestic products also rose to a peak of $74 million in that year. Even re-exports reached a postwar peak in 1818, although the increase over 1816 was negligible. Agricultural exports rose to $57 million in 1817 and to a peak of $63 million in 1818, advancing at a faster rate than domestic exports as a whole. Agricultural exports rose by $5 million in 1817 and $5.4 million in 1818, while aggregate domestic exports rose by $3.5 million and $5.6 million respectively. Cotton exports also reached a peak in the latter year.[42] Prices of export staples rose even more rapidly during this period. Cole's index of export staple prices at Charleston rose from 138 in March, 1817 to 169 in August, 1818. A similar rise occurred in Bezanson's cotton index.[43]

The net result in the balance of trade was a sharp drop in the trade deficit to $11.6 million in 1817, and a later rise to $28.5 million in 1818.[44] The large deficits of the postwar years are partly overstated, for some were offset by earnings of American shipping, which carried almost all American foreign trade—the earnings of which do not appear in the trade balance.[45]

Troubles and strains, however, began to pile up as the boom continued. The resumption of specie payments by the banks was increasingly more nominal than real. Obstacles and intimidation were the lot of those who attempted to press the banks for payment in specie.[46] As the Philadelphia economist, merchant, and State Senator Condy Raguet wrote to Ricardo:

> You state in your letter that you find it difficult to comprehend, why persons who had a right to demand coin from the Banks in payment of their notes, so long forebore to exercise it. This no doubt appears paradoxical to one who resides in a country where an act of parliament was

necessary to protect a bank, but the difficulty is easily solved. The whole of our population are either stockholders of banks or in debt to them. It is not the *interest* of the first to press the banks and the rest are *afraid.* This is the whole secret. An independent man, who was neither a stockholder or debtor, who would have ventured to compel the banks to do justice, would have been persecuted as an enemy of society. . . .[47]

The consequent loss of confidence in the banks was demonstrated by the emergence of a premium for specie on the market. The discount on bank notes made it more difficult for the banks maintaining specie payment to retain specie in their vaults, since people could redeem their notes for specie, and sell it for bank notes at a discount. Specie came to be at a premium in terms of Bank of United States notes, even though the Bank was required to pay in specie. This reflected a lack of confidence in the Bank's ability to continue specie payments. A premium on Spanish silver dollars—the major coin circulating in the United States—appeared in March, 1818, and reached 4 percent by June and 6 percent by November.[48] The specie drain from the Bank vaults increased, adding to the heavy external drain for payment of imports. It became evident that the Bank could not long continue expanding its notes and paying out specie at such a rapid rate. Importations of specie from abroad by the Bank, totaling over $7 million and purchased at a heavy price, proved only a temporary expedient. The problem was aggravated by the pressure resulting from rapid repayment of the Federal debt. The autumn of 1818 and early 1819 were the scheduled dates for the repayment of the "Louisiana debt," which had financed the Louisiana Purchase. Most of this debt—amounting to over $4 million—was owed abroad, and it had to be repaid in specie. The responsibility for meeting the payments fell on the Bank of the United States, the repository for the Treasury's deposits.

Faced with these threatening circumstances, the Bank of the United States was forced to call a halt to its expansion and launch a painful process of contraction. Beginning in the summer of 1818, the Bank precipitated the Panic of 1819 by a series of deflationary moves. The branches of the Bank were ordered to call on the state banks to redeem heavy balances and notes held by the Bank. The requirement that each branch redeem the notes of every other branch was rescinded, thus ending the liability of the conservative eastern branches to redeem the notes of expansionist branches. The Boston branch began this move in March, and it was made general for all the Bank's offices by the end of August. The contractionist policy, begun hesitantly under the presidency of William Jones and continued more firmly under the direction of his successor Langdon Cheves, sharply limited and contracted the loans and note issues of the branches. As a result, total demand liabilities of the Bank, including notes, private and public deposits, declined precipitately from $22 million in the fall of 1818 to $12 million in January, 1819, and to $10 million by January, 1820. Of this amount, notes outstanding of the Bank fell from a peak of $10 million in early 1818, to $8.5 million in the fall of 1818, less than $5 million by the summer of 1819, and $3.6 million by January, 1820. Particularly striking was the decline in the Bank's public deposits, consisting largely of bank debts accumulated from public land sales. They declined from $9 million in the autumn of 1818 to less than $3 million in January, 1819.[49]

Another result of contraction was a large rise in the Bank's specie reserve, which had been about $2.5 million during 1818 and early 1819. As loans were recalled, and the specie drain reversed, specie flowed into the Bank and reached $3.4 million in January, 1820. Specie reserves spurted to $8 million in the spring of 1821, at a time when total demand liabilities of the Bank were less than $12 million.[50]

The contractionist policy forced the state banks, in debt to the Bank, to contract their loans and notes outstanding at a rapid pace. Total bank notes in circulation were estimated at $45 million in January, 1820, as compared to $68 million in 1816.[51] The severe monetary contraction, lasting through 1820, led to a wave of bankruptcies throughout the country, particularly outside New England. In many cases, banks attempted to continue in operation while refusing specie payment, but their notes depreciated greatly and no longer circulated outside the vicinity of issue. The notes of most of the inland banks depreciated and fluctuated in relation to each other. New England, in contrast, was the only area little touched by bank failures or runs; the banks outside of Rhode Island remained solvent.[52] The entire hastily built private credit structure was greatly shaken by the contraction and wave of defaults.[53] The financial panic led, as did later panics, to a great scramble for a cash position, and an eagerness to sell stocks of goods at even sacrifice rates.

The severe contraction of the money supply, added to an increased demand for liquidity, led to a rapid and very heavy drop in prices. Although detailed price information is available only for wholesale commodities, there is evidence that prices fell in many other fields, such as real estate values and rents. Most important for the American economy were the prices of the great export staples, and their fall was remarkably precipitate. The index of export staples fell from 169 in August, 1818, and 158 in November, 1818, to 77 in June, 1819. A similar movement occurred in the price of cotton and in the Smith and Cole index of domestic commodity prices. Evidence of falling prices can be seen in freight rates and in the prices of slaves.[54]

The fall in export prices was aggravated by a fall in European demand for agricultural imports, occasioned by the abundant European crops after 1817 and the crisis and business contraction in Britain during the same period. Values of American exports declined sharply as well. Total exports fell from $93 million in 1818 to $70 million in 1819 and 1820. Re-exports did not contract, and the brunt was taken by domestic exports, which fell from $74 million to $51 million. Of this drop, $20 million was accounted for by agricultural exports ($10 million by cotton and $7 million by wheat and flour). It was a pure price decline, since the physical volume of exports continued to increase steadily during this period.[55]

Imports fell even more in value than did exports, reflecting the decline in American incomes. Total imports fell drastically from $122 million in 1818 to $87 million in 1819 and $74.5 million in 1820, thus practically ending the specie drain. Imports from Great Britain fell from $42 million in 1818 to $14 million in 1820, and cotton and woolen imports from Britain fell from over $14 million each in 1818 to about $5 million.[56]

During 1821, total exports and total imports are listed as almost identical, $54.6 million for the former and $54.5 million for the latter. Both were absolute low points, not only for the period of boom and depression but for America since 1815.[57] Import prices also fell with the advent of economic contraction abroad. They fell only slightly, however, and were a negligible factor in the reduction of import values, as compared to the decrease in money income at home. The index of import prices at Philadelphia fell from 126 to 112 from November, 1818 to July, 1819.[58]

The credit contraction also caused public land sales to drop sharply, falling from $13.6 million in 1818, to $1.7 million in 1820, and to $1.3 million in 1821.[59] Added to a quickened general desire for a cash position, it also led to high interest rates and common complaint about the scarcity of loanable funds.

Economic distress was suffered by all groups in the community.[60] The great fall in prices heavily increased the burden of fixed money debts, and provided a great impetus toward debtor insolvency.[61] The distress of the farmers, occasioned by the fall in agricultural and real estate prices, was aggravated by the mass of private and bank debts that they had contracted during the boom period. Borrowing for long-term improvements, farmers had been served by the new and greatly expanded banks of the South and West, as well as by the western branches of the Bank of the United States. Bank stockholders who had borrowed on the basis of unpaid stock found themselves forced to meet their debts. Speculators and others who had bought public lands during the boom were now confronted with heavy debt burdens. Merchants suffered from the decline in prices and demand for their produce and from heavy debts. Their debts to the British as well as to domestic creditors were often canceled by the ruthless process of bankruptcy. Niles judged that no less than $100 million of mercantile debts to Europe were eliminated by the bankruptcy during the depression. So low were prices and so scarce was the monetary medium in the frontier areas that there was a considerable return to barter conditions among farmers and other local inhabitants. Various areas returned to barter or the use of such goods as grain and whiskey as media of exchange.[62]

There was widespread resort to the bankruptcy courts and to judgments for debt payment. The plight of debtors in the West was well expressed by William Greene, secretary to Governor

Ethan Allen Brown of Ohio, in a memorandum to the Governor, in April, 1820:

One thing seems to be universally conceded, that the greater part of our mercantile citizens are in a state of bankruptcy—that those of them who have the largest possessions of real and personal estate . . . find it almost impossible to raise sufficient funds to supply themselves with the necessaries of life—that the citizens of every class are uniformly delinquent in discharging even the most trifling of debts.[63]

Manufacturers suffered from the general decline in prices as well as from the contraction in credit, and the panic served to intensify their generally depressed condition since the end of the war. However, the progressive factory at Waltham was able to withstand the buffetings of the depression, to continue profitable operations, and even to expand throughout the depression period.[64]

Evidence is very scanty on the behavior of wage rates during this period. In Massachusetts, the wages of agricultural workers fluctuated sharply with the boom and contraction, averaging sixty cents per day in 1811, $1.50 in 1818, and fifty-three cents in 1819. The wage rates of skilled labor, on the other hand, remained stable throughout at approximately $1 per day.[65] In Pennsylvania, woodcutters who averaged a wage of thirty-three cents per cord in the first half of the nineteenth century were paid only ten cents per cord in 1821 and 1822. Unskilled turnpike workers paid seventy-five cents a day in early 1818 received only twelve cents a day in 1819.[66]

One of the most significant phenomena of the depression was the advent of a new problem casting a long shadow on future events: large-scale unemployment in the cities. Although America was still an overwhelmingly rural country, the cities—the centers of manufacture and trade—were rapidly growing, and this depression witnessed the problem of unemployment for factory workers, artisans, mechanics, and other skilled craftsmen. These workers were often independent businessmen rather than employees, but their distress was not less acute. Concentrated in the cities, their plight was thereby dramatized, and they lacked the flexibility of farmers who could resort to barter or self-sufficiency production. In the fall of 1819, in thirty out of sixty branches of manufacturing (largely handicraft) in Philadelphia, employment in these fields totaled only 2,100, compared to 9,700 employed in 1815. There was a corresponding decline in total earnings—from $3 million to less than $700 thousand during the later year. Very drastic declines in employment took place in the cotton, woolen, and iron industries.[67] Unemployment also swelled the ranks of the paupers during the depression.[68]

By 1821, the depression had begun to clear, and the economy was launched on a slow road to recovery. The painful process of debt liquidation was over, and the equally painful process of monetary contraction had subsided.[69] The surviving banks, their notes returned to par, successfully expanded credit. The Bank of the United States, saved from imminent failure, was at last in a sound position. Its branches were again able to redeem each others' notes, and were now more firmly under strong central control. The premium on Spanish silver dollars over Bank notes dropped in June, 1819 from 4 percent to less than 2 percent, and par was restored by April, 1820. In states such as Kentucky or Tennessee, however, there was no general return to par and redeemability for several more years.[70] Business in Britain and continental Europe was also past the trough of depression, and American exports began to recover both in prices and in total values. Prices, in general, which had continued sluggish after the steep decline in 1819, began a slow rise. Export staples at Charleston, reaching 77 in June, 1819, fell to a trough of 64 in April, 1821, then slowly rose from that point on. In the same month a trough was reached by cotton prices, domestic commodities at Philadelphia, agricultural commodities, and industrial commodities, and each rose very slowly thereafter. Import prices, however, continued to fall slightly or remain at a stable level.[71] Credit began to be available, and new securities to be heavily subscribed, both at home and in the British market. Business and manufacturing activity began to rise again.[72]

Is the crisis of 1819 together with the preceding boom to be considered a modern business cycle? Wesley C. Mitchell, in his *Business Cycles . . . The Problem and Its Setting*, declared that

until a large part of the population is living by getting and spending money incomes, producing wares on a considerable scale for a wide market, using credit devices, organizing in business enterprises with relatively few employers and many employees, the economic fluctuations which occur do not have the characteristics of business cycles. . . .

in the modern sense.[73]

On the one hand, the boom, the crisis of 1818–19, and the depression until 1821 present many features akin to modern business cycles as interpreted by Mitchell. Although banking had previously been undeveloped, this period saw a rapid expansion of banks and bank money—unsound as much of the expansion may have been. The period also saw much of the typical characteristics of later financial panics: expansion of bank notes; followed by a specie drain from the banks both abroad and at home; and finally a crisis with a contraction of bank notes, runs on banks, and bank failures. A corollary to the contraction of loans and bank runs was the scramble for a cash position and rapid rise in interest rates during the panic. The diversity of bank notes and bank activity from section to section was hardly a modern characteristic, but there was an approach to uniformity in expansion and contraction because of the existence of the Bank of the United States. As in modern business cycles, the entire contraction and expansion cycle was fairly short-lived, totaling five or six years, and the period of crisis itself a short one. Furthermore, the sequence of phases was boom, crisis, depression, and revival as in the business cycle.[74]

Other modern characteristics were: the expansion of credit and of investment projects during the boom; the appearance of urban unemployment; and the marked expansion and contraction in prices.

On the other hand, there were many backward features of the economy that go counter to an interpretation of the period as a modern business cycle in the Mitchellian sense or the Panic of 1819 as a modern business crisis. Despite the growth of commerce, it was still true that the overwhelming preponderance of economic activity in that period was in agriculture. It has been estimated that 72 percent of the labor force in 1820 was engaged in agriculture.[75] Although statistics are not available, it seems from contemporary comments that urban construction increased in the boom and declined in the crisis. Physical agricultural production is not too responsive to cycles, however, and agricultural production represents overwhelmingly the greatest part of productive activity during this period.[76] Thus, physical production of cotton, rice, wheat, and flour continued to grow during the depression period.[77] Certainly farm employment is not a markedly cyclical phenomenon.[78] Furthermore, many farm households were self-sufficient, and carried on only local barter trade, or entered the monetary nexus occasionally. With such a prevalence of home sufficiency and barter conditions, the economy could hardly be classified as modern, or conditions the same as a modern business cycle.

Furthermore, the manufacturing and business enterprises that did exist were mainly small-scale. Modern business cycles are most characteristic in the sphere of large-scale business enterprises and large-scale manufacturing. Conditions in this period were quite the opposite. Small shops, small banks, small factories comprised the enterprises of the day. Rather than a sharp distinction existing between employers and numerous laboring employees, most workers, as we have indicated above, were craftsmen, who worked either in very small-scale firms or as independent businessmen, with not much marked differentiation. Such were the blacksmiths, shoemakers, tailors, printers, carpenters. More in the category of employees were sailors and unskilled road and canal workers.

One of the most vital points of difference between the economy of that period and of the modern day is the role of manufacturing. Not only was it small-scale, and even then largely (approximately two-thirds) in self-sufficient households,[79] but the conditions of the fledgling factories differed from the rest of the economy. The factories were depressed while the rest of the community was booming, due to the postwar import of manufactured goods; their depression was continued and intensified during the panic. A crisis occurring in the midst of a depressed period—as happened to much of manufacturing in 1819—is more a feature of early precyclical crisis as described by Mitchell.[80] Furthermore, in manufacturing fields other than textiles, there were not even glimmerings of large-scale factory production. The other leading branches of manufacture, such as pot and pearl ashes, iron, soap, whiskey, candles, leather, lumber products, flour, paper, were the product of household and small-scale neighborhood manufactures. An exception was the larger flour mills, which expanded rapidly during 1815–16 to supply the booming European market. The great preponderance of flour mills, however, continued to be small, local affairs using local streams for power.[81]

Transportation, so vital in the vast and thinly-populated country, stood just on the threshold of advances that would take it far beyond its current rude and primitive level. Inland transportation traveled mainly on the very costly dirt roads and down flatboats on the big rivers such as the Mississippi. The great improvements in transportation were just on the horizon: the river steamboats, the regular transatlantic packets, the canal boom and the great trade opened up by the Erie Canal, and the turnpike boom. But as yet, none of these developments had progressed beyond the early, hesitant stages.

With production and transportation in a relatively backward state, with such a large proportion of production on the farms and in self-sufficient households, and with the budding factory production facing a different course of economic conditions from the rest of society it is apparent that the National Bureau of Economic Research, within its own definitions, was correct in beginning its reference dates for American business cycles with the 1834–38 cycle and not earlier.[82] On the other hand, as the greatest and last major crisis before 1836, the panic of 1819 holds considerable interest for the study of business cycles and for the present day. It was an economy in transition, as it were, to a state where business cycles as we know them would develop. Its new shaky, banking structure provided a surge of bank notes, while bringing in its wake many modern problems of money supply, bank soundness, and bank failure. Its new manufactures were the beginning of a great industrial development, and initiated national concern with foreign competition and the prosperity of industry. Extensive foreign trade brought the country in direct relationship to the fluctuations and developments in European economic conditions. Finally, urban unemployment, that modern specter, first became an object of concern with this panic.

Faced with the new and burgeoning phenomenon of the panic, those Americans opposed to any governmental interference in the existing economic structure could take one of two courses: either simply deny that any distress existed, or face the facts of depression and argue that only individual acts could bring about a cure. The former position was the official reaction of the Monroe Administration.[83] In his annual message of December 1818, for example, President Monroe ignored the panic completely and hailed the abundant harvest and the flourishing of commerce.[84] In the following annual message, Monroe took brief notice of some currency derangement and depression of manufactures, but added that the evils were diminishing by being left to individual remedies.[85] By November, 1820, Monroe was actually rejoicing in the happy situation of the country; he admitted some pressure, but declared these of no importance. The best remedy for these slight pressures was simplicity and economy.[86] In his second Inaugural Address, on March 5, 1821, Monroe admitted at last to a general depression of prices, but only as a means of explaining the great decline in the federal revenue. Despite this, he asserted that the situation of America presented a "gratifying spectacle." [87] A few newspapers echoed this theme. An anecdote in the Detroit *Gazette* inferred that unemployment was nothing to worry about, being simply a consequence of the laziness of the worker.[88]

Of those who recognized the severity of the depression, there were scattered expressions of laissez-faire doctrine in opposition to all proposals of government intervention. We shall see below that the laissez-faire advocates developed their views and elaborated their arguments in the process of opposing specific proposals of government intervention: largely debtors' relief, monetary inflation, and a protective tariff.[89] Of general expressions of laissez-faire, not specifically related to proposals for intervention, one cogent exposition was that of Willard Phillips, young New England lawyer and leading Federalist. Phillips declared it outside the province of the legislature or of political economists to concern themselves with the state of trade or its profitability. For this "is a question which the merchants alone are acquainted with, and capable of deciding; and as the public interest coincides directly with theirs, there is no danger of its being neglected."[90] The New York *Daily Advertiser* set forth the laissez-faire position at some length. It stressed repeatedly that the depression must be allowed to cure itself. How could Congress remedy matters? It could not stop the people from exporting specie; it could not teach the people the necessary virtues of frugality and economy; it could not give credit to worthless banks or stop overtrading at home. The remedy must be slow and gradual, and stem from individuals, not governments. Any governmental interference would provide a shock to business enterprise.[91] As the New York *Evening Post* succinctly expressed it: "Time and the laws of trade will restore things to an equilibrium, if legislatures do not rashly interfere to the natural course of events." [92] Of the expressions of laissez-faire sentiment in Congress, one of the most prominent was that of Representative Johnson of Virginia in the course of his attack against a proposed protective tariff. His theme was "let the people manage their own affairs . . . the people of this country understand their own interests and will pursue them to advantage." [93]

Of the individual remedies proposed for the depression, the most popular were the twin virtues of "industry" and "economy." Regardless of what specific legislative remedies any writers proposed, they were certain to add that a necessary condition for permanent recovery was an increase in, or a return to, these two moral precepts. The ideas behind these proposed remedies were generally implicit rather than explained: "economizing" and living within one's income would prevent an aggravating debt burden from arising and reduce any existing one; "industry" meant harder work and hence increased production. Another cited advantage of economy was that most of the luxury items were purchased from abroad, so that an appeal to economy could ease the specie drain, and be urged by protectionists as a means of helping domestic manufactures. But generally these concepts were thought to need little analysis; they were moral imperatives.

The most extensive treatment of the economy and industry theme was a lengthy series of articles by Mordecai Manuel Noah, a leader in Tammany Hall and publisher of Tammany's New York *National Advocate*. Noah's theme was that the depression could only be remedied by individual economies in expenditure. He saw the cause of the depression in the indolence and lack of industry among the people and especially in the influence of the debilitating luxuries of high fashion. Noah had a Veblenian conception of the influence of the conspicuous consumption of the rich in encouraging extravagance by the poor. He advocated a return to family manufacture of clothing and an end to high fashion.[94] In imitation of Noah, who had signed himself "Howard" in writing these articles, the editor of the Philadelphia *Union*, signing himself "Howard the Younger," pointed out that it was the extravagant spenders who now complain of the "scarcity of money." [95] A quasi-humorous circular—printed in the Philadelphia *American Daily Advertiser*—called for a nationwide society to induce ladies to economize. It was signed by the "spirit" of many Revolutionary War heroes.[96]

Some writers went further to say that the depression was really having a good effect on the nation, since it forced people to go back to the highly moral ways of yesteryear—specifically to industry and economy. Thus, the New York *Daily Advertiser* saw much good from the depression; people had become much more economical and had established such channels for saving as savings banks and manufacturing associations. The New York *American* was even more emphatic, asserting that waste and indulgence had now been replaced by sober calculation, and prudence and morality had been regenerated.[97]

Similar to the theme that individual moral resurgence through industry and economy would relieve the depression was the belief that renewed theological faith could provide the only sufficient cure. The theological view, however, had no economic rationale. Typical was the (Annapolis) *Maryland Gazette*, which declared that the only remedy for the depression was to turn from wicked ways to religious devotion.[98] A similar position was taken by the General Assembly of the Presbyterian Church, which found the only effectual remedy in a resurgence of religion and its corollary moral virtues.[99]

If individuals are to economize, then governments should also. Drives for legislative retrenchment were generally based upon the decline of prices since the onset of the depression. Since the preceding boom and price rise had been used as justification for increasing governmental salaries, many lawmakers urged that these salaries now be cut proportionately in turn. The government, in short, was regarded as having an obligation to retrench along with its citizens.[100]

Many Americans, however, were not content with individual remedies and laissez-faire, and they pressed for the adoption of numerous proposals of government intervention and attempts at a remedy. One of the most striking problems generated by the panic was the plight of the debtors. Having borrowed heavily during the preceding boom, they were confronted now with calls for repayment and falling prices, increasing the burden of their debts. A discussion of the American search for remedies of the panic will deal first with proposals for debtors' relief.

II
DIRECT RELIEF OF DEBTORS

The plight of the numerous debtors during the panic was particularly arresting, and it inspired many heatedly debated proposals for their relief. One important group of debtors hit by the crisis were those who had purchased public land on credit from the federal government. Congress had established a liberal credit system for public lands in 1800. Purchasers were permitted to pay one-fourth of the total within forty days after the purchase date and the remainder in three annual installments. If the full payment were not completed within five years after the purchase date, the land would be forfeited.[1] In 1804, the minimum unit of land that could be purchased was reduced from 320 to 160 acres, thus further spurring public land purchases and debts. A growing backlog of indebtedness developed, as Congress repeatedly postponed the date of forfeiture for failure to complete payment.[2] The particularly strong boom in western land sales in the postwar period and the secular trend of extensive sales of public domain in the nation's expansion westward resulted in a heavy burden of debt owed to the federal government. By 1819, the debt on public lands totaled $23 million.[3] With the panic making the debt problem urgent, Congress continued to pass postponement laws, delaying forfeiture for a year—in 1818, 1819, and 1820—but these measures could, at best, temporarily postpone the problem.

What to do about this debt to the federal government was clearly a federal problem. President James Monroe, who is generally considered to have been completely indifferent to the panic and to any remedial measures by government, put the public land debt question before Congress in his annual message of November, 1820.[4] He brought to the fore one of the leading arguments used by all advocates of debtors' relief: namely, that the debtors had incurred their debt when prices were very high and now had to repay at a time when prices were very low and the purchasing power of the dollar unusually high. Monroe did not elaborate on this argument. He simply stated the fact and suggested that it might be advisable "to extend to the purchasers of these lands, in consideration of the unfavorable change, which has occurred since the sale, a reasonable indulgence."

Two days after the President's message, Senator Richard M. Johnson of Kentucky presented a resolution to permit debtors to relinquish a prorated part of the land which they had purchased, in proportion to their failure to pay, while obtaining title to the remainder of the land outright. Thus, a purchaser who was one-quarter in arrears could relinquish one-quarter of his land to the government and acquire clear title to the rest.[5] It quickly became evident that this measure was the major concern of the movement for relief of the public land debtors. Shortly afterwards, similar resolutions were presented by Senators John W. Walker of Alabama, James Noble of Indiana, and Jesse B. Thomas of Illinois.[6] The Walker Resolution provided for complete forgiveness of any interest due on the outstanding debt—a move to cancel the existing 6 percent interest charged on installments due. Important support for the bill came in the annual report to the Senate, on December 5, 1820, by Secretary of the Treasury William H. Crawford.[7] Crawford repeated President Monroe's argument that much of the public land had been bought at very high prices during a boom period. Crawford was at pains to separate such debt relief from legislative interference with private contracts. But it was certainly legitimate, he asserted, for the government, as a creditor, to relax its own demands. Crawford proposed to allow proportional relinquishment of the unpaid portion of land, a 25–37½ percent forgiveness of the total debt, and permission for the borrower to pay sums due in ten equal annual installments without interest.

The resolutions were referred to the Senate Committee on Public Lands and were the signal for a deluge of petitions on behalf of the measure from all of the western states, where the public land debtors were concentrated.[8] Several western state legislatures—Alabama,

Missouri, and Kentucky—sent resolutions asking for passage of the measure. The resolutions mentioned not only the decline of prices but also other aspects of the depression: The Kentucky legislature cited the unexpected depression of earnings, profits, property values, wages, and the depreciation of local currencies as helping to impose a burden on the debtors, and thus increasing the need for relief. The Alabama legislature cited the "great diminution of the circulating medium." The authors of the various resolutions did not engage in sustained reasoning to bolster their views.

The relief bill was reported to the Senate by Chairman Thomas of the Public Lands Committee on December 28. It followed the Crawford proposals closely. The major provision was the permission to relinquish the unpaid proportion of the land and attain clear title to the remainder for all those who had purchased public land before July 1, 1820. The bill also discharged the interest in arrears on the outstanding debt and added two further provisions: 1) the remainder of the debt could now be paid in eight annual installments, without interest charges, and payment of the full debt was extended for those who did not wish to take advantage of the relinquishment provision; 2) the grant of a special discount of 37½ percent for debtors who would pay promptly.

Senator Thomas, in his opening speech for the bill, warned that unless the relief were granted, all public land sold on credit would be forfeited to the government.[9] He emphasized that the "capacity of the community to purchase" was now greatly diminished, compared to the capacity at the time the land was obtained. At the time when most of the debt was contracted the "price of produce of every description was more than 100% higher than at present." Shortly after the bulk of the purchases, prices of produce fell to less than half their previous height. The burden on the debtors was aggravated by the fact that the banks, in their expansion during the boom, had liberally furnished money to the purchasers of public lands, inducing them to bid up the prices of the land to great heights. During the crisis, bank facilities were withdrawn, and banks were becoming bankrupt, their notes no longer receivable. The resulting destitution of the debtors, concluded Thomas, required governmental relief.

The major controversy over the bill was the question of which groups of debtors merited the relief. As reported by the committee, relief provisions would be restricted to those who had *originally purchased the land from the government.* They did not apply to those who had bought the public land with its outstanding indebtedness from the previous purchasers rather than from the government directly. Illinois Senator Ninian Edwards immediately called for the extension of the relief clauses to all public land holders.[10] Edwards insisted that the greatest sufferers were those latecomers who had bought the land at a very high price from the original purchasers; in many cases, the original purchasers had sold the land at a great profit to the newcomers, and yet only the original purchasers could benefit from the bill.

In his argument for the relief bill as a whole, Edwards went into great detail to excuse the actions of the debtors. The debtors, like the rest of the country, had been infatuated by the short-lived, "artificial and fictitious prosperity." They thought that the prosperity would be permanent. Lured by the cheap money of the banks, people were tempted to engage in a "multitude of the wildest projects and most visionary speculations," as in the case of the Mississippi and South Sea bubbles of previous centuries. Edwards sternly reminded the Senate that the government itself had encouraged public land purchases by making some of its bonds and other claims upon it receivable in payment for the lands.[11] He also pointed to the distress prevailing among the debtors citing: the bank failures; the great contraction of the money supply; the loss of property values; unemployment; and general despair, as well as the fall in prices, all highlighting the need for governmental relief.

Senator Thomas was apparently convinced by his colleague, and moved to extend the application of the relief bill to all holders of public land. The amendment was adopted by the Senate.[12]

The Thomas and Edwards arguments for relief legislation were repeated by Senator Johnson of Kentucky, who added specifically, in excuse for the debtors, that their distress was not caused by their "own imprudence" but by unforeseen changes in the economy, in prices, the money supply, and the state of the markets.[13]

Senator John Henry Eaton of Tennessee wanted a further restriction on the scope of the relief.[14] He moved an amendment to restrict relief to the *actual settlers only*, thus withholding relief from the mere "speculators" in the public lands. No one rose to defend his amendment, which was subjected to a storm of criticism from western Senators and from one New Englander.[15] Leading the attack was Walker of Alabama. He saw no reason why the government should discriminate among the purchases since they were sold to the highest bidders in good faith, and saw no reason why there should be a particular premium on settlement. His other major argument was that the government itself had fostered speculation on public lands. The Eaton Amendment was quickly rejected, but another amendment by Eaton drew more support and split the western delegation.[16] This was a provision to grant special relief to the actual settlers by forgiving them an additional 25 percent of their unpaid debt. The amendment, however, was finally rejected.

Aside from the passage of an amendment, offered by Senator Nicholas Van Dyke of Delaware, placing a maximum limit on the size of the purchase to which the relief would be applied, the bill passed through the Senate with little opposition. It passed by a vote of thirty-six to five, and none of the five opponents spoke against the principle of the bill.[17]

Meanwhile, Representative John Crowell of Alabama had taken the lead of the pro-relief forces in the House of Representatives by submitting a similar bill to the House Public Lands Committee soon after the President's address.[18] When the House received the Senate bill, the committee reported it out very quickly without amendments. The House debate was distinguished by the one reported speech in Congress opposing the *principle* of the entire bill.[19] Interestingly, this statement came not from some ultra eastern congressman far removed from the scene of the public land holders and their problems but from Representative Robert Allen of mid-Tennessee, a state that had been one of the centers of pro-relief agitation. Allen declared himself opposed completely to the whole principle of legislative interference with debt contracts. "If the people learn that debts can be paid with petitions and fair stories, you will soon have your table crowded," Allen charged. The next step would be debtors demanding refunds of their previous payments. Indeed, where was the line to be drawn? Furthermore, such legislation constituted special privilege for public land debtors. To the argument that the debtors had not got the money for payment Allen calmly retorted that, in that case, the government would get the land back, and would therefore not be the loser.

In addition to these general arguments against government interference with contract, Allen hit hard at the speculation issue, which had been prominent in the Senate debates. He declared that no group could be less deserving of relief than the bulk of the public land purchasers. Allen, indeed, used the same set of facts that had been employed by Thomas and Edwards to denounce rather than excuse the debtors. He declared that the debtors had formed companies, had borrowed heavily from the banks in order to buy public land, and thereby these speculators had bid the land away from the actual settlers. The speculators had gone into debt never intending to pay the price anyway, but only to sell them for a higher price to others. Allen was sure that the actual settlers were a thrifty lot who did not run into debt. In a later speech, Allen retorted that the advocates of the bill, in pleading for the wretched and the poor, did not realize that the really poor never bought land.

There was far more active opposition to the relief bill in the House than in the Senate, and it was a minority of western representatives that took the lead in the opposition. Besides Allen, Representatives William McCoy from wealthy, rural Fauquier County, Virginia, and Benjamin Hardin of rural Nelson County, Kentucky, worked hard to defeat or limit the bill, but without success.[20] Kentucky Representative George Robertson from rural Garrard County, tried to amend the bill to exclude speculators from its benefits and confine the bill to actual settlers, but the amendment lost by a small majority. Robertson was a leading lawyer who later became Chief Justice of the Kentucky Court of Appeals. The only victory for the anti-relief forces was the defeat of an attempt to make the reduction in debt unconditional instead of as a bonus for prompt payment.[21]

The only reply by the relief forces was that of Thomas Metcalf, from commercial Lexington, Kentucky, who declared that relief was called for particularly since the government's own policies had "beguiled" these debtors into error.[22]

The bill finally passed the House on February 28 by a vote of 97 to 40.[23] Following is a geographic breakdown of the roll-call vote in the House (bearing in mind that the negative was only the hard core of the greater opposition which had made itself felt in the voting on amendments):

Voting on Relief for Public Land Debtors

	For	*Against*
New England		
Maine	3	—
Vermont	2	1
New Hampshire	—	5
Massachusetts	6	3
Connecticut	2	4
Rhode Island	—	1
Total	13	14
Middle Atlantic		
New York	17	4
New Jersey	3	1
Pennsylvania	13	3
Delaware	—	—
Maryland	5	2
Total	38	10
South		
Virginia	14	6
North Carolina	2	4
South Carolina	3	2
Georgia	5	—
Total	24	12
West		
Tennessee	4	3
Other western States (Ohio, Illinois, Indiana, Kentucky, Louisiana, Alabama)	18	—
Total	22	3

The relief bill was thus supported by all sections of the country except New England—evenly split on the issue. The hard-core opposition sentiment was pretty widely scattered geographically, with the exception of the West, although proportionally greatest in New England. The opposition was fairly strong in the South, but not in the important large Middle Atlantic States of New York and Pennsylvania. The West, with the exception of Tennessee, was overwhelmingly for the measure, with even such sceptical Kentuckians as Hardin and Robertson joining in voting for final passage.

Since various proposals for debtors' relief legislation in the states caused indignant opposition in such places as New York City, one might be wondering why the New York representatives agreed to the measure. Perhaps one reason was that much of the public lands were held by eastern speculators. Another reason was that, after all, this particular debt was owed to the federal government itself, so that relief laws or changes in the contract by the government were directly the government's concern as one of the parties to the contract. There was not here a question of interference in *private* debt contracts. Hence the disposition, in Congress and out, was to let the relief advocates have their way in this case without much opposition.

Even Hezekiah Niles, influential editor of *Niles' Weekly Register*, who had no use for debtors' relief legislation, reluctantly approved of this bill, although he was critical of the public land speculators and apprehensive that the debtors would relinquish the poorest land to the government.[24]

And so the public land debtors gained their desired relief measure with little opposition. Large numbers of debtors took advantage of the relief relinquishment provision; half of the public land debt in Alabama—which in turn constituted half of the nation's total—was paid up within a year. Yet most of those who relinquished the land continued to cultivate it and treat it as their own.[25]

The major arguments for land debt relief—the plight of the debtors, the distressed conditions, lower prices—could be used on behalf of other, more far-reaching, measures for debtors' relief, private as well as governmental. They were so used, both for direct relief measures designed to aid the debtor directly and for monetary proposals aimed partly or sometimes wholly at debtors' relief. Against these proposals, the opposition was far more vocal and vigorous.

The immediate and pressing problem for debtors was the legal judgments accumulating against them for payment of their debts. Consequently, they turned to the state legislatures, which had jurisdiction over such contracts, to try to modify the provisions for payment. The proposed laws either postponed legal executions of property or prohibited sales of debtors' property below a certain minimum price. The moratoria were known as "stay laws" or "replevin laws," which postponed execution of property when the debtor signed a pledge to make the payment at a certain date in the future. Minimum appraisal laws provided that no property could be sold for execution below a certain minimum price, the appraised value being generally set by a board of the debtors' neighbors. Such laws had been an intermittent feature of American government since early colonial Virginia.[26]

The eastern states were heavily embroiled in controversy over debtors' and monetary legislation. Delaware, for example, was hard hit by the depression, and its relatively commercial New Castle County, in the north, had a particularly heavy incidence of suits for debt payments. As the Delaware legislative session opened at the beginning of 1819, New Castle County was a hub of agitation for debtors' relief legislation. Its Representatives Henry Whitely and Isaac Hendrickson submitted petitions from over 450 citizens asking for some sort of relief to debtors of banks. Finally, the Delaware House created a committee headed by Representative Henry Brinckle to consider the issues raised by these petitions, as well as banking proposals which will be considered below.[27] The committee took only a week to issue its report.[28] It noted that among the major relief legislation proposed were some acts that would prohibit execution of judgments completely, and some that would compel creditors to take such property at a minimum appraised valuation. The Brinckle Committee rejected all such proposals on grounds of unconstitutionality and because suspension of execution would endanger the position of creditors and impair the good faith of contracts.

As was the case in most states where relief proposals were debated, the report provoked a storm. Two members of the five-man committee, headed by New Castle's Representative John T. Cochran, moved rejection of the paragraph condemning relief laws. The motion was defeated by a vote of sixteen to four.[29] The dispute, therefore, cannot be simply described as a geographical split within the state, since the majority of each county voted down the amendment.

The large eastern state of New Jersey gave serious consideration to stay laws on executions. A Committee of Inquiry was appointed by the New Jersey General Assembly, 1820 session, to consider a stay law, which would have postponed executions if the creditor refused to accept the debtors' property at or above a minimum appraised value. A report strongly in the negative was delivered by Representative Joseph Hopkinson, and this served to send the bill down to a two-and-a-half-to-one defeat in the House.[30]

The arguments of the Hopkinson Report were a well-considered statement, typical of the opposition to debtors' relief legislation, as well as to proposals to increase the money supply. The report began with assurances that the committee was deeply sensitive to the prevailing financial embarrassments, and that they had given due weight to the numerous petitions for relief legislation. While the proposed legislation, however, would perhaps alleviate the condition of the debtors temporarily, it would, in the long run, make their distress worse. The contention that relief legislation would eventually intensify the depression was a central argument for the opposition in all the states. The Hopkinson Committee used a familiar medical analogy noting that "palliatives which may suspend the pain for a season, but do not remove the disease, are not restoratives of health; it is worse than useless to lessen the present pressure by means which will finally plunge us deeper in distress." They added that it was their duty to be truthful with the people and not delude them with promises that could not be kept—even at the expense of their "immediate displeasure."—an indication perhaps that the proposal was popular in New Jersey. The report remarked that suffering men were disposed to complain about their lot and look for rapid remedies rather than admit that the only cure was slow and gradual. As a result they would flee to patent-medicine panaceas, which would only make their condition worse.

Specifically, how would the proposed stay of execution law deepen rather than remedy the distress of the people? First, a stay law would not extinguish the debt, which would still remain outstanding. Second, the real reason for the depression was the lack of "mutual confidence." Only such confidence could lead to a revival of credit and activity. But it was clear, declared the Hopkinson Committee, that the distress would greatly increase if a potential creditor were prohibited by law from recovering his loan from a delinquent debtor. A stay law would eliminate rather than restore credit, confidence, and business activity.

Unsuccessful attempts to pass a minimum appraisal law and a stay law also took place in conservative New York State. Ultra-conservative Massachusetts considered but did not pass a stay law. The proposed New York minimum appraisal law, in 1819, provided that in all cases of judgments on houses and lands, the court officer shall appoint three disinterested men—one a representative of the creditor, one of the debtor and one picked by the court officer—to appraise the real estate at its "just and true value, in money." The creditor, in order to obtain payment, would be obliged to accept the property at such value. This bill was defeated by a three-to-one margin.[31] A proposal for a stay law was also offered and rejected by a two-to-one margin. A bill was later passed, however, relaxing the processes against insolvent debtors.[32]

Maryland, on the other hand, passed a stay law by a near two-to-one majority. It also passed a law in 1819–20 exempting household articles worth up to $50 from sales at execution—a considerable aid to harassed debtors.[33] There was much agitation for a special session of the Maryland legislature to enact a stay law. Citizens of rural Somerset County in southeastern Maryland, for example, called for a special session, citing the high proportion of enterprising citizens in serious debt.[34] The agitation drew the criticism of the alert, conservative New York *Daily Advertiser*, Federalist organ for merchants.[35] It pointed out that the distress of farmers and those trading with them, stemmed from the low prices of agricultural produce, and no legislative tempering with debt contracts could raise these prices in foreign markets. Furthermore, "the shock which business of every description . . . receives from [these] measures . . . is more than a counterbalance to any monetary relief." It went on to criticize the debtors for speculations and extravagance.

That the West had no monopoly on debtors' relief agitation is attested by the furious fight over stay laws in the Vermont legislature. In the fall of 1818, the Vermont House defeated numerous attempts to postpone consideration of the bill, and finally passed it by a three-vote margin.[36] The Senate failed to pass the bill in that session, and this precipitated another battle in the 1820 session. Repeated motions to postpone were rejected by two-to-one majorities, and the bill was passed by a similar margin, after limiting amendments to force the debtor to swear to inability to pay and to limit the bill to debtors with families had overwhelmingly failed.[37] The Senate still persisted in its failure to pass the bill, however, and so the House finally surrendered in the next session, by a three-to-one majority.[38] The legislature finally passed a law staying all executions for debt in the spring of 1822, after the crisis had ended. But that summer, the new law met the fate of many similar state laws, and was declared unconstitutional by the Circuit Court.[39]

In Rhode Island a unique situation faced the debtors. Since the establishment of Rhode Island's first chartered bank in 1791, a unique "bank process" privilege had been granted to banks of the state. When obligations to a bank fell due, the bank officers had only to give legal notice to the debtor. The courts were then forced to enter judgment against the defendant immediately and issue executions without the customary legal trial—although the debtor was permitted a trial if he denied the legality of the debt. All other debtors, including banks themselves, were entitled to the usual judicial proceedings. One of Rhode Island's first acts on the onset of the panic late in 1818 was to repeal the summary bank process laws.[40]

One of the most interesting of the controversies over the debtor's relief legislation occurred in Virginia—a stronghold of economic conservatism. Virginia's leading statesmen were noteworthy for their opposition to fiduciary banking, expansion of paper money, and government interference with the economy.[41] Yet, the Virginia General Assembly engaged in a spirited debate over a proposed minimum appraisal law. This law would prevent any sale of property under execution unless the property sold for at least three-fourths of its "value," as appraised by a governmentally appointed commission.[42] The chief advocate of the bill was Representative Thomas Miller, from rural Powhatan County. Miller concentrated on the plight of the large number of debtors.[43] In Virginia, he explained, most business was transacted on credit. The farmers, in borrowing to work on their crops, had done so when tobacco sold at $12 a pound, and wheat at $2 a bushel. Naturally they had anticipated that this prosperity would continue. Then, when they had to repay their debts, they were confronted with tobacco at $5 and wheat at $1. The value of the resources that they could use to pay debts had been reduced by more than half, yet the price of imported articles, such as woolens, sugar, and coffee had remained unchanged. This situation was general throughout the state.

Miller emphasized that the debtors could not be blamed for their plight. The change was a sudden one and was not due simply to their "extravagance." The expansion of banks and bank credit had raised the prices of property and produce, and induced the people to go into debt. Then, swiftly, the banks stopped expanding and contracted their loans and notes; the result was contraction of money and prices, and a great burden of debt. The responsibility for the debtors' plight was therefore that of the banks, and not of the debtors themselves. Miller laid blame on the state banks and the Bank of the United States; the latter for serving as an expansionist force from its inception, then initiating the contraction, thereby causing a multiple contraction by the state banks. Since extravagance was not the cause of the crisis, mere calls for "industry and economy" would not effect a rapid cure; and the legislature, which had assured the people that its chartered banks were good for the community, owed it to them to throw them a plank in the present sea of distress.

Miller's argument is particularly interesting in harmonizing the general anti-bank sentiment in Virginia with an argument for debtors' relief. The advocates of debtors' relief laws generally favored monetary expansion plans as remedies for the crisis. In many states the two were tied together, so that creditors were penalized with stay laws if they should refuse the new paper money, which would be loaned to debtors, to enable them to repay their debts. Yet, in this case, in a state of generally anti-paper money opinion, the leading advocates of debtors' relief linked together *anti*-bank ideas with pleas for a minimum appraisal law.

The same argument was advanced by another leading supporter, Representative William Cabell Rives of Nelson County.[44] He denounced the banks and called the relief law essential to the salvation of the people. In lurid terms he denounced the shylock creditors, who were bent on extracting their pound of flesh from the hearts of the people.[45]

The most comprehensive attack on the relief proposal came from Representative William Selden, of Henrico County, a middle-sized farming county adjacent to Powhatan and similar in the composition of its population.[46] He recognized that the value of money had changed, but asserted that it was not subject to regulation by the government. The value of money depended on the quantity of circulating medium and the quantity of goods; "money itself in an article of traffic" like any other. "Human legislation on this subject is worse than vain."

Selden proceeded to attack the idea of special privilege legislation for any class of citizens, such as farmers or debtors. The fact that debtors might be in the majority does not make such legislation just. Such class legislation would confiscate the property of the creditor and ruin the merchants who gave credit to their customers. Selden stressed the importance of personal responsibility for contracts and actions; the debtor should "pay the consequence of his own folly of imprudence." In short, freedom of contract must be maintained; "Leave men alone to make their own contracts, and leave contracts alone when they are made." [47]

Representative Robert T. Thompson, of wealthy Fairfax County, added another argument against the law. Objecting to the appraisement provision, he declared that property had only one value: the "price which it could command" at a fair public sale, and that its value could not be determined by any commission. Furthermore,

Thompson wondered why there was no pressure for acceleration of debt payment during boom periods. He concluded by urging that the legislature let the "cure . . . go on," this cure being the elimination of the common habits of extravagance and luxury.

The outcome of the debate was rejection of the minimum appraisal bill by a vote of 113 to 74.[48] The relief forces, however, tried again with two proposed stay laws in the 1820–21 session. These were rejected by a narrow margin.[49].

The conservative attitude toward the financial difficulties was reflected in the message to the Virginia legislature of Governor James P. Preston.[50] The embarrassments were caused by general imprudence, extravagance, love of ease, and an inordinate desire to grow rich quickly. Preston declared that the remedy for the crisis was a return to the old habits of industry and economy.[51]

North Carolina, plagued by a rapid fall in prices and land values, and beset by bankruptcies and failures, also saw a controversy over a stay law. Governor John Branch, in his message to the legislature in the 1820 session, proposed a stay and a minimum appraisal law to appraise the debtor's property at its "intrinsic value." There was too much opposition, however, for the bill to pass. Branch did succeed in passing a stay law for debtors who had purchased former Cherokee Indian land from the state.[52]

The pivotal state of Pennsylvania, which gave a great deal of thought to proposals for remedying the depression, considered stay laws and minimum appraisal laws. A minimum appraisal law was first suggested by two Representatives from widely separated rural areas, John Noble and James Reeder.[53] They urged a law forcing creditors to accept the real estate of debtors at a value set by an official. If they refused, execution of the judgment against the debtor was to be stayed for three years. Their major argument was that, while debtors generally had enough *paper currency* to have discharged the debt, the widespread depreciation of paper had placed a danger of forced sales on a great portion of Pennsylvania farmers and rural citizens.

The legislature never considered this bill seriously, despite the fact that Governor William Findlay urged its passage.[54] Attempts to pass such legislation were killed by the reports of several special committees on the economic distress in the next sessions of the legislature. One report was submitted by the fiery Representative William Duane, editor of the daily Philadelphia *Aurora*—the old stronghold of arch-Republicanism.[55] Duane, as chairman of the Special Committee on the General State of the Domestic Economy, declared that widespread distress prevailed among creditors, farmers, and mechanics throughout the state. In county after county, citizens testified to daily sacrifices of property and defaults on debts. Granting that a minimum appraisal law would afford some relief to specific debtors, such a law would be economically unsound, as well as an unjust special privilege for the debtor. Duane, like Hopkinson in New Jersey, declared that one of the greatest obstacles to a return of prosperity was the "absence of credit or confidence," and nothing could better delay a revival of confidence than such a measure.[56] The famous Raguet Report, in the 1821 session, also rejected such debtors' legislation, but, without engaging in analysis of the proposal, stated simply that it was impracticable and dishonorable.[57]

Despite this recommendation, Pennsylvania passed a minimum appraisal law in March, 1821, providing that bankrupt property must be sold for two-thirds of its assessed valuation, else the debt would be stayed for one year.[58] Further, the legislature, without controversy, modified the provisions of the execution laws in order to alleviate some of the burdens of the insolvent debtors. Specifically, a defendant could prevent sale of his landed property, if the property was considered to be unprofitable.[59]

One of the most acute and original critiques of stay and minimum appraisal legislation was the product of "A Pennsylvanian" writing in the conservative—formerly Federalist—Philadelphia *Union*.[60] "A Pennsylvanian" noted that these laws were being advocated in many petitions to the legislature. Aside from their impairment of contract, such laws would, rather than relieve the distress, have a "most pernicious effect." For the distress was caused by two factors, a lack of money and a lack of confidence. Such laws would not increase the amount of money in circulation, and therefore would not relieve the first cause. On the other hand, they would destroy the little confidence that now remained; they would induce the withdrawal of large amounts of capital now employed and mitigating the distress. The withdrawn capital would

> be either invested in the public funds or perhaps [be driven] to other states, where a higher rate of interest already holds out a sufficient temptation, and the people are too wise to destroy public confidence by laws impeding the recovery of debt.

"A Pennsylvanian" pointed to United States and City of Philadelphia 6 percent bonds being currently at 3 percent above par—indicating a great deal of idle capital waiting for return of public confidence before being applied to the relief of commerce and manufacturing. Thus, in the process of criticizing debtors' relief legislation, the "Pennsylvanian" was led beyond a general reference to the importance of "confidence" to an unusually extensive analysis of the problems of investment, idle capital, and the rate of interest.

In the heavily indebted agricultural states of the West, there was greater agitation for debtors' relief legislation. These states passed more such legislation than the eastern states, but generally only after an intense and continuing controversy. Although the relief sentiment was greater in the West, there were strong groups of advocates and opponents in each state.

Although Ohio was hit very heavily by the crisis, debtors' relief proposals did not make too much of an impact or generate great controversy. Ohio had had a minimum appraisement law since its inception as a state in 1803. The law set a minimum price at forced sale at two-thirds an official appraisal of the debtor's property—the appraisement to be performed by a board of the debtor's neighbors. If the auction sale brought less, the property would be retained by the insolvent debtor.[61] The laws were effective in shielding the debtor, although there were complaints that often the officials' appraisals were at a very low value, hardly higher than the market value itself.[62] In other cases, where appraisals were set at a high value, there were complaints in the press that creditors were being victimized. The Cleveland *Herald* cited one case of a creditor obliged by the law to accept miscellaneous articles of personal property (such as watches, dogs, barrels) at an inflated value or be forced to wait at least six months to collect. The *Herald* called for repeal of the appraisement law.[63] In sum, the plight of the debtors in Ohio was urgent, but their attention was concentrated on measures other than direct intervention in debt contracts.[64]

Thinly populated and overwhelmingly rural, Indiana was also heavily in debt and hard-hit by the economic crisis. As soon as the crisis struck, Indiana moved swiftly to pass debtors' relief legislation. The main argument was that such laws benefited debtor and creditor alike, since the creditors could only be harmed by the ruin of their debtors, a ruin inevitable should the rapid debt-collection system remain in effect.[65] In 1819, the Indiana legislature passed two relief laws; one increased the amount of personal property exempted from execution sales; the other stayed executions for one year unless the creditor agreed to accept at par the new paper money of the State Bank of Indiana, or to accept at par money of the other chartered banks in the state.[66] The measures passed in the Senate with only one dissenter.[67] On January 18, 1820, Indiana passed a minimum appraisal law providing for sales at a value of two-thirds of appraisal value and a one-year stay for creditors refusing these terms. The opposition to the Indiana relief laws centered on the banking proposals and the State Bank paper, rather than on the stay provision itself.

In the next session, the Indiana legislature passed a stronger minimum appraisal law, patterned after the Ohio measure. It provided that, in the case of insolvency, the sheriff request seventy-five freeholders to estimate the value of the debtor's property, and then the property could not be sold for less than two-thirds of this appraised value. If the property did not sell for at least this amount, the debtor was granted a year's stay. With almost all the freeholders being debtors, the appraisals were generally set at a very high rate, discouraging almost all forced sales.[68] In 1824, amid revived business activity, the anti-reliefers succeeded in repealing the appraisement law.

In Illinois, the major concentration in the state legislature was on the establishment of a new state-owned bank for issuing large amounts of paper money. The debtor's relief legislation was originally linked with the new bank. It provided that if creditors refused to accept the new state bank paper as payment for their debts, all executions would be stayed for nine months. Furthermore, the debtor would have the right to reclaim the property (to *replevy*) if he made full payment within three years. Thus, Illinois enacted the equivalent of a three-year stay of execution if the creditor refused to accept the new paper at par for payment of the debt.[69] Even if the creditors accepted the notes, however, the debtors could claim rights of replevy for sixty days and judgments were stayed for one month. Debt contracts explicitly made in gold and silver, and which therefore had to be repaid in kind, were stayed for a period of one to five months. As further relief for all debtors immediate judgment could only be rendered against one-third of a debt, while all real estate, except that previously mortgaged, was exempted from judgments.[70]

Interestingly enough, the most bitter opponent of the inconvertible bank paper plan—Representative Wickliff Kitchell, of rural Crawford County in eastern Illinois—introduced a substitute debt-relief program of his own, albeit more modest than the three-year replevy law. Kitchell proposed a flat one-year stay on all executions for pending judgments on past debts. The execution would apply if the creditor swore that the property was in danger of being lost, in which case the debtor would have the right to replevy the property for one year, and for two years for debts over $500. There would be no stay or replevy for debts contracted in the future. The substitute bill was rejected in the Illinois House by a vote of 16 to 10. However, the legislature passed an additional mandatory nine-month stay law on all pending executions.[71]

Extreme western Missouri, just in the process of becoming a state, was the scene of one of the most comprehensive programs of relief legislation, and also of one of the most vigorous controversies over relief. Missouri had had particularly widespread speculation in land, and incurred heavy indebtedness in the course of this speculation.[72] Most of this speculation during the prosperous postwar years, in town lots as well as in farms, was predicated on a continued heavy wave of migration to the West by men with money to spend. The wave came to a halt during the depression, adding to the crisis and fall in prices, and spreading insolvency among the debtors and landholders in the state.[73] One striking result during the era (and this was also true in Illinois) was the large number of ghost towns—built during the boom—now mute evidence of the highly erroneous expectations of a few years before. As was the case throughout the West, a good part of the indebtedness was committed in public lands and was owed to the federal government. We have already seen the action that the government took to relieve this problem. This relief did not solve the problem of the private land-debtors or of the merchants deeply in debt, who had anticipated heavy demand from relatively well-to-do immigrants. The press reported widespread imprisonments for debt and noted that few could afford to attend the sheriff's sales to purchase the debtors' property. There were many cases of forced sale of land for tax delinquency. Close to the barter of the frontier, it is not surprising that many business firms announced their willingness to take produce in payment of debts.

In the spring of 1821, public pressure erupted for relief legislation by the state, and the pro-relief forces agitated for a special session of the legislature.[74] Many newspaper articles, in April and May of 1821, cited the mass of unpayable debts and urged governmental relief. The author of one such article signed himself "Nine-Tenths of the People." [75] There had been rumors of a special session since early March, and the supporting articles were responses to these rumors.

Opposition to such legislation, however, was also vocal. As early as August 16, 1820, thirteen members of the grand jury of St. Louis—the urban center of Missouri—denounced any stay or minimum appraisal law. They declared that stay laws for *land* debts alone (which were being proposed) would be special privilege for landholders.[76] Opposition was expressed on constitutional grounds also. A citizens' meeting in May at Boonville, Cooper County, in central Missouri, denounced any debt interference legislation as immoral and unconstitutional. The sacredness of contracts was emphasized in an article in the *Missouri Gazette*, in March; the author declaring that only regular bankruptcy laws were just, and that the only leniency should be by voluntary act of the creditors themselves.

Other writers stressed the pernicious economic effect of stay and other debtors' relief laws. They declared that creditors would cease to lend their money, and that such laws would interrupt business calculation and discourage regular trade. The laws would only aggravate the crisis further.[77]

Despite this strong opposition, on April 24 the Governor called a special session to be conveyed on June 1, ostensibly only to consider imminent statehood. The conservative forces sensed that the major aim was relief, however, and became very vocal in opposing the expected storm. The Jackson *Independent Patriot,* from rural southeastern Missouri, and the St. Charles *Missourian* took the lead in expressing fears of a replevin law. This opposition was echoed by most of the other leading newspapers, such as the *Missouri Intelligencer* and the St. Louis *Enquirer.*[78]

The fears of the conservatives proved justified. In his message of June 4, Governor Alexander McNair cited the "Pecuniary embarrassments . . . heretofore unknown to us," and five days later a debtors' relief bill was introduced in the House.[79] The bill, which became law in this session, provided for a two-and-one-half-year moratorium for executions on *land* debts only. Under the law, the debtor could at any time replevy all land sold at sheriff's auction by a mere payment of his debt plus 10 percent interest. The theory of the legislation was that most Missourians in the state were landholders, and that therefore this form of relief was particularly needed. It was hoped that in two and one half years revived prosperity would permit the farmer-debtors to keep their land. The special session also established a state loan office to issue paper money, reduced the penalties of imprisonment for debt, and exempted various personal necessaries from forced sales at auction.

The major act of the special session was the establishment of the loan office. When the fall session convened in November, the relief forces were anxious to enlarge the system through a strong stay and minimum appraisal law. This law was desired for its own sake, as well as to assist circulation of the new notes, and to supersede the previous law that applied only to land. The proposed law became the most vehemently debated issue of the fall session. Governor McNair's opening message was extremely cautious. He hoped for "some effective plan of relief" which would "blend with our humanity for the unfortunate debtor a due respect for the principles of the Constitution and the rights of creditors." [80] On this hotly controversial issue, the Governor was leaving the initiative strictly to the legislature. The battle was extremely close in the House, which at one time rejected the bill by a tie vote of 21 to 21, but the bill finally passed, after high pressure by the relief forces, on a vote of 23 to 18. The bill barely passed the Senate by a vote of 7 to 5 and became law.[81] The voting on the stay-minimum appraisal law, as well as on the loan office bill, cut sharply across sectional lines. The constituencies, such as St. Louis, Jackson, and Boonville, were closely divided within themselves.[82]

Considered by the relief forces—headed by Representative Duff Green—as the climax of the relief program, this law featured a minimum appraisal provision.[83] In each township, the county court was to appoint three people to appraise the worth of the debtor's property. The creditor was forced to accept the property at least at two-thirds of the official value. On the other hand, if, at the public sale, the property sold for *more* than two-thirds the official appraisal, the creditor was still entitled to only two-thirds of the sale price, while the debtor could keep the remainder. If the creditor refused to accept the property under this provision, the debtor was granted a stay of two and one half years in payment.

This was a very strong minimum appraisal law, yet the relief forces were not satisfied. They were disappointed that the law did not force the creditor to accept the new loan office certificates as an alternative to the two-and-one-half-year stay. Without such a clause the law was too narrow of application. Consequently, the relief forces were able to pass a supplementary stay law, which gave the creditor the choice of accepting two-thirds of the appraised value of the property *in loan-office certificates* at par or suffer a two-and-one-half-year stay.[84] Again, the division in the legislature was very close, 17 to 15 in the House and 6 to 4 in the Senate, and again the voting cut across sectional lines in every county.[85]

During the course of relief agitation in the summer and fall of 1821, the bulk of the Missouri press swung over to support the relief program. The opposition branded the relief laws as the work of selfish groups of "spendthrifts" and "big speculators" working their influence on the state legislature. The theme of the opposition, as in the case of public land debtors described previously, was that the law was being pushed by bankrupt speculators and spendthrifts, and not by the "honest" debtors, although no criterion was laid down to distinguish between these groups of debtors.[86] The speculators were also accused of buying the support of the press.[87] Another common opposition theme held that pressure for relief came from the *wealthy* debtors rather than from the mass of poor. Thus, the *Missouri Republican* declared that the relief legislation was intended to preserve the "wealthy debtor in his palace," and that, in general, it benefited the dishonest man and burdened the just.[88]

As was the case with most debtors' relief and monetary expansion laws passed in this period, the stay laws ran into trouble with the courts and were declared unconstitutional by the State Circuit Courts in July, 1822. The furious relief advocates called for a purge of the judiciary, and the battle over the relief issue continued to rage.[89] In the fall of 1821, before the climactic stay law legislation, the elections, drawn on the relief question, had yielded victory for the relief forces. Thus, in October, 1821, Pierre Chouteau, merchant and son of an eminent family in the state, ran as a debtors' relief candidate. He defeated Robert Walsh, running in opposition in a special election for State Senator from St. Louis. A similar victory for the relief forces was gained in Howard County, a rural district in central Missouri, adjacent to Boonville. Now, after the court decision and a turning of the tide in public opinion, the general election to the legislature on August 7, 1822 hinged directly on relief as the critical issue. The relief forces advocated constitutional amendments to smash judicial opposition to the relief laws, while the opposition advocated repeal of the entire relief structure. The elections were a victory for the anti-relief forces. The pivotal city of St. Louis returned three reliefers and three anti-reliefers in the House, and John S. Ball, an anti-reliefer, to the State Senate; and in another special Senatorial election in St. Louis, in October, 1822, an anti-reliefer triumphed.[90]

Sensing the political currents, Governor McNair, who had started it all the previous year, strongly recommended, in his opening message of November 4, the elimination of the chaos by repealing all of the relief laws.[91] He declared that they had not proved successful in alleviating the financial distress, and that, furthermore, the crisis was ending from natural causes. In final analysis, the only true remedies were the gradual ceasing of speculation, a change from luxury to economy, avoidance of debts or extravagance, and a growth in industry and enterprise. The legislature lost no time in complying with McNair's wishes. On November 27, a bill to repeal the stay-minimum appraisal laws was introduced and passed by a large majority.

In early 1821, Louisiana passed—with little or no controversy—a stay law suspending execution sales for two and one half years and imposing a minimum of personal property which could be retained by the debtor.[92]

Relatively developed, compared to the other western states, were Tennessee and Kentucky. These were the best known centers of debtors' relief agitation and legislation. Tennessee had experienced a pronounced boom since the war with the opening of new lands, increased production of cotton at booming prices, and a great expansion of the credit system.[93] The monetary contraction and the fall in the cotton price wreaked extensive damage on the numerous debtors, particularly in the cotton-growing regions. Insolvencies and forced sales abounded.[94]

As in many other states, debtors turned to the state legislature for aid.[95] The center of relief agitation was the predominantly cotton-growing middle Tennessee, particularly Nashville, the most populous city in the state. The acknowledged leader of the relief agitation was the wealthy, influential merchant and politician, Felix Grundy of Nashville. Grundy, formerly Chief Justice of the Kentucky Court of Appeals and a leading Representative in the Tennessee legislature, became a candidate again for his old post as State Representative in the summer of 1819, basing his campaign on a relief platform.[96] The relief proposals centered on the banking system and on stay laws for debts. Many other legislative candidates also ran on a relief platform and were active in proposing plans of action. Many of the candidates gathered in the Davidson County courthouse (Nashville is in Davidson County), on July 19, to discuss the need for relief. They were supported by the influential

Nashville *Clarion*, which urged the legislature to suspend execution of debt judgments.[97] Grundy and numerous other reliefers were elected, and, soon after the legislature opened, Grundy opened the relief struggle by introducing a set of resolutions.[98] The resolutions began by pointing to the distress prevailing in the state, which "requires the early and serious attention of the legislature." The Grundy resolution did not mention a stay law, but implied it and urged that creditors be prohibited from forcing debtors to pay in *specie*. It advocated forcing creditors to accept the notes of state banks at par or forfeit their debt.

Following up his resolutions, Felix Grundy introduced a bill in the Tennessee House staying all executions of judgments for two years, unless creditors accepted notes of the leading banks in the state at par.[99] Passage of this bill in October, 1819, by an overwhelming vote of 24 to 10 in the House and a similar majority in the Senate, constituted the first major victory for the debtors' relief forces in Tennessee.[100] Another conditional stay law passed in the 1819 session was one introduced by Representative William Williams, of Davidson County. This provided that when a *bank* was the creditor and refused to accept at par, in payment of a debt judgment, either its own notes or the notes of the two leading banks in Tennessee, the execution would be stayed for two years. This bill was passed overwhelmingly with very little opposition. Another aid to the debtors passed in this session was a bill by Williams tightening the usury laws, by setting maximum rates of interest on loans.[101]

During early 1820, relief agitation grew in strength, this time centering on proposals for a new state loan office or bank to issue inconvertible paper along with further stay provisions. The reliefers called for a special session in the spring of 1820. It is interesting to note the Nashville *Clarion* proudly proclaimed that several men of wealth had taken the lead in the call for an extra session. Typical of the appeals for a special relief session was the petition of citizens from Williamson County, adjacent to Davidson.[102] The petition pointed to the great decline in the price of produce, to the contraction of bank credit, and to the consequent multiplying suits for debt payment. Blame was laid on the "avidity of the creditors to collect," which seems to increase "in an inverse ratio to the ability of the debtor to pay." Unless relief were offered quickly, warned the petition, most of the citizens would suffer insolvency and ruin. East Tennessee, the region centering on Knoxville as its leading city, was largely opposed to the relief program and to the proposed special session.[103] Typical was the vigorous disapproval of the Knoxville *Register*.[104] It declared that the people were opposed, and charged that the huge number of petitions for relief and a special session, as described in the Nashville press, had come from only three counties endorsed by "but half a dozen signatures." The honest, the industrious, the prudent citizens needed no relief and desired no special session. The demand for relief, charged the *Register*, was coming from those who had made purchases without capital, and lived in luxury beyond their means. "Now that they have run their race, they wish the Legislature to pass a law that they may keep their honest creditor from recovering his debts." A grand jury from Sumner County, adjacent to Davidson County, declared that those seeking relief were not the poor and needy but those large businesses and speculators who had extended their credit with the banks; moreover, only these wealthy debtors would benefit from relief.[105] The *Courier*, from Murfreesboro, a town near Nashville, replied that the debtors' distress was not owing to their own imprudence but to a "fall of foreign markets, and the domestic scarcity of a circulating medium," resulting in a great fall in the value of property. Legislative interference, it concluded, was necessary to save the people from bankruptcy and ruin.[106] The East Tennessee opposition had a different view of the consequences of stay legislation. Thus, the Knoxville *East Tennessee Patriot* admitted that a stay law might give temporary relief to some people, but warned that its impairment of contracts would lead to increased rather than diminished bankruptcies.[107] The East Tennesseans had even made a strong but unsuccessful effort to nip the debtors' relief campaign in the bud by sending Enoch Parsons, losing gubernatorial candidate in 1819, to Nashville to campaign against Felix Grundy's election.[108]

While the opponents of debtors' relief charged that wealthy debtors were behind the movement, the relief forces made a similar charge. The Nashville *Clarion,* ignoring the eastern Tennessee opposition and its own praise for the wealthy supporters of relief, bluntly charged that the only opposition to relief came from land speculators and the "monied aristocracy of Nashville" opposed to the relief of the people.[109] In fact, much vigorous opposition to debtors' relief centered in Nashville and Davidson County itself, despite the fact that the relief forces stemmed from that area. The Nashville *Gazette* retorted to the *Clarion's* charge that in the opposition there were "men who have money—and men who have none." The opposition to relief legislation cut across lines of wealth.[110]

Governor Joseph McMinn, elected in 1819, granted the wish of Grundy and the relief forces, and called a special session for June 26.[111] In his opening address,[112] McMinn pointed to the unprecedented general pressure and urged that debtors be saved from destruction. "The people should be made to see," he declared,

> that public agents . . . have not abandoned them in their affliction. Men's confidence in each other's solvency will be restored; the thirst for purchasing at sheriff's sales will be allayed; treasures which are now hoarded up to be used in fattening on calamity will be drawn out and again circulated in the ordinary channels of useful industry.

Thus, McMinn emphasized the ending of hoarding as a prime element in recovery. The relief advocates agreed with their opponents that the restoration of confidence was important to recovery, but urged that only aid to debtors would accomplish this end.

To gain the objective of relief, Governor McMinn advocated a loan office measure to increase the supply of paper money, a stay law, and a minimum appraisal law. The major controversy in that session was the loan office bill. He recommended a stay law as a corollary to the loan office bill, providing for a stay of execution for two years, unless the creditor were willing to accept the new paper notes at par in payment for the debt. McMinn further suggested a minimum appraisal law which would compel the creditor to accept the debtors' property at a valuation fixed by a governmentally appointed committee of arbitration.

The next day, June 27, Felix Grundy moved to refer the three proposals of the Governor to a Joint Select Committee on the Pecuniary Distress. The committee included the leading anti-relief stalwarts in the legislature, in addition to Grundy. But the McMinn-Grundy leadership counted on Representative Samuel Anderson, from Robertson County in mid-Tennessee, to cast the deciding vote in favor of the relief proposals. Instead, Anderson turned against the stay and appraisal bills and caused alarm in the relief camp by submitting the committee report on the next day, rejecting any stay or minimum appraisal law as "inexpedient and unpolitic." [113] Grundy acted swiftly, however, and a day later succeeded in "packing" the committee with four more of his supporters, with Grundy himself becoming chairman. Backed by petitions from citizens of Warren and Smith Counties (in mid-Tennessee) supporting the relief proposals, Grundy reported the stay and loan office bill to the House on July 4. He allowed the minimum appraisal bill to die in committee, rejecting it as too extreme.

In the debate on and eventual passage of the bills, most of the effort was centered on the loan office. The stay law was opposed almost singlehandedly by Representative Williams, now a staunch opponent of relief. He moved to strike out the requirement that the creditor must receive loan-office notes or suffer a two-year stay in execution. This amendment was overwhelmingly defeated by a vote of fourteen to three, despite a petition from rural Giles County of mid-Tennessee, condemning the law as "impolitic and improper."[114] Williams tried a similar motion a week later, but lost by a vote of eleven to four, and the stay provision became law along with the new state bank.[115]

Although the relief movement triumphed in 1819 and 1820, the climate of public opinion had changed sharply by mid-1821. The new state bank and its paper were not faring well, the nationwide depression was receding, and the Supreme Court of Tennessee handed down a decision in June declaring the stay provision unconstitutional for compelling acceptance of the new bank notes. In the gubernatorial campaign of the summer of 1821, *both* candidates vigorously opposed the relief program. Colonel Edward Ward and William Carroll were wealthy merchants and prominent citizens of Nashville, and both were firm friends of Andrew Jackson. It is instructive that Carroll ran his campaign as the "people's candidate" against the wealthier Ward.

Carroll's decisive victory in the gubernatorial race did not intimidate Governor McMinn, who, in his farewell message to the legislature, again urged a minimum appraisal law, and also suggested a replevin law, so that the debtors could win back their forfeited property.[116] McMinn's proposals were referred to Felix Grundy's Committee on Pecuniary Embarrassments, and Grundy's report signaled the turn of the tide for the relief movement in Tennessee. Grundy noted that the greatest distress during the crisis had been caused by the large accumulated debt. He declared that, since 1819, three-fifths of the debt owed to easterners had been liquidated, and that this relieved the pressure on the numerous Tennesseans in debt to eastern creditors. The economy was reviving, and the situation was no longer grave. He therefore rejected an appraisal law as a violation of contract, but staunchly defended the worth of the stay law in averting debtors' ruin.[117] Later, Grundy attacked the courts for ruling against the stay laws, and was joined by the Knoxville *Intelligencer* and the Nashville *Whig*.

The anti-relief tone of the new administration was set by Governor Carroll's opening address.[118] It was mainly devoted to paper money, but he also attacked the stay and proposed appraisal and replevin laws as violations of contract.[119] Carroll declared that the relief measures had brought momentary relief for some, at the expense of increasing the general distress, and had caused the ruin of thousands through sudden fluctuations of credit and extreme depreciation of currency. The debtors' situation was still troublesome despite Grundy's optimism, and the press continued to advertise many sheriff's sales. The relief forces again tried to pass a stay and an appraisal law, but without success. As a matter of fact, Grundy managed to push through another minimum appraisal law in October, 1823, but the court decision effectively ended any such stay law in Tennessee. By the fall of 1822, Governor Carroll could report a virtual ending of the economic crisis in Tennessee.[120]

The citizens of the state of Kentucky found themselves heavily burdened with insolvent debtors and forced sheriffs' sales for execution of suits against debtors.[121] As in Tennessee, the major focus of agitation on the state level was the banking system; but agitation over stay laws was also widespread. In Kentucky, a stay law had long been embedded in the state's legislation. As early as 1792, the state had passed a minimum appraisal law; and it had passed a stay law in 1814–15, providing a twelve-month stay should any creditor refuse to accept at par the notes of the state's leading bank—the Bank of Kentucky—and a mandatory three-month stay even if the creditor accepted the notes.[122]

The campaign of the relief forces was waged largely over stay-replevin legislation, and the elections in the fall of 1819 were an overwhelming victory for the relief forces. In the bitter fights over proposed stay legislation, two new newspapers were inaugurated in the city of Frankfort: the *Patriot*, to support the relief program, and the *Spirit of '76*, to oppose it.[123] The first relief act to pass was an "emergency" stay law, staying all executions for sixty days; this was passed on December 16, 1819.[124] Governor Gabriel Slaughter, opposed to relief, vetoed the law, but the legislature was able to override the veto. A very strong stay law was passed the following February 11, providing a mandatory one-year stay of execution *if* the creditor accepted Bank of Kentucky notes at par in payment, or a two-year stay if the creditor refused.

The crisis was intensified by the alarm felt by creditors at this law and by their growing reluctance to lend.[125] The depression continued in full force during 1820, and the reliefers began to concentrate their attention on proposals for a new state bank. Postponement of payment does not after all liquidate the debt burden, and it has been estimated that over $2 million of debt was under execution in this period. A bank was expected to grant indirect but effective relief by supplying new money to debtors. Passage of such a measure was assured by the election of Governor John Adair, a leader of the relief forces. A bank was established and, further, a new stay law passed on Christmas Day, 1820. The new law extended existing provisions, but now provided a stay of two years, unless the creditor accepted either Bank of Kentucky or the new state-owned Bank of Commonwealth notes. The law gave preference to the new bank by continuing the mandatory one-year stay even if the creditor accepted Bank of Kentucky notes, while only imposing a three-month stay for acceptance of Bank of Commonwealth notes. This was succeeded by a full mandatory twelve-month stay in February,

1820. Further relief to debtors was granted by a law exempting various tools and implements from forced sale for debt payments and by special stays for executions on real estate.

Throughout 1820, the cherished goal of the relief forces was the passage of a general "property law," which would have been the most drastic relief legislation in the nation. This would have indefinitely postponed all sales of property under execution. However, this ambitious attempt never came to a vote. In the fall of 1821, the legislature moved again to block the infuriated creditors; by December, 1821, a minimum appraisal law was passed. It prohibited the sale of property at forced sale for less than three-quarters the value set by a jury, unless the creditor agreed to receive Bank of Commonwealth or Bank of Kentucky notes in payment.[126]

For a few years, the debtors reaped a substantial harvest from the stay and from bank legislation. The Bank of Commonwealth notes soon depreciated to half, as compared to specie. The juries and judges of Kentucky during 1821 and 1822 adopted a "scaling system" in their verdicts on damages and executions for debt contracts. For example: if a creditor sued a debtor for payment on a debt of a hundred dollars, and the debtor had already paid fifty dollars, the magistrate or jury "assumed" that the fifty "dollars" paid consisted of specie rather than notes (which, of course, was not the case), on the ground that there was no proof to the contrary. Then, as a one dollar specie was now worth two dollars of Commonwealth notes, the debt was judged fully canceled, and, in addition, a judgment for court costs was levied against the creditor.[127]

The proponents of debtors' relief argued that the legislature was obliged to provide relief in times of distress. Indeed, they considered themselves generous for not going so far as to repudiate all private debts completely.[128] The opposition assailed the measures as repudiating contracts, and asserted that the only remedies to help the debtors in the long run were thrift and industry. Stay laws were attacked as leaving the creditors' property in the hands of speculators and as greatly hampering credit.[129] The bitterness of the opposition increased as the relief system continued, and, as the economy recovered, it succeeded in turning the relief tide. As early as the 1822–23 session, the legislature reduced the stay provision from two years to one year, and by 1824 the stay laws were repealed.[130] In the meanwhile, the decision of the state courts that the relief legislation was unconstitutional precipitated a vigorous and prolonged political controversy over the judiciary, the anti-reliefers finally winning by 1826.

One of the most interesting approaches to the problem of debtor's relief was that of Amos Kendall, at this time editor of the influential Frankfort *Argus of Western America*, and later one of the chief theoreticians of the war against the Second Bank of the United States. Kendall, though not completely opposed to relief, was disturbed at some of the extreme stay legislation, particularly the proposed property law, which would have repudiated all debts. In a series of articles in the *Argus*,[131] Kendall considered one of the favorite relief arguments: that debtors were unduly burdened because they had borrowed when the money unit had a lower value in purchasing power, and must now repay their debt when money had a higher value. Kendall began with a discussion of utility, developing in essence the subjective theory of value and the law of diminishing utility. He deduced that, since value depended on the desires of men, and since these desires were always changing, desires and values could not be reduced to any standard of measurement. A unit of measure was always fixed, and yet all values were continually changing. Hence, there was no such thing as a standard of value, and money could not be used for such a standard. Turning to money, Kendall traced its deveolpment from barter and indirect exchange, until the money-commodity became a general medium of exchange. This process revealed that money was simply a commodity, albeit the most useful and exchangeable one—a commodity the value of which was always changing. Therefore, money could by no means serve as a standard of value, and from this Kendall deduced that the relief argument, resting on the assumption of money as a standard of value, was untenable.[132] In the following year, Kendall denounced wasteful governmental expenditures and concluded emphatically that the legislature could not relieve debts. "The people must pay their own debts at last." They must rely on their own power and resources and not on that of the banks or legislature.[133]

Thus, faced with widespread debts and insolvencies, states in every region were confronted with, and wrangled over, debtors' relief proposals. Stay laws were considered in the eastern legislatures of Delaware, New Jersey, New York, Maryland, Vermont, Massachusetts, Pennsylvania, and Virginia, as well as in the western states of Ohio, Indiana, Illinois, Missouri, Louisiana, Tennessee, and Kentucky. Minimum appraisal laws were also considered in almost all of these states. Stay laws were passed in Maryland, Vermont, Ohio, Indiana, Illinois, Missouri, Louisiana, Tennessee, and Kentucky; minimum appraisal laws were passed in far fewer states: Ohio, Indiana, Missouri, Pennsylvania, and Kentucky.

If final passage is considered, the western states were the stronghold of relief measures. However, Pennsylvania passed a combined minimum appraisal and stay law, and there were at least sizable minorities demanding stay and minimum appraisal laws in such important and conservative states as Delaware, New Jersey, New York, and Virginia. Vermont and Maryland passed stay laws, and New York modified its judgment procedure slightly to ease the strain of insolvent debtors. Rhode Island eased the burdens of debtors to banks. Neither was the western experience uniform. Ohio and Indiana, for example, passed their legislation overwhelmingly, while there was bitter controversy in Missouri, Tennessee, and Kentucky. Four of the western states passed appraisal laws, while they could not pass in Illinois and Tennessee.

Within the states there was a noticeable lack of sharp division along sectional lines in controversy over this legislation. Within urban centers and rural counties, there was sharp controversy over relief, and tides of opinion impressed themselves in turn up on all sections.

Debtors' relief proposals were often tied to schemes for monetary expansion, which furnished one of the richest areas of controversy during the depression.

III

STATE PROPOSALS AND ACTIONS FOR MONETARY EXPANSION

Much of the response of the American people to the depression centered on monetary problems. One major group of proposals advocated that governmental measures—federal or state—combat the monetary scarcity. Since the banks were chartered by the states, the supply of money was largely a state problem, and the bulk of the discussion was waged at the state level.

The new state of Alabama, which entered the Union in 1819, had been a particular beneficiary of the postwar boom, with its great rise in cotton prices and its influx of immigrants. Alabama was the major center of speculation in public land purchases. Of the $22 million of public land debt outstanding in 1820, half was located in Alabama. Speculation in public lands was financed by the banks and spurred by the high price of cotton. Credit in Alabama was financed by three banks chartered in 1816 and 1818. It was also financed by new banks in Tennessee and Kentucky, the debtors migrating from these states to Alabama in the boom years.[1] The opinion was common in Alabama that banks were great engines for developing the country's resources, particularly the potential cotton lands of the area. Banks were expected to create money and increase capital.[2]

Alabama was divided into two separate trading areas, with little connection between them. Northern Alabama was connected with the Tennessee Valley and used Tennessee bank notes; its farmers sold in local markets or floated produce to New Orleans. Southern Alabama sent its cotton to Mobile and used Georgia and South Carolina bank notes. The chief bank in northern Alabama, the Merchants' and Planters' Bank of Huntsville, was greatly affected by the suspensions of specie payment of the Tennessee banks during the crisis of 1819 and was forced to suspend specie payments in 1820. The notes of the Huntsville Bank depreciated rapidly with respect to specie although they continued to circulate at par with Tennessee bank notes. Specie and par bank notes began to pass from circulation into hoards. Northern Alabama suffered from a depreciating currency. Southern Alabama, on the other hand, possessed two sound banks, but they were very small and were of little importance. This area used the notes of solvent banks in South Carolina and especially Georgia. Both regions abounded in complaints of a "scarcity of money."

As a remedy for the monetary scarcity, business houses began to print "small change tickets," declared to be worth twenty-five cents, and municipalities also engaged in this practice. There were widespread irregularities and forgeries. Finally, the Alabama legislature, in 1821, prohibited the issuance of private change tickets, leaving the issue of small notes to municipal governments.[3]

One particularly important monetary problem was the suspension of payment by the Huntsville Bank and the consequent depreciation of its notes. In 1821, the legislature refused to abide by the existing law which forbade accepting notes of non-specie paying banks in taxes. The decision to accept the depreciated notes was defended by Governor Thomas Bibb as necessary to avoid excessive harshness toward the citizens of northern Alabama.[4] This state forbearance bolstered the acceptance and raised the exchange rate of the Huntsville notes throughout the state. The Alabama legislature went further and issued Treasury notes payable in the depreciating currency of the Huntsville Bank. Under the government umbrella, the Huntsville Bank issued large quantities of notes, which sank to a 25–50 percent discount. The Treasury warrants depreciated correspondingly.[5]

With such disappointing results, the legislators began to look to another solution for the monetary difficulties: the establishment of a large, state-wide, state-owned bank. The constitution of Alabama in 1819 had specifically authorized the establishment of a state bank, with the state to own two-fifths of the stock.[6]

The legislature therefore chartered the Bank of the State of Alabama, on December 21, 1820, with a very large authorized capital of $2 million to which the state would subscribe $800 thousand. Unfortunately for the plan, however, the constitution had also provided that half of the capital stock must be paid in specie before beginning operations, and no such public subscriptions were forthcoming. The Bank remained a stillborn project.[7]

The legislature adopted another plan the following year: to consolidate the three private banks of the state into an amalgamated state bank. This bank plan was vetoed by the new Governor, Israel Pickens. The ostensible reason for the veto was that the plan linked a state bank with private banks. Actually, Governor Pickens was politically powerful in Southern Alabama, a region that had been angered by the actions of the Huntsville Bank and at the favoritism shown toward it by Governor Bibb and the previous legislators.[8] For his veto, Pickens was hailed by many of his followers as the savior of Alabama. Pickens's veto was followed by barring the depreciated Huntsville Bank notes from acceptance in taxes. The result was a further rapid depreciation of Huntsville notes.

It is true that Pickens's actions removed the state prop from the non-specie paying Huntsville Bank and defeated one plan for a state-owned bank. But Pickens was not necessarily opposed to state measures for monetary expansion. On the contrary, he advocated a state bank that would be wholly state-owned, non-specie paying, and would use forthcoming public land revenue for eventual redemption. Such a bank was finally established in December, 1823, but came too late to be considered an anti-depression measure. While Pickens and the Huntsville group each favored some form of monetary expansion, many in the commercial communities were opposed to the whole idea, in particular the newspapers of the metropolis Mobile.

The Alabama experience highlights the two basic measures for monetary expansion advocated or effected in the states: 1) measures to bolster the acceptance of private bank notes, where the banks had suspended specie payment and where the notes were tending to depreciate; and 2) the creation of state-owned banks to issue inconvertible paper notes on a large scale. Of course, the very fact of permitting non-specie paying banks to continue in operation, was a tremendous aid to the banks.

State-owned banks also existed in the neighboring state of Louisiana and in the territory of Mississippi, but these had been established prior to the crisis, and played a conservative rather than an expansionist role. The Bank of Mississippi, the only bank in the infant territory, had been formed from a private bank in early 1818, and was partially government-owned. The bank was partly independent of the government, but its notes were the legal tender for the territory. The major struggle in the Mississippi legislature occurred over a bill by Representative Harman Runnels, of Lawrence County in central Mississippi, to authorize the receipt in taxes of bank paper from Alabama, Georgia, and South Carolina. This passed the legislature after a largely sectional fight between the eastern and central sections of the state, on the one hand—oriented toward the southeastern states—and more wealthy, commercial Natchez, leading town in the state and oriented toward Louisiana and the Mississippi River. Governor George Poindexter vetoed the bill, and it failed to pass over his veto.[9]

The Louisiana State Bank, established in early 1818,[10] continued to be conducted with great caution. The Report of the House Committee on the Louisiana State Bank, in the 1819 legislature, praised the bank for its conservative discount policy and declared that the bank was necessary because of the great scarcity of specie in Louisiana and adjoining states.[11] In fact, the Committee suggested that the bank could perhaps be more liberal in granting loans.

In Louisiana the crisis and the scarcity of money led to a tightening of credit rather than expansion. Typical was the reaction of the New Orleans *Louisiana Gazette*, which feared that "too much regulation" was becoming the order of the day, with "paper systems to substitute for gold and silver"—"one of the hobby horses of our times." [12]

The state of Georgia had invested in private banks from the establishment of its first bank of 1807.[13] These investments were for revenue purposes, however, rather than efforts to expand the supply of money. Before the war, revenues from the state's investment in banks had nearly covered the total state expenditure, so that, after the war, the state increased its investment, culminating in the largely state-owned Bank of Darien, established in 1818. The latter bank was the depository of state funds, capitalized at $1.6 million of which over $600 thousand was paid up, and had branches throughout the state.[14] A proposal for an agricultural bank, however, was turned down by the legislature at the same time.[15] Banks were welcomed also for their aid in supplying money and credit to the merchants and planters of the state, and the Bank of the United States branch at Savannah was originally welcomed for the same reason. The branch expanded credit, while the Georgia banks engaged in heavy expansion of credit for purchases of Alabama public lands. When the panic struck, the Bank of the United States pursued a policy of forced contraction of the notes of its branches, leading to calls on the state banks to pay their balances due to the United States Bank. In Georgia, these balances were particularly heavy, because of the widespread use of Georgia bank notes in payment for the Alabama lands, and the deposit by the federal government of these funds in the Bank of the United States branch at Savannah.

The contraction policy of the Bank of the United States resulted in mounting bitterness against it among the local banks and the population of the state. A joint committee of local banks charged a plot on the part of the bank to destroy them.[16] In 1820, the Georgia legislature suspended the legal 25 percent interest penalty provision for nonpayment of specie by its banks, in so far as the nonpayment applied to debts owed to the Bank of the United States.[17] In the summer of 1821, the two Savannah banks (the Planters' Bank and the Bank of the State) took advantage of this provision to suspend specie payments to the Bank of the United States, while continuing them to individual noteholders. In December, 1821, the Georgia legislature again voided the interest penalty on nonpayment of notes to the Bank of United States and extended this action to all cases of nonpayment. In recommending this action, the joint committee on the state of the banks of the Georgia legislature attacked the Bank of the United States Savannah branch for refusing to expand its note issue, and for draining the state banks of specie.[18]

The Bank of the United States sued in the courts, and the Supreme Court of the United States voided the Georgia law in 1824, whereupon Georgia repealed the law.[19] Meanwhile this severe action by the Georgia legislature and banks disturbed Secretary William H. Crawford, one of Georgia's leading politicians, and he took steps to ease the Georgia monetary situation. He ordered the Treasury office in Alabama to deposit all its funds in the Bank of Darien instead of the Bank of United States branch at Savannah. In its new role as Treasury fiscal agent, the Bank of Darien was able to continue the expansion of discounts and note issues, that it had originally based on the state's stock subscription at the opening of the bank. In 1822, when the depression was over, the Treasury removed its funds from the Bank of Darien and returned them to the Savannah branch of the Bank of the United States. As a result of its previous expansion and renewed pressure by the United States Bank, the Bank of Darien suspended specie payment, its notes depreciating rapidly by 1824.[20]

The justification for the Georgia government's action in protecting the banks against the specie demands of the Bank of the United States was provided by Governor John Clark in his message to the legislature of November 7, 1820.[21] Countering fears of depreciation, Clark admitted that the action might cause Georgia notes to depreciate outside the state, but justified it as preserving an important source of state revenue—the state's bank investments—and as insuring "a circulating medium sufficient to supply the real wants of our citizens."[22]

By the end of 1822, however, Clark had changed his mind on banks, which by now had all suspended specie payments. He declared his readiness to dispense with them altogether. Clark asserted that "the opinion . . . almost universally prevails, that the pecuniary embarrassments of the citizens is greater in proportion as you approach the vicinity of a bank."[23]

Permitting banks to continue operations without redeeming their notes in specie was one basic means for a state to maintain or expand the supply of money in a time of financial crisis. The important neighboring state of South Carolina already had as its fiscal agent, a large state-owned bank, established in 1812 with a capitalization of $1.1 million. This Bank of the State of South Carolina, while conservatively operated, suspended specie payment on October 1, 1819, and continued operations until its resumption in 1823.[24]

Anger in the state was directed against the Bank of the United States, for the pressure on the state banks, and for the general monetary contraction.[25] Some South Carolina leaders envisioned a general suspension of specie payments in the state. Robert Y. Hayne, then Attorney General of South Carolina, anticipated that the state would be forced onto an inconvertible paper system.[26] He declared that the banks, with notes depreciating, must suspend specie payments, and he denounced agents of Virginia banks for buying up bank notes and coming to Charleston to redeem them. Hayne declared:

It seems to me that the final result will be a stoppage of specie payments by all the banks and then we will find it necessary to follow the example of Great Britain and deal on paper. The time is approaching rapidly when gold or silver will be regarded as merchandize only and bill will become the current coin.

Hayne thought that each bank could be required to maintain $1 million of government bonds ("stock") and to limit its note issue to $1.5 million. "Might not such bills constitute a circulating medium and be a legal tender?" Hayne added that the legally or constitutionally required limit would be sufficient check on the danger of an excessive issue of the inconvertible paper, and that the notes of borrowers would be as good a backing for the bank notes as specie. He recognized that to secure a stable paper it would be necessary for the states—and perhaps the nations—to act in concert. Stephen Elliott, wealthy landowner and head of the Bank of the State, also advocated an inconvertible nationwide currency, based on land for stability of value.

On the other hand, there was considerable opposition to any suspensions of specie payment. A leader in opposition was Jacob N. Cardozo, influential editor of the leading Charleston daily, the *Southern Patriot*.[27] He attacked state-owned banks including the one in his state, for a tendency to overissue their notes, and to cause excessive spending and speculation. On the other hand, he defended the Bank of the United States and its branches, the existence of which prevented excessive note issues by state banks. Cardozo was particularly angered at plans for inconvertible paper money. He denounced these alleged remedies for the crisis as the "grossest quackery." Cardozo maintained that inconvertible paper issues would aggravate rather than cure the distress. According to Cardozo, the economic difficulties were largely caused by the banks "having chocked the channel of circulation with paper." This distress had to be relieved, and the only way that this could be done was to "return to a free exchange of bank notes for specie." "There is but one mode of relief," he declared, "and that is the rigid enforcement of specie payments." The excess of bank notes raised prices of staples and other products too high, and this had practically ended the American export trade. Only rigid enforcement of specie payment would permit removal of the excess paper and the consequent revival of exports.[28]

There was a considerable amount of controversy in adjacent North Carolina over the actions of the banks in continuing operations while suspending specie payments, and over the role of the Bank of the United States. One of the leading advocates of inconvertible paper was the prominent Archibald D. Murphey, Chairman of the Legislative Committee on the Board of Internal Improvements. Murphey wrote to Colonel William Polk, of the State Bank of North Carolina (a private bank), attacking the Bank of United States branches for ruining banks and individuals, and calling for paper unredeemable in specie.[29] To Murphey, the Bank of the United States constituted the "greatest crime in years." Murphey squarely faced the problem of depreciation:

> [The] true interest of the state [is] to have a paper that has a par value at home . . . given to it by . . . the confidence of the people, and which will not pay debts or [circulate] distant markets without a loss. . . . The true mode of fixing our permanent prosperity is to adopt a system of policy as will give us a home market. Our money will easily sustain its credit among its own citizens, and if we had markets at home it could not travel much abroad.[30]

To help put this plan into effect, Murphey recommended that the legislature "throw" money into circulation in expenditure on public works, to the extent desired by the banks.

The North Carolina banks were not penalized by the legislature for suspending specie payments to those it considered "brokers," while maintaining payments to others. North Carolina was particularly exercised over the problem of the "money brokers," who were generally denounced in the press. This institution grew up, almost inevitably, in response to the universally varying depreciation of bank notes. Money brokers, centering in the large cities, would buy up the notes of distant banks at a discount, and then send agents to these banks with packets of notes to claim redemption in specie at par. Banks with depreciating notes liked having as wide a circulation for their notes as possible, but naturally did not like out-of-town brokers descending upon them claiming payment. Many citizens were tempted to agree, since they found it easy to blame foreign brokers for their plight and the plight of the local banks.

Thus, the influential Raleigh *Star*, early in the crisis, denounced northern money brokers and accused them of being responsible for the monetary contraction and suspensions of specie payments in North Carolina.[31] The *Star* suggested that the banks should refuse to pay these demands for specie and advocated outlawing the buying and selling of coin at a premium for bank notes. The paper accused the brokers of being speculators, amassing princely fortunes, and of being obstructionists. The *Star* also went so far as to suggest a state loan office to issue inconvertible Treasury notes eventually redeemed out of the revenues from taxes and the sale of state lands. The *Star* presented a detailed plan for the number of branches and suggested the sizable note issue of $30 thousand to be loaned at low rates of interest, covering only the expenses of the institution.

Typical of the attack on money brokers was an article by a "Gentleman in North Carolina," pointing to the recent withdrawal by two New York City brokers of $100 thousand in specie from the state. "Gentleman" charged that the "brokers are trying to break every bank in the country." [32]

Defending the actions of the banks, "A Citizen" wrote to a friend in the North Carolina legislature that it should not compel them to resume specie payment. The banks had not overissued their notes, he declared; if they had, why was there still a general complaint of scarcity of money? [33] The writer also made a point similar to Murphey's, that the fact that North Carolina bank notes were not depreciated *within* the state proved that they were not overissued.

Backed by government and much of public opinion, an agreement not to pay specie to brokers or their agents was made at Fayetteville, in June, 1819, by the three leading banks—the state bank, the Bank of New Bern, and the Bank of Cape Fear. Their notes immediately fell to a 15 percent discount outside of the state. The banks, however, continued to insist that their debtors pay them in specie, although they loaned out depreciated notes. Further, the banks themselves began to send agents to New York City and elsewhere to buy up their own depreciated notes at a considerable discount and then to retire the notes.[34]

Controversy over the North Carolina bank action raged in the states. One Washington writer commended the banks as saving banks and public, and stated that unsound banks should only liquidate gradually. He suggested this action to all the states.[35] The North Carolina banks were vigorously criticized in the neighboring state of Virginia. One article in the leading Virginia newspaper, the conservative Richmond *Enquirer*, defended the brokers and asserted that the banks would suffer from the partial suspension.[36] The brokers, "Philo-Economicus" maintained, "were the only persons who kept up the value of the paper." A Virginian would take a North Carolina note at par if he knew that at any time he might sell them to brokers for Virginia paper at a 2 percent discount. Should the brokers refuse to purchase the paper, the notes would depreciate and disappear from circulation to return to the issuing bank. "Few people will be willing to take it at a loss of 8 to 10 percent, and it will therefore be driven back to the counter where it first saw the light." Thus, the individual noteholders themselves would more quickly return the notes to the bank, and the banks' partial suspension would be of little avail.

The action of the North Carolina banks also drew sharp criticism from the influential New York *Daily Advertiser,* which denounced this innovation in banking as unjustly discriminating in favor of banks as compared to ordinary debtors.[37]

In Virginia, a stronghold of financial conservatism, there was little agitation for, or consideration given to, plans for government to bolster or increase the supply of money. We have seen that Representative Miller, leader of the debtors' relief forces in Virginia, took an *anti*-bank position, as contrasted to the situation in other states. A typical Virginia attitude was expressed by a writer in the influential Richmond *Enquirer*. "Colbert" observed that all sorts of monetary and relief projects had been proposed, and that he was "alarmed at the idea of legislative interference in any form or shape." Such governmental interference would, in the long run, aggravate rather than mitigate the evil. Paper money schemes could only cause loss of confidence by driving specie out of circulation. Furthermore, bankruptcies were eliminating the evils of rashness and avarice. And if the current increase in the value of money were allowed to continue unhampered, specie would return to circulation. At this point, just when the evil paper system was being liquidated through bankruptcies, there were proposals urging Congress or the states to issue large amounts of treasury notes, benefiting only the speculator.[38]

The situation was more turbulent in Maryland. Maryland had been the scene of considerable expansion in banks and bank notes, and the Baltimore branch of the Bank of the United States was perhaps the most irresponsible of the branches, its officers engaging in lax practice and outright dishonesty. The practice of stockholders paying only the first installment of their nominal capital in specie, or the notes of specie paying banks, and the remainder in stock notes, was particularly prevalent in Maryland, notably in the country banks outside Baltimore, as was the practice of heavy borrowing by directors.[39] The panic, as a result, brought about a large number of failures of the country banks and what has been estimated as a reduction of one-third of the bank capital in the state.

The legislature moved quickly to bolster the position of the banks. As in North Carolina, there was bitter criticism of the money brokers; and the legislature, in 1819, moved to require a license of $500 per annum for money brokers, in addition to a $20 thousand bond to establish the business. A milder requirement was soon substituted, however, after the legislature realized that this law was ineffective against out-of-state brokers. More stringent was an 1819 law prohibiting the exchange of specie for Maryland bank notes at less than par value for the notes. The law—repealed after the crisis was over, in 1823—was always readily evaded, the penalty merely adding to the discount as compensation for the added risk.[40] The New York *American* aptly pointed out that the undervaluation of specie by this law would cause specie to be exported from the state and discourage its import.[41] In 1821, the legislature imposed a penalty for passing any note of a non-Maryland bank.[42]

There was considerable agitation for and against various expansionist proposals in Maryland. In the summer of 1819, three such widely scattered counties as Washington, in the north; Somerset, far down on the eastern shore; and Prince Georges, near the District of Columbia, were all the scenes of citizens' meetings, petitioning for a special session of the legislature to permit suspensions of specie payment by the Maryland banks. The banks were to be allowed to continue in operation despite the suspension.[43] A Baltimore writer pointed to England as reason for abandoning slavish devotion to specie payment in an emergency.[44] "A Farmer of Prince Georges County," in the influential Baltimore *Federal Republican*, called on all of the state to follow the example of the three counties.[45] To permit the banks to suspend specie payments would relieve the distress of the people. It was sufficient, the "Farmer" declared, for the banks to be able to pay specie for their notes at the expiration of their charters. Another writer, signing himself "Specie," was quick to reply.[46] His letter is particularly interesting as being evidence that the agitation for suspension was not an overwhelming movement in the grass-roots. "Specie" was interested in defending Prince Georges County from any inference that its citizens were anxious for such a special session. The "Farmer," he asserted, was probably a bank director; otherwise he was a propertied debtor wishing to evade payment of his just debts or to pay them in a spurious "rag" currency. Suspension of specie payment he denounced as improper, unjust, and absurd. The device, he admitted, might produce a "slight degree of temporary ease," but in the end would eventually increase our depression and distress. The writer also declared that far from the citizens' meeting of the county endorsing the proposal, the opposite was true. The meeting was called, he declared, by a few "discontented, meddling, unknown persons." At the meeting, however, the people wre unanimously opposed. He also accused the "Farmer" of obtaining his cue from "Homo"

(Thomas Law, the leading advocate of a federal inconvertible paper currency), whom he called a "notorious advocate . . . of the rag system." [47]

Typical of the opposition to banks permitting suspension of specie payment was a public meeting at Elkton, in the extreme northeastern corner of the state. The meeting was held at the very beginning of the crisis, in the fall of 1818, and was given widespread publicity by the staunch hard-money Hezekiah Niles in *Niles' Register*.[48] Niles termed the meeting a gathering of "respectable" farmers, mechanics, and laborers of Cecil County. They resolved to refuse the paper of non-specie paying banks and to receive no small-denomination notes. It was declared that refusal of the country's banks to pay specie while continuing to pay large dividends to their stockholders was a violation of their trust.

The legislature did not act to permit suspensions of specie payment. It did consider a proposal for a state loan office to increase the supply of money. A report of the proposal was given to the Maryland House by a prominent Federalist legislator, Representative Josiah F. Polk.[49] Polk supported a loan office on the grounds that the cause of the depression was reduction in the currency. The restoration of the supply of currency to its former amount would raise prices, but would not, as critics charged, hinder our exports. In fact, declared Polk, exports from the state would be *greater in monetary value,* although the quantity of goods sold might be diminished. Polk presumably believed that the demand for American exports was inelastic. The price rise would enable debtors to pay their debts on just terms equal to the terms they had originally contracted, and would also bring about more diligent cultivation of the soil. Polk's support of a state loan office, however, was very cautious in practice, since he advocated a paper currency redeemable in specie, with heavy specie reserve.

The Delaware legislature, as we have seen, rejected pleas for debtors' relief legislation, but it did permit banks to suspend specie payments during the panic and continue operations. The citizens of New Castle County, who were in the forefront of pleas for debtors' relief, also led in asking for monetary expansion. Their proposal, signed by 139 citizens, suggested that the Farmers Bank of

Delaware and the Commercial Bank of Delaware be granted renewal of their charters with the proviso that they extend all of the loans to their present debtors for three and one half years.[50] This plan was never considered by the legislature.

In the next session, however, the House Committee on Banks recommended a new system of banking in the state.[51] Under this plan, the private banks were to merge in one central bank, with branches throughout the state. The capital of the new bank would consist partially of the existing capital of the private banks and partly of new capital to be subscribed mainly by the state itself. This proposal would extend banking capital by state action, but did not involve the issue of inconvertible state paper. The proposal was amended in committee to be a planned merger of three private banks into the fourth—the Farmers' Bank of Delaware—with some capital added by the state. In the amended plan, the additional capital was scaled down from $500 thousand to $200 thousand, compared to the existing nominal bank capital of $1.1 million. The bill passed by a vote of 11 to 8 in the House, but the Senate refused to concur.

Delaware did, however, pass a law in 1820 similar to Maryland's, making it illegal for any person to exchange any bank note for less than its par value.[52] Ironically, as passed by the House, this bill was originally designed to abolish the circulation of notes of non-specie paying banks by closing down banks whose notes were not at par in Philadelphia. The Senate reversed the intent by shifting the onus for depreciation on the noteholders rather than on the banks.

In New Jersey, serious consideration was given to a state loan to persons in need, mainly debtors, upon security presented for repayment. This borderline measure—between monetary expansion and direct debtors' relief—was rejected in the same Hopkinson Report which ended the possibility of a stay law in the state.[53] Hopkinson objected that the "state has no money to lend." Only a very large sum, say half a million, could appreciably affect the situation, and this could only be obtained through borrowing. Yet, heavy taxes would be required to pay the annual interest. Furthermore, there would be a social loss of the interest earnings, during the time that must elapse between the state's borrowing and its reloaning to debtors, and, in addition, there would be losses due to expenses of distribution and expenses of recovery. Furthermore, how could the neediest give the required security? Even more fundamental was Hopkinson's objection that the loan to needy debtors would only be temporary; the debtor would simply change his creditor, and the time of debt would be extended. Addition to state debt and taxes, he declared, was no cure for the depression; the only remedies were industry, economy, and a favorable change in the European situation.

New York opinion was highly critical of all inconvertible paper schemes. Typical was an editorial in the New York *Evening Post* declaring that at least there would be no suspensions of specie payments in New York City. The attempt to raise prices by increasing the circulating medium would only make the same quantity of produce pass for a greater nominal amount in paper.[54]

Financially conservative New England also remained generally free of controversies over monetary expansion proposals.[55] It was necessary for the Joint Committee on Banks of the Massachusetts legislature, however, to consider and turn down proposals to prevent circulation of bank notes in the state at a discount. It curtly declared that the exchange value of notes must be regulated by the community itself, according to public wants and needs.[56]

In Vermont, the desire for increased money supply took the form of advocating charters for several new banks, and the battle over these charters raged furiously. Leader in the fight for the new banks was the wealthy, influential Cornelius Peter Van Ness.[57] Particularly controversial was a proposed new Bank of Burlington—the leading town in northwest Vermont. The bill was heavily favored by citizens of this area, which was a Federalist stronghold in the state. Van Ness piloted the bill through the General Assembly, passing the House in November, 1818 by a vote of 97 to 81.[58] Even so, many restrictions were imposed on the new bank. There was a penalty of 12 percent interest and forfeiture of the charter for suspending specie payment. Furthermore, the note issue was to be limited to the amount of specie plus three times the *paid-in* capital, and there were provisions for strict supervision. Even so,

Governor Jonas Galusha vetoed the bill, and the veto was sustained.[59] By a slim margin, the House refused to charter a new bank in Windham County, and five other proposed banks were rejected or refused consideration. In fact, in the three years of agitation from 1818–21, only one bank was chartered, the Bank of Brattleboro, and that over heavy opposition.

A clue to the determined opposition to new bank charters lies in the annual message of Governor Galusha to the state legislature, in the fall of 1819.[60] Galusha pointed to the general distress, the scarcity of circulating medium, and the inability of debtors to pay their debts. He reasoned that the cause of this distress was the multiplicity of banks, and that therefore adding new banks would merely aggravate the problem. Observing the various states, he declared:

In those states where the banks are the most numerous and the means of credit the most easy, the recent cry of scarcity of medium, and its consequent distresses, have been the most heard and felt.

Pennsylvania was hit heavily by the crisis and was particularly noted for extensive investigations by its legislature into the extent of, and the possible remedies for, the depression. Most notable was the special committee headed by State Senator Condy Raguet of Philadelphia. Raguet received reports of widespread depression throughout the state. After studying written testimony, sheriff's records, petitions, and answers to committee questionnaires by members of the legislature, Raguet concluded that the economic distress was unprecedented. The distress took the following forms: ruinous sacrifices of landed property at sheriff's sales for debt; forced sales of merchandise; bankruptcies in agriculture, trade, and manufacturing; a general scarcity of money, making it almost impossible to borrow; a general "suspension of labor"; general stagnation of business; suspension of manufactures, and unemployment.

Raguet tended to be conservative in his economic views. His committee report brusquely rejected any direct debtors' relief or stay law legislation. On the other hand, Raguet advocated a State Loan Office to lend paper money to distressed debtors. He suggested that the state form a $1.5 million loan office to lend to the largest possible number of sufferers, particularly farmers and manufacturers, on landed security. The loans would be at long term (from five to ten years) and the attempt would be made to exclude speculators. Raguet declared that in this crisis the paternal care of the government was necessary. Not all individuals could be saved, but many unfortunate farmers and debtors could be greatly relieved. Although the details of the plan were never clarified, it appears that, unlike the loan office plans in the western states, this proposal did not involve inconvertible state paper but rather the borrowing of money from the public and relending it to debtors. Raguet declared that such a scheme would diffuse capital and greatly benefit the community. Money would be more plentiful, for

> the plenty or scarcity of money depend no less upon the rapidity or slowness of circulation, and upon the expansion or contraction of confidence, than upon its absolute quantity.[61]

The greater the turnover of money, the more debts it could cancel.

A loan office for Pennsylvania had originally been suggested the month before by Governor William Findlay, in his annual message to the legislature.[62] Findlay suggested a state loan office fund, to draw money away "from comparative inactivity" to be loaned on landed security. This would help to check the sacrifices of property and would also "aid in giving new life and activity to numerous pursuits of productive industry, and facilitate the progress of restoration from the embarrassments." Thus, the government would cooperate in providing the citizens with relief.

Despite the initial impetus to the loan office proposal by the State Administration and the support of such an influential legislator as Raguet, the proposal met with powerful opposition. One of the most influential newspapers in the state was the Philadelphia *Aurora*, traditionally the organ of ultra-Jeffersonianism. Its editor, William Duane, was a staunch conservative on monetary matters and was in bitter political opposition to the Findlay administration.[63] In the House, Duane, a representative from Philadelphia, was named chairman of the Special Committee on the General State of the Domestic Economy.[64] In his report, Duane also stressed the widespread extent of the distress in all economic occupations throughout the state. Rejecting debtors' relief proposals as did Raguet, Duane also firmly rejected a state loan office. He declared that such proposals had always aggravated rather than removed the depression. Furthermore, pointed out Duane, lending only on landed security would be unjust and would discriminate against those who did not own landed property. Those in most distress were the speculators who had little land to pledge in security. But more important, a loan office would extend the very evils of "fictitious capital" largely responsible for the depression, would give false new hope to debtors, and would delay the vital restoration of domestic thrift. Also, Duane was highly critical on political grounds, fearing that a large class of debtors to the state would always manage to avoid repayment of their loan. Thus, the public debt would increase with no corresponding increase of capital.

Duane's report aroused a storm of controversy in the House. Leading the angry opposition was Representative Henry Jarrett, from rural Northampton County in eastern Pennsylvania. Jarrett, a minority member of the committee, who had originally called for the committee investigation to establish a loan office, objected that the Duane report opposed all the petitions from his constituents. These constituents were in great distress and were demanding some relief.[65] As a result, the House voted to prevent the official printing of the report; the vote was a narrow one, 49 to 40. Heaviest support for the Duane Report in the vote came from the city of Philadelphia, and from nearby Bucks and Chester Counties, all voting unanimously for printing. (Yet, in the previous session, citizens of Chester County had petitioned for a state-owned bank.) On the other hand, while rural York County, for example, voted heavily against printing, so did the representatives from Philadelphia County.[66]

Emboldened by this success, Representative Jarrett submitted, on February 1, a substitute report of his own on the pecuniary distress.[67] Interestingly enough, in his analysis of the *causes* of the depression, Jarrett was as conservative as Raguet and Duane, in attributing it largely to excessive bank credit in the boom. But their agreement on causes did not prevent a sharp disagreement on remedies or on the specific question of a loan office. Essentially the controversy was whether now—in the depression—a dose of money and credit would considerably alleviate distress or would aggravate matters by adding more of the alleged original poison leading to the present ills. To Jarrett there was no question that some relief to debtors was needed. At present, he declared, there was a great burden of unpaid debt, and this burden was causing loss of confidence by potential creditors and a consequent near prostration of all private credit. Jarrett conceded that the most important remedy was not new money but restoration of confidence. But he reasoned that if the government established a loan fund, granting loans on ample security, this would tend to re-establish confidence and credit in general. Furthermore, he visualized a similar pump-priming effect as did Raguet. A dollar thus loaned would rapidly circulate, and tend to repay many times itself in outstanding debts. As Jarrett stated:

An inconsiderable sum of money, for which the most ample security could be given, being loaned to a single individual in a neighborhood, by passing in quick succession, would pay perhaps a hundred debts.

Furthermore, the impetus to confidence and credit would "thereby bring into action additional sums that are now dormant, and give renewed impetus to industry." He therefore called for a $1 million state loan office.

Faced with this controversy, the House tabled the entire issue. Finally, a loan office bill, providing for $1 million-$2 million of state loans on landed security, failed to pass by the narrowest possible margin—a tie vote. According to the well-informed *National Intelligencer*, much of the support for the loan office bill came from the "log-rolling" of those eager to advance a bill for the appropriation of state money for extensive internal improvements.[68] The loan office issue continued to be a lively one in the state, however. A year and a half later, the Philadelphia *Union*, a paper of Federalist leanings and a notable stronghold of conservatism on monetary matters, warned that in Pennsylvania the "rage is for a loan office."[69] The loan office, it asserted, was being advanced as the sovereign panacea—for the payment of debts, to end speculation, to encourage industry, and even to reorganize society. The *Union* declared that Pennsylvania had about fifty banks, five hundred brokers, and from five thousand to fifty thousand private lenders of money. Yet they were not willing to lend to all who would like to borrow, so a loan office was supposed to be necessary. Yet, since overextension of credit was the cause of the distress, the loan office would attempt to cure the evil "by forcing still further the causes to which they owe their existence . . . instead of looking for relief in the restriction of the credit system, we are to look for its extension."

The *Union* pointed particularly to the plan of a local newspaper in Paradise—in Lancaster County—a small town close to Philadelphia. The Paradise editors advocated a $3 million-$5 million fund loaned for twenty years to distressed persons. Their argument was simply: why shouldn't the legislature grant such relief "when it is in their power to do so?" The *Union* attack was directed at the losses that would accrue from unwise lending by government. Private lenders were willing to risk continued fluctuations in the value of money. With proper security, there were plenty of lenders available, and no forcing was required. If a man could not borrow privately, he was really bankrupt and could not put up the security envisioned in the loan office plan. In sum, the *Union* could only see in the plan a sacrifice of permanent prosperity for mere temporary relief.

The *Union* added the argument that it was necessary for the crisis to run its course further, since there were still some basically unsound bank notes circulating in some of the counties. When the true value of the currency became evident, its total supply would contract even further. The paper also developed an interesting reply to the loan office claims of bolstering confidence. Lack of confidence and idle capital, it stated, were due not to purely psychological factors but to the simple fact that there was no good security available. Furthermore, as the state would borrow its sums in bank paper the circulation of the banks would increase, and their issues extended. Eventually, the process of cessation of monetary expansion, calling in of loans, and contraction, would be set in motion again. Countering the argument of beneficial increase in velocity of circulation, the *Union* declared that increased velocity would only lead to further depreciation of the already unsound currency.[70]

The West was the major center of state monetary expansion. Yet, Ohio, very hard hit by the panic and in great monetary difficulties, was very spare with such legislation. It directed its attention instead to its famous conflict with the Bank of the United States, which came to a head during this period. Ohio, a thinly populated state, had experienced a great boom in the postwar years, and contained twenty-four banks by the beginning of the crisis. Heavily in debt, much of Cincinnati was foreclosed during the crisis by the branch of the United States Bank. By 1819, only six or seven of the state's banks were redeeming their notes, the others struggling to continue with their notes greatly depreciated.[71] The scarcity of money led to barter in many interior areas. Yet, Ohio did not seriously consider a state bank or loan office plan. Governor Thomas Worthington, in his message to the legislature in December, 1818, did propose a state bank because of the disordered state of paper currency and the difficulty in collecting taxes, but nothing came of this suggestion.[72] A bill to this effect was introduced in the Senate, but never came to a vote. Governor Ethan Allen Brown, however, in the next annual message, abjured all such remedies for the crisis.[73] He added that there must be further contractions of bank notes rather than an expansion. Brown continued in this position throughout the depression, reaffirming, in December, 1821, his opposition to any system of bank and paper credit as remedy for the distress.

The one Ohio act to bolster the money supply was, in February, 1819, to prohibit buying or selling of bank notes below their par in specie. This futile attempt to halt the depreciation of bank notes was not enforced and was finally repealed in January of the following year.[74]

Most of the banks in Ohio failed during the depression, but, as we have seen, the legislature tried to maintain their notes at par, despite their suspension of specie payments. In December, 1819, a committee of citizens of Cincinnati issued a report backing the suspension of the banks and urging continued circulation of the notes.[75] The report absolved the banks from all blame for their plight and attributed the distress to the contractionist pressure of the United States Bank, much hated in many states for similar reasons, and to the machinations of eastern money brokers. These expressions of confidence, however, did not keep the bulk of the banks from failure. It is interesting that this point of view was not seconded by the Cincinnati *Gazette* itself, which blamed the banks for unwarranted extensions of their credit and even noted that the United States Bank had been extremely patient with the banks' failure to redeem in specie.

The neighboring state of Indiana suffered severely from the depression. The state's major money-making export—grain to New Orleans—declined greatly in value. Land values plummeted, and some formerly flourishing towns became uninhabited.[76] As a result, half of the state taxes were in arrears, and the Indiana legislature petitioned Congress not to prosecute its citizens for non-payment of federal taxes.

The banking situation in the state was unique. The Indiana Constitution of 1816 had prohibited any further incorporation of banks, except for a possible state bank, which would require a minimum specie subscription of $30 thousand.[77] This provision effectively confined chartered banking in the state to the two banks established two years before, the Bank of Vincennes and the Farmers' Bank of Indiana at Madison. In January 1817, Indiana adopted the Bank of Vincennes as a state bank, and its authorized capital was tripled to $1.5 million with the state contributing $375 thousand of the increase.

By the fall of 1818, the Farmers' Bank at Madison, under pressure by the United States Bank and others, suspended specie payment and wound up its operations by 1820.[78] Meanwhile, the grandiose plans for a state bank at Vincennes, with fourteen branches throughout the system, could not be consummated. Most of the leading politicians of the state were stockholders of the state bank and the state itself subscribed heavily. With only seventy-five thousand people—almost all farmers—in the state, and a scarcely developed capital market, such a large bank could hardly be floated. The state had therefore no success with an attempted sale of over $2 million in bank stock. Only three branches were finally organized. The bank participated heavily in the boom and received the benefit of federal deposit in the state; but it suspended specie payments during the crisis, and the federal government removed its deposits in July, 1820.

Indiana, in the monetary sphere, thus differed from most other states. While elsewhere people could call for a state bank as a remedy for the crisis, the people of Indiana had already had a state bank and were disgruntled with its record. In Indiana, state banking was on the defensive rather than the offensive. Among the leading opponents were the large numbers of incoming settlers from other states. These settlers exchanged their specie and Bank of United States notes for state bank notes at the frontier, only to find their value greatly depreciated at the next town. A meeting denounced the banking system of the state as injurious, fraudulent, and dangerous, and decried its political influence. The members vowed not to support any bank director for public office.[79] Leader of the opposition to the bank was Elihu Stout, editor of the Vincennes *Western Sun* in Indiana's leading town. Born in New Jersey, Stout had worked for years in Kentucky and in Nashville, and there had become a personal friend of Andrew Jackson. The leading force on behalf of the state bank was the Vincennes *Sentinel*, the editor of which was an officer of the bank. The "aristocrats" of the Vincennes area, such as United States Senator James Noble, Jonathan Jennings, and William Hendricks, supported the bank.[80] The opponents were later to be leaders of the "Jacksonian Democrats" in the state. The opposition pointed to the heavy loans to directors and to leading political figures. It grew more and more exercised because the state continued to accept the unredeemable notes of the bank, notes that continued to be issued in defiance of the bank's charter. The opposition also pointed out that the state's receiver of public dues was an officer of the bank. Further, the state, in 1819, deposited $10 thousand of irredeemable bank notes. This was done at a time when the state was short of specie to pay its own officers.[81] In late 1818, the legislature had all but unanimously decreed a stay of execution for one year should creditors refuse to accept at par the paper of those banks of the state, whose "money was current with the markets."[82] Finally, the opposition, headed by General Samuel Mulroy, introduced in July, 1820, a resolution in the legislature to investigate the state bank. The resolution failed.

The opposition was particularly angry because the bank was obligated by its charter to pay specie, yet was continuing operations while refusing to redeem. Representative John H. Thompson moved a bill to require the state bank to pay in specie or forfeit its charter, but the bill was defeated. Leader of the pro-bank forces was Representative Thomas H. Blake of Knox County, the county which included Vincennes. Blake's major arguments were the dependence of governmental salaries on the notes of the state bank and the assertion that no western banks were paying specie. The state election of 1820 was waged on the bank question. The issue was whether or not the state bank should be compelled to redeem its notes in specie. The voters chose overwhelmingly in the affirmative, and there was a heavy turnover of members of the legislature, even in areas that were formerly strongholds of the bank.

Actually the bank was on the edge of bankruptcy, and had been subject to considerable embezzlement by its officers. The election forced its demise. The bank suspended operations on January 2, 1821, and was forced to end its affairs completely by the following year.[83] Richard Damil, at a banquet in honor of General William Henry Harrison, at Vincennes, toasted its demise: "The State Bank of Indiana; more corruption than money." [84]

Although the commerce of the neighboring frontier state of Illinois was hardly developed, it chartered four private banks in the postwar years, two of which loaned heavily for public land speculation. The Bank of Illinois, at Shawneetown, was a particular favorite of the state government. As early as the beginning of 1817, Illinois had passed a stay law, postponing all executions for one year unless the creditor agreed to accept the notes of that bank and of several other banks in surrounding states. When the crisis came, the banks began to fail. There was a mass of unpaid debts, and Illinois noteholders suffered from the wave of bank failures in Ohio, Kentucky, and Missouri, the notes of which also circulated in Illinois. The Bank of Illinois failed by 1823, and another leading bank, the Bank of Edwardsville, which had begun business in the fall of 1818, failed in 1821.[85] The other two banks—the Bank of Kaskaskia and the Bank of Cairo—never began operations.[86]

Illinois was thus confronted not only with a heavy debt burden but with failure by its own and neighboring private banks. Furthermore, the Illinois State Constitution, ratified in 1818, provided that no further banks be chartered in Illinois except a state-owned bank. The route seemed paved for a state-owned bank to come to the rescue. The first step of the legislature was to establish a specie paying bank.[87] In the spring of 1819, it chartered the State Bank of Illinois, to be half owned by the state, half by private individuals. Authorized capital was to be the huge amount of $2 million from private sources, plus $2 million from the state, with the state to choose half of the directors. The bank was to have ten branches. Ten percent of the stock would be paid for directly in specie or specie paying bank notes, with a 12 percent interest penalty for any failure to redeem the bank's notes in specie on demand. Not only was this capital not forthcoming but the new bank could not even attract the $15 thousand in specie capital legally necessary to begin operations. Even a supplementary act declaring state warrants the equivalent of specie could not attract the needed capital. As a result, the bank never began operations, and the charter was rescinded in 1821.

Meanwhile, the fall in prices of land and other property, and the bank failures and contraction of the money supply, added to the distress and to the burden of unpaid debts. A clamor began to arise for a wholly state-owned bank, which would not be hampered in its operations by any specie paying requirement. The agitation was led in the Illinois House in the 1819–20 session by Representatives Richard M. Young and William M. Alexander, both from Union County in the southwestern tip of Illinois. Union County citizens submitted a petition for the establishment of a new State Bank of Illinois to issue inconvertible paper.[88] After the defeat of an amendment to reduce the bank's nominal capital, and to increase the proportion of paid-in capital, the bill passed the House by the narrowest of margins, fourteen to twelve. Two weeks later, an unusual protest was filed in the House against the bank bill by four Representatives: Wickliff Kitchell and Abraham Cairnes from Crawford County, Raphael Widen of Randolph County, and Samuel McClintoc of Gallatin County.[89] These counties are in widely scattered areas of the state: Crawford in the East; Randolph in the West; and Gallatin, a more populous county, in the Southeast containing the town of Shawneetown. The protest assailed the bank bill as unconstitutional. But, in addition, it assailed all banks—even those redeeming in specie—as dangerous, and as creators of false and fictitious habits, corrupting morals by providing "quick and easy access to every luxury and vice." The proposed state bank, without one cent of specie capital, was far worse. For it was clear that its credit had to depreciate, thus deceiving those who would accept its notes. The paper bank would inject "a false and fictitious currency, which has no intrinsic value, which must depreciate" like the old Continentals. The second economic argument was that the general embarrassments were due to bank credit expansion, and therefore that the bank would also aggravate the depression as well.

Citizens' meetings in the previously mentioned counties protested against the bill, as did citizens of Bond County, a small county in western Illinois. The Bond County resolution met the relief problem squarely. It stated that the legitimate object of banks was to afford a convenient medium for granting credits on solid capital, and that they were not suited for projects to create funds for needy individuals.[90] It warned against depreciation of the new bank notes. On the other hand, a citizens' meeting in adjacent Madison County, containing the important town of Edwardsville, supported the new bank as an expression of the state's duty to afford relief. Support for relief was also given by the Edwardsville *Spectator*, Edwardsville's influential newspaper.

Passing both Houses by a very close margin, the bill was vetoed by the Council of Revision, which consisted of Governor Shadrach Bond, who had opposed such a bank in his opening message, and the judges of the State Supreme Court.[91] The Council vetoed the bill unanimously, on the grounds of unconstitutionality, and issued a prediction that the bank notes would depreciate, and thus be an unsatisfactory medium, especially for interstate purchases.[92]

The House lost no time in countering the veto message. It referred the bill to a select committee, weighted with supporters of the bank, and the committee recommended overriding the veto in its report a few days later.[93] The committee report, in addition to defending the constitutionality of the proposal, admitted that the bank paper might not be received outside the state, but hailed this development as beneficial. "If other states did refuse to receive Illinois paper, the citizens of Illinois would have more for their own use." Despite the fact that Speaker John McLean, from Gallatin County, temporarily resigned his chair in order to combat the bill, the House overrode the veto (only a simple majority being needed) by seventeen to ten, a far greater margin than before. The Senate also overrode the veto, and the new State Bank of Illinois was established.[94]

The state bank was installed at Vandalia, in middle Illinois, with five branches, and a total nominal capital of $500 thousand. The only specie capital was $2 thousand from the State Treasury to pay for the cost of printing an issue of $300 thousand in inconvertible notes. The notes were distributed to the branches in the various districts with instructions to lend as fast as applications came in, in proportion to the number of inhabitants in each district. They were declared receivable in all debts due either to the bank or to the state. Loans above $100 were securable by mortgage on real estate and by personal security for loans under $100. The maximum loan to any one person was $1,000. The rate of interest was 6 percent, and the loans were renewable annually, with the payment of 10 percent of the principal—the bank was envisioned as operating for ten years. The bank notes were backed by a stay law, delaying all executions for three years unless the creditor agreed to receive the state bank notes. Thus, the state did its best to place the notes on as close to a legal tender basis as constitutionally seemed possible. All the funds of the State Treasury were, of course, deposited in the bank.

The bank lost no time in issuing and lending the notes. There was little concern about security or chance of repayment; in practice, anyone with an endorser could borrow $100.[95] The officers of the bank, political figures appointed by the legislature, borrowed up to the legal limit, and thus were not averse to depreciation of the notes, a depreciation which would lighten the burden of repayment. The notes began to depreciate immediately, and fell rapidly from 70 percent, to 50 percent, and 25 percent and finally ceased circulating by 1823. In January, 1823, with the notes rapidly losing value, the House overwhelmingly rejected the option of issuing an additional $200 thousand.[96] No notes beyond the $300 thousand were ever issued, and the bank closed in 1824. Very few debtors ever repaid the loan; there was no prosecution for failure to pay. Specie, of course, was completely driven from circulation by the quasi-legal tender bills, while they continued in operation.

Despite the argument of the House Committee, the legislature was alarmed at the depreciation. It was particularly chagrined at the refusal of the land offices of the United States Treasury to accept the notes, and it formally petitioned the Treasury, without success, to accept the new bank notes as equal to specie. While attempting to bolster the value of the bank notes, however, the legislature took the expedient if ironic step of authorizing issue of auditor's warrants by the state. These warrants exchanged on the market at three times the same nominal amount in bank notes. These warrants were specifically used to pay the salaries of state officials and of the members of the legislature, and arose from refusal of state officials to accept their salaries in the bank notes at their par value.[97]

In the frontier Michigan Territory, the territorial and local officials issued paper money, or scrip. The Governor and judges first issued paper in 1819 in small-denomination bills, from two to twenty dollars. The paper bore interest at 6 percent and was to be redeemed out of the sale of certain public lands, but these lands had already sold at a much lower price. As a result, the paper passed at a 10 percent discount as early as 1820. Wayne County, the site of the town of Detroit, found its taxes largely in arrears in 1819 and 1820, and so the county commissioners issued paper money to be redeemed out of future taxes. No tax at all was levied in 1821, however, and by March 1822, Wayne County was $3,000 in debt. As a result, the scrip depreciated at a 25 percent discount.[98]

Missouri, as noted previously suffered from a burden of debt, particularly in land speculation. With the halving of migration during the depression and the general fall in prices, land value plummeted. The monetary situation intensified the difficulties.[99] Missouri's first bank, the Bank of St. Louis, had opened at the end of 1816, and expanded credit heavily, particularly in real estate loans. Harassed by defaults of its debtors and the failure of other banks, the Bank of St. Louis failed in the summer of 1819. Much the same thing happened with the other major bank, the Bank of Missouri, which failed in 1821. The monetary contraction and resulting distress was intensified by the failures of banks in neighboring states, many notes of which circulated in the state. With notes vanishing or becoming worthless and with specie having been previously drained to the East, a demand arose for the state to furnish needed currency. Typical of the rising agitation for a state bank or loan office to provide paper money was a letter to the St. Louis *Enquirer* in the spring of 1821.[100] The letter pointed to the sudden creation and withdrawal of a large amount of currency that had taken place in Missouri in recent years. The writer estimated that the total paper circulation in Missouri had risen as a result of the boom—including bank notes of Missouri, Kentucky, Ohio, and the Carolinas—to $1 million. Now, in two years time, the total circulation remaining amounted to only $100 thousand. This 90 percent contraction in the money supply, according to the writer, benefited the creditor tenfold, since the value of his credit had increased to that extent. The writer concluded that a state bank was needed for relief of the people. Many newspapers presented similar letters urging a state bank.[101]

Representative Duff Green, soon to emerge as leader of the pro-relief and pro-loan office measures in the legislature, set the stage for a loan office, placing the responsibility for the "hard times" squarely on unemployment caused by a shortage of currency.[102]

Although the legislature had discussed a loan office in the regular 1820–21 session, nothing had been done, but with the upsurge of interest in the spring of 1821, rumors of a special relief session of the legislature began to circulate. A special session was finally called for June 4, amid vigorous protests from anti-reliefers. Governor Alexander McNair revealed the major purpose of the special session in his call for relief from the pecuniary troubles, and his submission of the relief proposals. The major bill submitted at this session was a loan office bill. Support was bolstered by the report of a legislative committee investigating the failure of the Bank of Missouri, which urged a new state currency; the committee estimated that the money supply had contracted to one-sixth of the 1818 total. The opponents of the loan office bill liked neither an inconvertible currency based on the state's credit, nor the two-year stay provision for those creditors who refused to accept the notes in payment. The stay section was therefore eliminated from the bill, although it passed as a separate bill the following January. The loan office bill, after spirited opposition, narrowly passed the House on June 21, by a margin of three votes.[103]

There was no discernible sectional division in Missouri on the loan office or relief measures, either in the legislature or among the public. Each territorial district of the state was closely divided on the issues. Leading the opposition was United States Senator Thomas Hart Benton, later to be dubbed "Old Bullion" because of his staunch advocacy of hard money at Jackson's side. Benton declared that the only satisfactory money was metallic and urged the citizens to end the specie drain to the East themselves by shifting their custom to a barter trade with New Orleans. Benton also suggested that the United States recognize the revolutionary Mexican government, in order to spur an influx of silver from Mexican mines.[104]

The loan office was established with four branch offices throughout the state. It aimed to provide an expanded circulating medium to relieve the shortage of money and to furnish loans, particularly on land, for relief of the burdens of the debtors. The law authorized the issue of $200 thousand of inconvertible paper, in denominations from fifty cents to ten dollars. The state agreed to receive the notes in payments of all taxes and other debts due, and to pay them out to its officers for salaries and fees. A large portion of the law was a description of how the public could obtain loans of the new notes on their land. Loans were to be for one year at 6 percent interest, but the borrower had the right to renew the loan every year, and the state could not call in more than 10 percent of the principal every six months. However, the state was required to call in 10 percent of the notes annually. The loans were to be divided among the districts in proportion to their population. Maxima to each borrower were $1,000 on real estate and $200 on personal property, the landed property to be worth at least twice the amount of the loan. The similarity is obvious between this loan office act and the State Bank Law of Illinois earlier in the year.

The leading issue of the legislative session of the fall of 1821 was the loan office system. The expansionists and relief forces were eager to enlarge the scope of the loan office. The reliefers wanted strong stay laws, for their own sake and to give the notes a quasi-legal tender effect, and the battle over the stay legislation is recorded previously. They also suggested bills for expanding the loan office note issue, for longer loans, and for the use of the notes to finance internal improvements in the state.

Many petitions arrived in the legislature to enlarge the note issue. The St. Louis *Enquirer* declared that the $200 thousand issue would not be enough. That amount, it asserted, was highly inadequate "to the great purpose in contemplation." [105] Governor McNair, however, was noncommittal and left the initiative to the legislature. On November 9, a bill was introduced authorizing the State Treasury to redeem its auditor's warrants in the new notes. The bill passed the legislature, and the scope of the notes was enlarged. Not only were they now receivable by the state for taxes and used in paying its officers, but it was now a means of paying the state's debts. Furthermore, since the State Treasury "Auditor's warrants" could be exchanged for loan office certificates at par, they were now usable as money. To enable this backing, the law authorized a further $50 thousand issue of loan office notes.[106]

Others wanted the state to furnish the capital to build factories and mills with loan office certificates. New wealth would thus be created, people would obtain new products, and prosperity would be restored. The expanded money supply was in this way conceived as a method of increasing the capital and productive activity of the country, as well as simply of relieving debtors. James Kennedy, George H. Kennedy, and Ruggles Whiting petitioned the legislature to lend them money to build a steam mill. Duff Green, leader of the relief forces, sponsored the project, which needed a special law, since the loan office was legally limited to a $1,000 loan for each person. Furthermore, the loan required landed property, whereas these men and others wished to engage in manufacturing activity. The legislature passed this special bill, lending the three men $10 thousand in new loan office certificates. They used $10 thousand of the $50 thousand which had been previously set aside to redeem the auditor's warrants. Emboldened by this move, the legislature also agreed to use the other $40 thousand in similar loans for internal improvements. Money to redeem the state's warrants could wait on loan office receipts coming in from taxes.

Now all the authorized new money was spent. The legislature passed another special act for the issuance of yet another $50 thousand in certificates and the loan of them to a Neziah Bliss for the establishment of an iron works, with mortgaged real estate as security. Governor McNair recommended that new issues of loan office paper be made and be given to each district for lending to enterprisers to erect such factories as they deem most beneficial to the people of the district. The legislature balked, however, at any further increase in note issues. McNair's proposal was endorsed in resolutions by both houses, but no law was passed to enact it. Various other plans were offered for increases in note issue, but few came to a vote. The major bill in the House was Green's proposal to emit another $300 thousand in note issue, but the bill was defeated. A similar bill in the Senate lost by a two-to-one vote. The door was emphatically closed on further emissions in this session when the House declared any further issue inexpedient. Authorized issues had totaled $300 thousand. The major action of the session was stay laws bolstering the credit of the loan office notes. As in the case of the stay laws, the voting on the loan office bill revealed no sectional division, but rather a division of opinion within every area and county.

As the loan office swung into action in the summer and fall of 1821, the proponents were hopeful of success. Most of the papers in the state had supported the bill, and they declared that the need for more circulating medium had been met. The *Missouri Intelligencer* went to the extent of urging that specie be permanently replaced by the new paper.[107] The same paper argued obscurely that these certificates would meet the need for currency within the state, while interstate debts could be met with farm produce, thus giving the farmer a better chance of marketing his produce. Opponents, led by the Jackson *Independent Patriot*, branded the law the work of sinister selfish groups, particularly speculators and bankrupt spendthrift debtors, who wanted to obtain large amounts of "rag money." The opponents charged that the inconvertible paper would soon depreciate and drive "real" money from circulation. The advocates of the loan office retorted that the paper was soundly backed by the future resources of the state, by expected future revenues from taxes and land sales.

By January, 1822, the loan office notes began to depreciate. The relief advocates met in January at St. Charles to discusss means to bolster the value of the certificates. To no avail, however. By March, the loan office notes had depreciated to such an extent as to have practically disappeared from circulation. Unreconstructed advocates asserted that the depreciation was due to deliberate attempts of merchants to force down the value for speculative purposes.[108] It is true that merchants generally refused to accept the notes, but it seems evident that the reason was serious doubts on their present and future value. Some merchants took the notes only at a discount, others not at all. Several merchants in the town of Franklin banded together to announce a boycott of the loan office paper, attacking it as "calculated to injure us materially in our business." One Thomas Willis, a barber of St. Louis, advertised in the press that he would not accept a loan office note "on any terms whatever." [109]

The extraordinary rapidity of the collapse of the notes was partly due to unfavorable judicial decisions that spelled the writing on the wall for the loan office. The loan office law was declared unconstitutional by the courts in February and in July, 1822, and the stay laws were overthrown in the same period. In the course of his St. Louis Circuit Court decision in Missouri on February 18, 1822, declaring the loan office act unconstitutional,[110] Judge N. Beverly Tucker shed light on some of the reasons behind the loan office legislation. He declared that Kentucky's inconvertible paper scheme had stimulated exports from there to Missouri, presumably because of low export prices resulting from depreciating Kentucky paper. Missouri, he declared, attempted a paper system to exclude Kentucky imports, a goal which was accomplished.[111]

The elections, as we have seen, were fought bitterly during 1821 over the loan office and stay measures. The reliefers sought a constitutional amendment to eliminate judicial opposition, and charged that the judges were prejudiced against the notes because they were forced to receive them in salaries. Anti-reliefers called for repeal.

The elections were won overwhelmingly by the anti-relief forces. Governor McNair followed the straws in the wind by not only calling for complete repeal, in his November 4 message to the legislature, but also by stating that the measures had proved unsuccessful in alleviating the financial distress. McNair concluded that the only effective method of relief was private "industry" and economy. Swiftly, the legislature acted to repeal the loan office law, acting after only $200 thousand had actually been issued. The problem of disposing of the existing notes remained. One proposal to fund the notes at half their nominal value was given scant consideration, and, in a law of December 16, the legislature decided that no renewals of loans would be made, and that all borrowers would be required to pay 10 percent of the principal to the state every six months until the debt was completed. The notes would no longer be received in payment of dues by the state and would be destroyed as repaid.

Banking became a matter of controversy in Tennessee as early as the years of the postwar boom. Many small banks were established in the small rural towns of the state, and these were supported in the rural areas. The press in the two big towns of Knoxville and Nashville, however, sharply criticized this development as dissipating the capital that rightly belonged in the larger, commercial areas.[112] Most of these small banks were consolidated in 1818 into branches of one of the leading banks, the Nashville Bank.

As insolvencies developed in the crisis, the banking affairs of the state became swiftly disordered. The Nashville Bank, the Farmers' and Merchants' Bank of Nashville, and the Bank of Tennessee (Nashville Branch), all had to suspend specie payments during June, 1819. On June 21, the day before the Nashville Bank suspended, citizens of Nashville had recommended immediate suspension of specie payments by all banks of Tennessee.[113] On June 23, the leading bankers of Nashville met at the courthouse and passed an almost identical resolution, urging all the banks to suspend specie payments—while continuing their operations. They insisted that while the banks should suspend specie payments the public should not allow such a step to "impair the credit" of bank paper. By July, every bank in mid-Tennessee had suspended specie payments, and the only major bank continuing to redeem was the Knoxville branch of the Bank of Tennessee. The Nashville banks issued a statement to justify their suspension. They pointed to the increased demand on them for specie; to meet these calls they would have had to press their debtors and ruin them. The Bank of the United States was blamed for the destructive pressure, as were easterners who turned in Tennessee bank notes for redemption. Therefore, the bank's suspension while continuing operations was really a humanitarian gesture to shield their debtors and to prevent specie from being drained from the state.[114]

While the banks quickly found themselves forced to suspend payment, the public was not so eager to maintain the credit of their notes. Creditors such as merchants Willie Barrow and Thomas Yeatman advertised in the press their unwillingness to accept bank notes in payment.[115] People turned to the legislature for debtors' relief legislation and for methods of bolstering and expanding the money supply of the state. As has been stated, the leader of the relief forces, in both fields, was one of the dominant political figures in the state: Felix Grundy, now newly elected Representative from central Davidson County (including Nashville) on a relief platform. In Grundy's resolutions, presented to the legislature on September 20, he stated that the "present deranged state of the currency . . . requires the early and serious attention of the legislature." His major concrete proposal at that time was a virtual legal tender law, aimed at bolstering the money supply and aiding debtors—a law to compel creditors to accept bank notes of the state or forfeit the debt.[116] Grundy's bill staying executions for two years unless creditors accepted notes of state banks passed in the fall of 1819.[117]

East Tennessee was generally a more rural, less commercial area than the central region, but its main distinction was the relative absence of cotton and slave plantations, as compared to mid-Tennessee. East Tennesseans considered the suspension of specie payments by the banks, while continuing in operation, as a plan to evade meeting the banks' just obligations. There was also a great deal of opposition to the bank suspension in mid-Tennessee. Citizens of Warren County, in that area, petitioned the legislature that banks be placed upon a "constitutional equality with the citizens" in paying their debts, by compelling the banks to redeem their notes in specie as promised. Henry H. Bryan, running for Congress from mid-Tennessee, declared in a campaign circular that

> banking in all its forms, in every disguise is a rank fraud upon the laboring and industrious part of society; it is in truth a scheme, whereby in a silent and secret manner, to make idleness productive and filch from industry, the hard produce of its earnings.[118]

During 1820, the crisis continued to intensify; prices of produce fell, sheriff's sales increased, and the bank notes, not redeemable in specie, continued to depreciate despite the stay law and the exhortations of the bankers. The cry began to spread that the great evil of the times was the continuing diminution of the currency. Davidson County, especially Nashville, was the center of the agitation. These advocates also began to criticize the banks bitterly for continuing to call on their debtors for payment. The legislature began to be considered the source from which new money should be produced. In the late spring and early summer of 1820, the chorus swelled for a special session of the legislature to supply an increased circulating medium. Typical of the agitation for increased currency at a special session was a petition from citizens of Williamson County, adjacent to Davidson.[119] It declared that the banks were contracting credit rather than affording relief. Relief must be speedily effected to avoid the "ruin" of most citizens of the state. The Nashville *Clarion* lauded the "several men of wealth" who had taken up the "fight for relief." [120] On the other hand, the Nashville *Gazette* opposed the plan.

Grundy prevailed upon the newly elected Governor Joseph McMinn to call the special session for June 26. The Governor, in his message to the legislature, recommended a plan for a state money. He first cited the diminution in the supply of money and the need for its increase. In his plan, the state treasury would issue certificates through a loan office, resting vaguely on faith in public responsibility, and on the usual general pledge for eventual redemption from revenues of public land sales and taxation. Three hundred thousand dollars in notes would be emitted by a loan office under control of the legislature, which would have many branches in the various counties. Its notes would be receivable in dues to the state.[121] The proposal was shepherded and considerably expanded in the House by Felix Grundy.[122] His bill provided for two loan offices, one in Nashville and the other one in Knoxville, with eight branches between them. Total note issue would be $750 thousand; $488 thousand in the Nashville area, and $262 thousand in the Knoxville area. This, he declared, might be insufficient, in which case the note issue should be increased. The notes would be loaned to individuals on real estate and personal security, at 6 percent; the maximum loan for each person would be $1,000. The maximum denomination note was to be $100, to insure plenty of notes in circulation, and to prevent seepage of large denomination notes out of the state and into the hands of eastern creditors. The notes were to rest on "public faith" and the eventual proceeds of land sales, and were to be receivable in payments to the state. Grundy asserted that the object of the legislation was to aid the wealthy as well as the poor, and that both groups were ardently for the legislation.

To the criticism that the loan office notes would not be accepted by the New York and Philadelphia creditors of Tennessean merchants, Grundy retorted that this would be so much the better, since the notes should stay at home. When that happened, surplus produce of the state could be the medium of traffic, rather than gold and silver. Grundy, in conclusion, lauded his proposal as positive and for the benefit of the community.

Representative William Williams, also of Davidson County, led the opposition to the Grundy plan. He offered two amendments to the bill: one to reduce authorized issue to $500 thousand, and the other to pledge in redemption a definite quantity of treasury surplus, thus effectively converting the plan into a far more limited operation. Both amendments were turned down by almost two-to-one majorities.[123] Another major leader of the opposition was Representative Pleasant M. Miller, from Knoxville, who submitted a series of amendments to reduce the branches or add funds for redemption, but all were overwhelmingly defeated. Finally, the Grundy bill passed by a two-to-one vote.[124]

The passage of the Grundy bill engendered a great deal of bitterness. Protesting legislators submitted two separate resolutions against the bill. On the day of the passage, Representative Sampson David of Campbell County, in East Tennessee, submitted his reasons for voting against the bill. Among them he charged that this was an "untried and dangerous experiment," that all paper institutions were ruinous to the best interests of the country, and that one man's property would be used to pay the debts of another. A week later,[125] Miller submitted a protest signed by six of the other opponents of the bill, with the result that eight of the thirteen voting against the bill felt it incumbent on them to register a protest. Miller's statement was more reasoned than David's. Miller stated that the loan office notes would only be exchangeable in the bank notes of the state, which continued to depreciate. Therefore, the loan office notes would not be higher in value than the bank notes. In fact, they would be lower, since no funds for redemption would be possible for at least five years. Miller warned that the banks, which were the bulk of the creditors, would not receive the new notes, so that the notes would depreciate still further.

The loan office bill reached the Senate floor on July 14. Senator Samuel Bunch, from East Tennessee, moved to reduce the issue to $500 thousand, but this motion was defeated, and the amendment to make the notes redeemable in specie or specie paying bank notes was rejected by almost three to one. A stay provision for two years, if creditors refuse to accept the notes, was retained by a large margin despite an effort to strike it out. Another limiting amendment was approved, however—Nashville's Adam Huntsman's proposal to eliminate the Grundy provision to establish branches in every county. However, amendments to prohibit loans either to directors of the office or to members of the legislature were overwhelmingly rejected.[126]

A famous incident occurred at this point. General Andrew Jackson, a wealthy cotton planter from Nashville, and several other citizens of that town, sent a very vigorous memorial to the Senate denouncing the loan office bill as unconstitutional and ruinous. Senators Adam Huntsman and David Wallace denounced the memorial and successfully had it tabled by a vote of 11 to 5. However, it did have the effect of changing the cast of the bill. Instead of a loan office bill, it was converted into a bill for a Bank of the State of Tennessee. The measure was, however, in fact made more expansionist by eliminating even the pledge of future revenue and simply basing the notes on the "faith of the state." [127] The House forced a reversion to the eventual pledge of public revenue, but it also raised the maximum note issue by $1 million, although the final bill passed by only one vote. The Senate proposed striking out the maximum limit, but the House by a large majority failed to concur. Finally, after a most vigorous controversy, the bill passed the legislature on July 27.[128]

Andrew Jackson had been most determined in opposing the legislation.[129] In his memorial, he leveled a far-reaching attack against the bill.[130] Jackson asserted that the loan office notes would not maintain equivalence with specie. All inconvertible notes depreciated down to a negligible value, and as evidence the memorial cited the old Mississippi Bubble. Jackson also cited the "judicious political economists," who had established that "the large emissions of paper from the banks by which the country was inundated, have been the most prominent causes of those distresses of which we at present complain." The abundant money supplied by the banks raised prices and led to extravagant expenditures. The increased paper money and higher prices depressed manufactures by artificially raising the high price of labor and making American products overpriced in foreign markets. If, Jackson and his associates concluded, "the paper issued by the banks upon a *specie* basis had been the prolific parent of so much distress, how greatly must this pressure be augmented by the emission of loan office notes." Furthermore, these notes would not only burden tradesmen and farmers but would give a special privilege to the imprudent speculative debtor.

The remedy offered by Jackson and his associates for the depression was the same as that advanced by so many others; a return to industry and economy, an abandonment of extravagance and excessive debt. A return to industry and simplicity would restore confidence and bring back much of the hoarded specie into circulation.

The meeting which sent this memorial was organized by Jackson in Davidson County on July 15. He also organized meetings in adjacent Sumner and Wilson Counties. His friend Major William Berkeley Lewis tried to throw cold water on his moves by writing Jackson that the proposed legislation was really not much worse than private banks, and that the majority of Nashville citizens favored it. Jackson countered that the people were overwhelmingly opposed. The Jackson efforts met with bitter criticism both in the legislature, and from a grand jury of Davidson County, which accused the memorialists of attempting to thwart the will of the people.[131]

The final act establishing the Bank of the State of Tennessee was very similar to the loan office proposal. Nominal capital was $1 million, bank notes were to be in denominations of $1 to $100, and the notes were to be eventually redeemed by public funds. All public money was to be deposited in the bank. Loans were to be for one year, at 6 percent interest, and personal loans to be limited to $500. The bank could not call in more than 10 percent of a loan when due, except after sixty days' notice. Personal loans would be renewable every three months. Notes were authorized up to $1 million. A stay provision held up executions for two years unless the creditor accepted the bank's notes.

The new bank was never popular in Tennessee. The proponents were disgruntled because they felt the 6 percent interest charge to be too high. On the other hand, the notes immediately depreciated to a great extent. The Nashville Bank and the old private Bank of Tennessee refused to accept the notes of the new state bank. Furthermore, they did their best to thwart inflation of the currency by calling their loans and contracting their note issue.[132] In June, 1821, the bank received a severe blow when the Supreme Court of Tennessee declared the stay provision unconstitutional. The handwriting for the bank was on the wall.

Both gubernatorial candidates in the 1821 elections staunchly favored rapid return to a specie basis. One of the candidates was Colonel Edward Ward of Nashville, a conservative planter and the leading cosigner of the Jackson memorial. He issued a circular to the people during his campaign denouncing the emission of paper by the new bank. Ward admitted that a large supply of paper might help the debtor, but only through injuring the creditor. Furthermore, the depreciation of currency had brought evil results to the whole country. The remedy, then, was for each individual to practice thorough economy, and for a prompt return to specie payments.

His successful opponent, Major-General William Carroll, a Nashville merchant, had practically the same views. He also advocated a prompt return to specie payment. As a matter of fact, his basic view, even though he himself was a director of the Farmers' and Merchants' Bank of Nashville, went beyond Ward's in opposing all banks. He also attributed the crisis to the previously undue increase in the volume of bank notes.[133] In his Inaugural Message, Carroll denounced the evil consequences which had resulted from the state bank:

> When floodgates are thrown open . . . there is no safe criterion to regulate . . . emission. The moment you issue more than is necessary, it depreciates . . . [particularly] . . . beyond our own neighborhood. . . . Every specie dollar that can be obtained from the vaults of the banks is . . . hoarded.

He called for gradual resumption of specie payments to restore confidence; prompt resumption, he concluded, would put undue pressure on debtors.[134]

Carroll acknowledged that distress existed, but declared the only remedy to be industry and economy; these remedies had to be put into effect by the individual. By 1822, Carroll declared that the pecuniary embarrassments had "greatly diminished" due to the industry of the citizens.[135]

The Bank was not ended quickly, however, as Grundy managed to battle the Administration for many years. A bill was passed in 1821 providing for resumption by all the banks by 1824, but the Grundy forces managed to postpone the full resumption of specie payments in Tennessee until July, 1826.[136] It ceased to be an important factor, even though its formal existence was extended to 1831, when it ended with a shortage of funds of $100 thousand.

The state of Kentucky had a checkered banking history before the crisis of 1819. Since 1806, the dominant bank in the state had been the Bank of Kentucky, with $1 million capital stock. This bank was half owned by the state, and half the directors were government-appointed; consequently, its operations were intimately associated with the government. During the postwar boom, the legislature chartered, in one session of 1817–18, no less than forty-six new banks with a total capitalization of $10 million. This contrasted to the total of two banks previously in existence in the state. The legislature made the entire banking structure very weak by authorizing redeemability of their notes in the notes of the Bank of Kentucky, as well as in specie.[137] The new banks expanded their credit and note issue greatly during the summer of 1818, and large speculative loans were lavishly granted. The crisis of 1819 hit Kentucky severely, and monetary difficulties figured prominently in the debacle. During 1819 and 1820, all of the new banks failed; they were not able to redeem in Bank of Kentucky notes or in specie. Still more significant was the suspension of specie payments by the Bank of Kentucky itself in November, 1818. The Bank of Kentucky had expanded its issue during the boom, too, and much of the pressure for redemption came from balances which had accumulated against it in favor of the Bank of the United States, some of them receipts of the government land office.[138]

Representatives of the leading banks of Kentucky met at Frankfort on May 17, 1819, and pledged to cooperate among themselves to increase the circulating medium, without suspending specie payments. Suspensions, however, continued apace.[139]

In this troubled monetary situation, a group of citizens of Franklin County, containing the city of Frankfort, met on June 4, to take into consideration the present state of the country and devise means to avert impending distress.[140] They drew up a set of resolutions which became famous throughout the country, drawing comment from the presses of Washington, Philadelphia, and New York. This was probably due to the eminence of the sponsors, unusual for county meetings of this type. Chairman of the meeting was Jacob Creath, an outstanding minister and orator, and also present were such leading political figures as George Adams, George M. Bibb, John Pope, and Martin D. Hardin.[141] It is interesting that even the bitter eastern opponents of the resolutions admitted the unquestioned respectability of the participants. The Frankfort Resolutions began by pointing to the economic distress, the "scarcity of money," the pressure of debtors, the "smaller employment," lack of confidence, and disruption of trade. The resolutions first charged the banks with largely causing the distress by expanding loans and note issues, thereby encouraging speculation and extravagant spending, and leaving themselves vulnerable to runs for specie. After this analysis, the resolutions called upon the banks to do their proper share to remedy the depressed conditions. What should the banks do to fulfill the responsibility? They should "suspend specie payments and make moderate paper issue." Furthermore, the legislature should meet in special session and take steps quickly to permit the banks to continue in operations while suspending specie payments. This was a curious charge indeed upon the banks. It was not without justice that the New York *American* charged that from the proposals one would think the meeting was a convention of bank directors.[142] The resolutions did suggest, however, a maximum legal regulation on the amount of bank paper that could be issued during the suspension, violation of which would forfeit a bank's charter.

The Frankfort Resolutions created a great stir, notably in Kentucky but throughout the country as well. In Kentucky, county-wide meetings of citizens immediately mushroomed, some supporting, some opposing the Frankfort proposals. In nearby Bourbon County, a citizens' meeting passed nearly unanimously similar resolutions calling for a special session to permit suspension of specie payments, and liberal note issue by the banks. Adjacent Shelby and Scott Counties also endorsed the proposals.[143] Nearby Harrison County issued a similar resolution, but along slightly more conservative lines. It called for the banks to make new issues of paper, postpone their demands on debtors, and for the government to permit suspensions of specie payments. It refused, however, to endorse the demands for a special session.

The Frankfort Resolutions provoked vigorous reactions by conservative papers in the East, especially in New York City. William Coleman, editor of the New York *Evening Post* and the former "Field Marshal of Federalism," issued an editorial denouncing the proposals.[144] After proudly proclaiming that in New York City there would be no suspension of specie payments, the *Post* declared that any new monetary issue would simply depreciate proportionately. "The attempt to raise prices by increasing the circulating medium is only to make the same quantity of produce pass for a greater nominal amount in paper." The best course for the banks would be to stop and issue no more irredeemable paper, and to redeem the notes which they had already issued. To refuse to redeem notes and to continue issuing more, declared Coleman, "under the pretext of keeping up the value of property," would be just as wise as it would be for farmers to establish a bank in every field of corn to keep up the price of grain by issuing notes to facilitate purchase. Other papers attacking the Frankfort Resolutions were the New York *American*, New York *Daily Advertiser*, and the *National Intelligencer*. The *American* and the *Intelligencer* conceded that the participants at the Frankfort meeting were highly respectable citizens.[145]

Although the Frankfort Resolutions were denounced in the eastern press, the controversy over the resolutions must not be conceived as an East-West conflict. The debate within Kentucky was spirited and determined, and the opposition was centered in the same geographical area as the proponents. Thus, the resolutions were attacked by two leading Kentucky newspapers—the Frankfort *Kentucky Argus* and the Lexington *Kentucky Herald*—which denounced the proposals as "shielding the extravagant debtor from his honest creditor," and as trying to "interfere in individual transactions, and thereby . . . to destroy confidence." [146] The *Argus* maintained that most Kentuckians opposed the resolutions.[147] "Franklin" conceded a shortage of specie in the West, but stated the reason to be lack of confidence in the banks."This want of confidence induces every man . . . who gets possession of a *fund of dollars*, to lay it by." The proper remedy commended to his fellow citizens of Louisville was a law exacting penalties on banks for so much as whispering the idea of suspending specie payments. This would restore confidence in the banks and their "specie will be abundant." [148] A citizens' meeting in Jefferson County, containing Louisville, passed by a large majority a resolution that the banks ought to continue redeeming their notes in specie and opposing a special session. On the other hand, a citizens' meeting in rural Bullitt County, adjacent to Jefferson, advocated suspension of specie payments, especially for the Bank of Kentucky.

Several rural counties in Kentucky issued anti-Frankfort resolutions. Nelson, Washington, and Green Counties in the more southern part of the state, and Mason County on the northern border, attacked the proposals for legislative sanction of suspensions of specie payment and further bank note issue. Niles, perhaps over-optimistically, estimated that the large majority of citizens' meetings throughout Kentucky believed that the banks "should pay their debts or shut up shop." [149] The Washington County resolution asserted that distress was not as great as generally represented, and that it was due to speculation and extravagance.[150] A suspension of specie payment would unjustly withhold their rightful property from the creditors. Furthermore, it would weaken public confidence in the banks and would subsidize extravagance and imprudence. The increased issue of paper, the resolution declared, would, in the end, increase the economic difficulties. The best remedy was for the debtors to "bear the chastisements they bring on themselves."

Mason County, in a meeting of six hundred citizens, passed a set of resolutions almost unanimously.[151] A suspension, it pointed out, would destroy confidence in the state's circulating medium. The Mason County resolution maintained that bank credit expansion had led to the panic, adding, in opposition to the Frankfort view, that they "contemplate with horror . . . a resort to that very policy as a remedy, which has produced so much distress . . . and which, instead of alleviating, must lamentably increase the evils which it pretends to remedy."

A special session was not called. The major battle over relief, in the fall elections, was over proposed stay legislation. The victorious relief forces passed a stay law in February, 1820, granting a one year extra stay to debtors whose creditors refused the paper of the Bank of Kentucky, which had suspended specie payments.

By mid-1820, it had become clear that some remedy was needed for the troubled monetary situation. In effect, the legislature had granted the desire of the relief forces to permit banks to continue in operation while suspending specie payments, and had also granted special privileges to notes of the Bank of Kentucky. Yet, the bank notes continued to depreciate rapidly. The *Kentucky Gazette* warned its readers in the summer of 1819 not to receive any bank notes except with great caution, and with the help of appraisals by professional brokers, nor to exchange specie and specie paying notes for Kentucky notes. Even the banks themselves began to refuse each others' notes.[152] The public began to lose faith in all of the state's bank notes. The tavern keepers and merchants of Frankfort decided not to receive the bills of any bank below the denomination of one dollar, and a meeting of butchers of Lexington decided to refuse any paper not acceptable to the banks of that town. As a result, one by one, the "independent" banks, those that had been chartered during 1818, were forced to close their doors. Public opinion generally held the banks responsible for the crash (as could be evidenced even in the Frankfort Resolutions), and this sentiment, coupled with the difficulties of the independent banks, resulted in repeal of all those bank charters in February, 1820.[153] Consequently, the only bank still operating by mid-1820 was the Bank of Kentucky. In the meanwhile, the very severe monetary contraction added to the great economic difficulties in the state as debts mounted and prices plummeted. Finally, in August, 1820, the conservative administration of Governor Gabriel Slaughter, which had done its best to block relief measures, was replaced by the pro-relief advocate, Governor John Adair. The expansionist forces moved rapidly toward the climax of their effort in Kentucky, the establishment of a wholly state-owned bank issuing inconvertible paper, the Bank of the Commonwealth of Kentucky.[154] The Bank of the Commonwealth, enacted on November 29, had a nominal capitalization of $2 million. The legislature elected all the directors and the bank had branches throughout the state. The notes were inconvertible, but the state pledged future revenues from sale of its public lands in the West and other surplus revenue. The notes were receivable in all debts to the state. Loans were to be made on mortgage security, proportioned to the population of the district. It was stipulated that borrowers must use their notes either to repay debts or to buy stock and produce. The maximum individual loan was $200. To these ends the bank was authorized to issue up to $3 million in notes. The appropriation by the legislature consisted simply of $7,000 to purchase the plates and paper for printing the notes. The object of the act was providing cheap money for debtors for repayment of their debts. As we have seen, the legislature obligingly passed several stay laws to grant preferential treatment to its Bank of the Commonwealth. Courts favored debtors' payment in Bank of Commonwealth notes.

Expansionist forces in the legislature had to struggle to beat down many amendments for making the new institution a specie paying bank. The hard money leader in the House was Representative George Robertson, who for fourteeen years had been Chief Justice of the Kentucky Courts of Appeals. In the House, an amendment, defeated by a small margin, would have imposed an interest penalty on all notes not redeemed in specie. The provision for the state to pledge a redemption fund in the vague future, rather than provide it at present, only passed by a small margin. Another rejected amendment would have prevented the bank from opening until the state had subscribed $100 thousand in specie or in the notes of specie paying banks. The conservative forces managed to defeat a provision permitting the bank to lend money on personal property as well as real estate—this was defeated by a two-to-one vote. The final bill passed the House by a vote of 54 to 40. There was also a sharp fight over the authorized note issue. The House had originally agreed to a $2 million limit, but the relief forces managed, by a three-vote margin, to increase the maximum to $3 million; they failed, however, in an attempt to extend it further to $3.5 million.[155]

In the Senate, the battle against the non-specie paying bank was led by John Pope, who had shifted from his previous inflationist stand. Pope's amendment to begin penalties for non-redemption in specie after three years was defeated by one vote. On the other hand, an attempt by extreme pro-relief forces to *prevent* any future possibility of redemption was beaten down by a two-to-one vote. Also, a provision to reduce the maximum interest rate on the banks' loans from 6 percent to 3 percent was heavily defeated. The final bill passed the Senate by a vote of 22 to 15.[156]

The establishment of the Bank of the Commonwealth was a measure of the dissatisfaction of the expansionist forces with the semi-private Bank of Kentucky, for the conservatism of its operations. The charter of the latter bank was due to expire in 1821, and it was clear that the expansionists were aiming for non-renewal of the charter, thus closing the bank. The Bank of Kentucky reacted belligerently, contracting its loans and notes and refusing to accept the notes of the Bank of Commonwealth.

During 1821, the Bank of Commonwealth rapidly issued close to its authorized $3 million in notes, and the hopes of its proponents were high. At the opening of the October, 1821, session of the legislature, Governor Adair hailed the Bank of the Commonwealth and attributed an extensive relief of the "pecuniary embarrassments" of the state to the increased currency provided by the new bank.[157] In particular, many heavy debtors had been saved from ruin. Adair pointed to the general scarcity of money, particularly the scarcity of specie, and the scarcity in circulation of the specie-backed notes of the Bank of the United States as evidence that specie did not suffice for the currency needs of the country. Banks, in order to obtain enough specie, were forced to make heavy calls on their debtors. With specie and Bank of the United States notes insufficient, and the Bank of Kentucky suspending specie payment, a state currency was needed. The duty of every government, declared Adair, was to supply a sound and sufficient circulating medium and to "prevent as far as practicable the evils of a fluctuating currency." He admitted that, left alone, the condition of the people would gradually improve and commerce revive. But the government must not become an accessory to the distress of its citizens by refusing to perform its monetary duties. Pursuing the approach that the government should stabilize the value of its currency, Adair pointed out that specie itself was not of invariable value; that value was the price which the products of labor bore in relation to money. This value fluctuated in inverse proportion to an increase or decrease in the quantity of the circulating medium. The debtor and creditor should then receive, on repayment of the debt, money of the same value as of the time the loan was made. "To coerce a literal obedience to contract" when the value had greatly changed would be against true equity. The duty of the legislature in depressed times was to apply appropriate remedies and not await the slow growth of more favorable conditions. The clearly proper system was "an increase in the circulating medium." A private specie paying bank could not successfully accomplish this, because of the demands upon it for specie should its notes increase. Therefore, only use of the resources and faith of the state itself could establish a general paper system.

Adair did not contemplate a permanent inconvertible paper system. He conceded that such would be impossible to establish, but felt that this bank merely "anticipated" the future revenues of the state. Adair warned, however, that it was important to sustain the credit of the paper, and that therefore there should be no further note issues which might weaken public confidence.

Legislative satisfaction in their creation was bolstered by a report, a few days later, of the eminent John J. Crittenden, president of the new bank.[158] Crittenden reported that, since April of the year, when the bank had begun operations, it had issued $2.5 million in notes and was preparing to issue half a million more. He reported that the bank had decided not to lend for too long a period, in order to avoid the evils of the unlimited time granted by banks during the boom. The present loans were, in contrast, from four to six months' duration. The bank also decided to call the principal of their loans in gradually, at the rate of 1 percent per month. Crittenden also stated that since, unfortunately, only a limited number of people could obtain the benefit of the loans, the bank, as soon as it received payment from one set of borrowers, would lend again to another set.

Crittenden recognized that when the immediate debts were paid there would be less demand by debtors for the notes, and so he asserted that the regular rate of calls would support the credit of the notes until the legislature eventually made the notes redeemable.

Crittenden concluded that the bank was being highly successful in furnishing a circulating medium enabling debtors to repay their debts, and to transfer their debt burden to the bank, repaying the latter gradually.

The bank was also commended in a report by Representative Samuel Brents, chairman of the House committee on the Bank of the Commonwealth.[159] Brents, from Green County in southern Kentucky, pointed out that, before the current year, most citizens were very heavily in debt, and there was little or no market for their produce to enable them to repay. The bank and its note issues had enabled rapid liquidation of the debt burden. The report commended the bank and all of its decisions.

In their triumph, the relief forces failed by only a few votes to repeal the Bank of Kentucky charter immediately and to transfer all state funds to the new bank.[160] They did pass a resolution urging the federal post office to receive the new notes in Kentucky in payment for postage. This resolution was attacked by Representative Thomas Speed of Nelson County, who asserted that this action implied that the inconvertible paper was permanent rather than temporary. He pointed out that the notes had already depreciated considerably.[161]

In his legislative message in the spring of 1822, Governor Adair continued to eulogize the bank; he declared that it had saved the community from severe suffering, permitted payment of debts, and helped the restoration of commerce.[162] Adair also added that the increased currency had restored activity to construction of improvements and provided capital for depressed industry. A note of alarm was distinctly sounded in this message, however. Already the Bank of Commonwealth notes were beginning to depreciate rapidly. In fact, they sold at 70 percent of par as soon as they were first issued.[163] Adair exhorted everyone to trust the new bank notes—backed by the faith of the state and advanced for the general good of Kentucky; he stated that he could not understand some people's distrust of the new bank notes, a distrust that cast discredit on the fair name of Kentucky.

Before the session had opened, the bank, anxious about the depreciation, had decided to try to bolster its credit by increasing the rate of calls on its loans to 2 percent per month. This action ignited fervent controversy in the legislature. Three legislators moved rejection of the change: Representative Tandy Allen of Bourbon County, a rural county adjacent to Lexington; Representative George Shannon of Fayette County, containing commercial Lexington; and Representative Speed. One legislator moved approval, and two others urged provision of some funds by the state to enable redemption in specie. Representative Hugh Wiley of Nicholas County advocated that the bank issue no further notes.[164] Dominant sentiment was for the restoration of the more gentle 1 percent call, and resolutions to that effect were submitted by Representative Charles H. Allen and Representative Shannon from the Committee on Currency. Allen represented Henry County in western Kentucky.

On May 21, a frankly grave report was submitted by President Crittenden and the Board of Directors, on the "present depreciation of the paper of this bank" and the means to correct it.[165] The report declared that for the past several weeks there had been constant and rapid depreciation of the bank notes in the main commercial centers of Lexington and Louisville, and that, at this time, it had depreciated to about 62 percent of par. In contrast to the optimism of the previous fall, Crittenden declared that there was no prospect of preventing further rapid depreciation, unless the cause were removed. The major cause was the "super-abundance of bank paper, compared with the demand of the community." The original heavy debt burden had been extinguished, while the circulating medium had "increased to a degree hitherto unknown." Thus, the demand for use of the notes had decreased just at a time when its amount had been rapidly increasing. Once the redundant paper came "into contact with" specie and the various commodities, it instantly depreciated. Crittenden deprecated the alleged influence of brokers in bringing about the decline, asserting that the depreciation would have occurred without them. The final consideration for Crittenden was that Kentucky, being a part of a great, interconnected nation, could not maintain a purely local inconvertible currency without suffering the evils of depreciation as well as great fluctuations in its value, especially since the surrounding states were either on a specie basis or were rapidly returning to one. Unless checked by drastic action, Crittenden warned, the depreciation would proceed, and end circulation of the paper entirely, destroying the bank. The people, already fearing such an eventuality, were accelerating the very depreciation. Farmers and mechanics were beginning to realize that such a depreciated currency was ruinous to their interests, and that the increased prices of imports from other states and countries constituted a virtual tax upon their industry. In self-defense they would soon completely reject the paper of the bank.

Thus, its president virtually repudiated the basis of the bank's operations. He maintained that the only means of saving the bank would be to cease lending, and heavily contract, thus sharply reducing the notes in circulation.

The legislature, however, was in no mood as yet for such blunt messages. On the contrary, the House passed the Allen Resolution submitted by Representative Tandy Allen of Bourbon County, to reduce the rate of calls to 1 percent per month, by a two-to-one margin, and beat down by slim margins modifying amendments to reduce the note issue of the bank, and to begin providing funds for redemption of the notes. The Senate, however, refused to agree to this resolution, and the 2 percent recall rate was finally allowed to stand.[166]

The state, in the meantime, was in turmoil over the bank notes. Actually the notes had never been at par, and by the spring of 1822 were depreciated by 50 percent. Dispute was bitter on the merits of the bank notes. One critic wrote caustically that the only good quality of the notes was that they were too valueless to be worth counterfeiting.[167] Many people refused to accept the Commonwealth notes at any price, and this included many stock raisers, hemp and tobacco growers, commission merchants, and stage drivers. In fact, by 1822, it was impossible to use the notes in any everyday transactions. This included postage, which had to be paid in specie or United States Bank notes.

Bitterly and increasingly, opponents denounced the bank as destroying confidence, commerce, credit, and trade, and leaving the poor with a heavy debt to the state as well. Many had opposed the bank from its inception on the ground that it was no concern of the state's to help debtors, and that thrift and industry were the only remedies for the crisis, as well as on predictions of inevitable depreciation. On the other hand, the advocates of expansion continued to declare that the depreciation was really a blessing, since the very fact that imports from other states were cut off encouraged manufacturing in the state. The *Kentucky Gazette* went so far as to declare it good that the federal government did not accept the new notes in payment for public lands, since there would now be no great incentive for good Kentuckians to emigrate further West. It added that the depreciation "protects" Kentucky from imports of iron, leather, wool, and hemp.[168]

The end of the state bank experiment was signaled by the capitulation of the leader of the relief forces, Governor John Adair.[169] In his message to the legislature in October, 1822, only a year after his warm approval of the bank, Governor Adair concluded that legislative intervention could not really aid financial troubles. The only remedies, he asserted, were economy, industry, and the trade of foreign commerce. It was true, he declared, that government aid was often useful in emergencies, but to continue such measures would be destructive and demoralizing. The relief measures succeeded in alleviating distress, but now they must be ended. Adair recommended rapid contraction of loans and notes, and immediate withdrawal of one-sixth of the total outstanding. In this way, the exchange value of the notes would appreciate. Adair recognized that diminution in the money supply would be inconvenient, but he concluded that the state would be more than compensated by the re-establishment of credit and the "freedom of circulation" of the appreciated currency.

The legislature moved more than enthusiastically to implement these recommendations. It provided for the calling in of $1 million of Commonwealth notes in twelve months, with one half to be immediately recalled, and the received notes to be burned. The burning of Bank of Commonwealth notes took place in public bonfires in Frankfort throughout the ensuing year, to the plaudits of such conservative observers as Hezekiah Niles, and to the discomfiture of the expansionists, who complained of the injustice to debtors. In January, 1823, more than $770 thousand worth of notes were publicly burned.[170] As the notes diminished in quantity and half were withdrawn from circulation, they gradually approached par.[171] A proposal to repeal the Bank Act immediately failed by a two-to-one vote, but the bank ceased to play an active role, although it continued formally in existence until the Civil War.[172]

Another monetary experiment was performed in March, 1822, by the city of Louisville. Louisville issued an inconvertible city currency in small denominations, from six cents to one dollar, to an amount totaling $47 thousand. This currency was receivable for all taxes and debts due the city; future city taxes and property were pledged for future payment. These notes soon depreciated to a negligible value, and all were retired and burned by the end of 1826.[173]

In sum, the most spectacular expansionist measures were the establishment in several western states—Tennessee, Kentucky, Illinois, and Missouri—of new state-owned banks to issue inconvertible currency. In each of these states, all the banks had suspended specie payment during the depression. After controversy, they had been allowed to continue in operation, but their notes depreciated rapidly. The legislatures then turned, despite heavy opposition, to establishing the new state-owned banks.

All of these monetary ventures began in high hopes to issue large quantities of notes. But all came quickly to grief, despite such aid by the states as legal tender provisions and penalties against depreciation. The notes depreciated rapidly almost as soon as operations began, until the public began to refuse acceptance. In Missouri and Tennessee, the depreciation was spurred by court decisions adverse to the constitutionality of the notes or the accompanying stay laws. Opinion in each of the states swung sharply against the new paper, and where the notes did not disappear from circulation, steps were taken to halt and eventually to liquidate the projects.

This record of monetary expansion should not lead us to label the West as simply "soft money" and the East as "hard money." Many western states were monetarily quite conservative during the depression. And those that adopted loan office projects did so only over bitter opposition. Nor were the other states, especially in the South, free from expansionist proposals or policies. In some southern states, banks were allowed to suspend specie payment completely and continue operations, while in others, banks were allowed to suspend payment to suspected "money-brokers." These brokers were money-changers who purchased bills of shaky or remote banks at a discount and then attempted to redeem the mass of notes at par. They performed the function of a rudimentary clearing system, and were naturally hated by the banks whose notes came home to roost.

Only staunchly hard money Virginia remained free from expansionist agitation. Maryland and Delaware passed anti-depreciation laws over bitter opposition, in vain attempts to bolster the credit of suspended banks by outlawing depreciation. Loan office proposals were considered in several eastern states, but were turned down in all of them. On the other hand, many eastern states enforced specie payment on most of their banks, and New York and New England remained largely free of expansionsist agitation or policy. Massachusetts, however, considered, and rejected, an anti-depreciation measure.

Thus, one of the sharpest and most interesting controversies generated by the panic centered on the money supply. One group urged various plans for monetary expansion, some of which were adopted; while the majority of articulate opinion advocated restoration of specie payments and abstinence from inflationist schemes. Leading figures on both sides were propelled to engage in trenchant economic analysis in finding support for their positions. Although it is true that the inflationists were relatively stronger in the West, it must not be overlooked that bitter disputes raged within each region, state, and locality. Neither was there a discernible class, or occupational, demarkation of opinion, and both sides were headed by wealthy, respectable men.

IV

PROPOSALS FOR NATIONAL MONETARY EXPANSION

Since state banks were a state responsibility, the discussion of monetary remedies for the depression took place mainly on a state level. Some people, however, envisioned inconvertible paper currency on a national scale, and put forward proposals to that effect.

The simplest method of attaining a national inconvertible paper currency, given the existing situation, was a general suspension of specie payments, including suspension by the Bank of the United States. The bank's inconvertible notes would then have been the basic national currency—a less radical course than the governmental creation of a new type of inconvertible paper. Some suggestions for this relatively moderate approach appeared. "A Mercantile Correspondent" advanced a cautious plan for a five-year suspension, with the bank to purchase one to two million of specie per annum, so that the bank would own five to ten million in specie at the end of five years, a sum which the writer deemed ample to resume payment.[1] The writer advocated a quasi legal tender plan, through an enforced stay of execution should the creditor refuse to accept the notes. "Mercantile Correspondent" proposed a maximum limit of $35 million on outstanding sums of United States Bank notes, which would function as standard money. The other banks would need no statutory limitation, since each bank would be required to pay its obligations daily to every other bank, this interbank competition acting as a check on their respective issues.

Emergency suspension of specie payments by the bank was advocated by the highly influential Oliver Wolcott of Connecticut, formerly Secretary of the Treasury. Wolcott offered no detailed plan.[2]

Another writer more boldly advocated permanent abandonment

of specie payments and use of the bank notes as standard currency.[3] "One of the People—A Farmer" asserted that the credit of the bank and confidence in its notes depended on its capital and skill rather than on the quantity of its coin. A critic calling himself "Agricola" attacked this position, asserting that the credit of a bank is determined precisely by the quantity of its specie.[4] Confidence in a bank, declared "Agricola" shrewdly, is dependent on public opinion concerning the amount of specie that the bank possesses. Specie, after all, was the means for banks to pay their debts. The writer decried excessive, and therefore depreciating, note issue. Banks, he stated, could not add to the national wealth or capital. Their sole legitimate object was to furnish facilities for exchange and to transfer money from one place to another.

One of the most detailed proposals for an inconvertible paper based on the existing Bank of the United States was put forward by "Anti-Bullionist" in a pamphlet.[5] The author attributed the crisis to the external drain of specie, particularly to the East Indies, which had caused a deficiency of the currency supply within the country. The solution was to substitute for specie a "well-regulated" paper money. This purely domestic money would enable development of the nation without danger from foreign competition or influence. Notable in "Anti-Bullionist's" approach was his attempt to guard against excessive issue of the notes and subsequent depreciation. His goal was stability in the value of money; he pointed out that specie currency was subject to fluctuation, just as was paper. Moreover, fluctuations in the value of specie could not be regulated; they were dependent on export, real wages, product of mines, and world demand. An inconvertible paper, however, could be efficiently regulated by the government to maintain its uniformity. "Anti-Bullionist" proceeded to argue that the value of money should be constant and provide a stable standard for contracts. It is questionable, however, how much he wished to avoid excessive issue, since he also specificially called a depreciating currency a stimulus to industry, while identifying an appreciating currency with scarcity of money and stagnation of industry. One of the particularly desired effects of an increased money supply was to lower the rate of interest, estimated by the writer as currently 10 percent. A lowering would greatly increase wealth and prosperity. If his plan were not adopted, the writer could only see a future of ever-greater contractions by the banking system and ever-deeper distress.

The "Anti-Bullionist" therefore proposed that the Bank of the United States issue non-redeemable paper, with the notes of the state banks redeemable in the new notes. In contrast to England, where the central bank was not subject to any legal check on its issue, the bank's notes would be limited by a certain ratio to a Treasury issue of inconvertible notes, bearing interest of 3 percent. In this elaborate plan, while the bank notes would be redeemable in Treasury notes or in specie at the bank's option, because of their interest-bearing quality the Treasury notes would not be money and would not enter into circulation. The Treasury notes would also be redeemable, at the option of the Treasury, in specie or in the par value of 6 percent government bonds. Thus, the bank notes would have a roundabout if tenuous connection with specie and would supposedly be supported at par to specie.

The author, however, was not sure about the efficacy or desirability of the specie check, and advocated in addition a direct check on the bank's issue, by a Board of Commissioners appointed by the federal government. The Board would engage in careful study of the foreign exchange market, and would require the bank to keep its note issue limited to that amount which would tend to preserve the average foreign exchange rate of the dollar at approximately par, never depreciating more than 5 percent below. In this way, the author proclaimed, in an early version of a specie exchange standard, that since the European currencies would be kept at par with specie, the American currency would also be kept at par, though not directly redeemable. The writer finally envisioned a Treasury note supply of $20 million supporting a total monetary circulation of $100 million at par value in foreign exchange.

The outstanding advocate of a national inconvertible paper money was unquestionably Thomas Law, one of the leading citizens of Washington.[6] Law came from a remarkable English family. His father was a bishop, patron of the famous Dr. William Paley, and his brothers numbered two bishops, an M.P., and Edward Law, Lord Chief Justice of England. Thomas Law himself had been a top-flight civil servant in India and had married a daughter of Martha Washington. He was a friend of the leading Washington figures, including John Quincy Adams, William Crawford, John C. Calhoun, and Albert Gallatin. Law had first propounded his plan years before the depression began, but the advent of the panic spurred him to truly zealous efforts on its behalf.[7] His influence in Washington was such that despite the poor opinion held of his scheme by the editors of the leading semi-official *National Intelligencer* they gave him space to expound it in almost every issue.[8] Law's articles are to be found under various pseudonyms, the most prevalent being "Homo," and others being "Parvus Homo," "Philo Homo," "H," "Statisticus," "Justinian," and "Philanthropus." He also carried on debates between his various pseudonyms on his monetary views.

Law criticized the Bank of the United States, which he considered an evil source of restriction on monetary expansion. He proposed to substitute a National Currency Board, to be appointed by the President and Congress.[9] The board was to issue an inconvertible national paper currency, in denominations above one dollar, with mixed coins to be issued for small change. A daring feature of the plan was that the new notes were to be loaned in perpetuity, with no necessity for repayment of principal while the interest payments were maintained. The board would lend the notes in perpetuity to the state governments at an interest of 2½ to 4 percent, in proportion to their population, on condition that the states in turn lend them to individuals at 5 percent in perpetuity.

Law asserted that these notes would not be issued in unlimited amounts. Their supply would be limited by the maintenance of the interest rate at 5 percent. When the rate of interest for loans prevailing on the market fell below 5 percent, the board would cease issuing its notes, since no one would come to the government to borrow. In fact, Law believed that if the market rate of interest fell below 5 percent debtors to the government would borrow on the market on cheaper terms in order to repay their debt at 5 percent. In this way, there would presumably be a stabilizing of the money supply and of the rate of interest. One flaw in Law's plan was that debtors to the government would hardly borrow at

4 percent to repay their debts, since they need never repay the principal in any case. Such generous terms could never be received from private lenders. Law's limits, therefore, would have proved in practice to be virtually non-existent.

Law envisioned the loans of the board and state governments to consist of subscriptions to corporations for roads, canals, and bridges; purchase of government and private stocks, and private loans. The principal object of the plan, according to Law, was "for the community to have a sufficiency of the circulating medium, without fluctuations in value by excess or scarcity, and that the interest of money may be low." [10] Law pointed to England–his birth place–as a model of prosperity, because it had sufficient (and inconvertible) currency to keep its rate of interest low.[11] Law asserted it undeniable that a certain quantity of money was necessary for current expenses.[12] This included pocket money, money for purchase of raw materials and goods, and money to build factories. Law ignored the classical economic position that in the long run any quantity of money serves as well as any other. Instead he estimated that the minimum monetary requirement was $15 per capita, i.e., $150 million for the country's ten million population. In one sense, Law agreed with the "hard money" critics of the banking system that the banks caused ruin through first encouraging credit and investments, and then curtailing their loans and bankrupting their borrowers. His objection, however, was solely to the curtailment. What was needed, he concluded, were permanent loans at low interest, in order to increase productive capital and stimulate industry. Contrasting the National Currency with a system of bank notes, he declared that while banks issued promises to pay specie that they did not have, the board would issue notes on the "property of the nation," notes which did not have to be redeemed. While bank notes could be refused by other banks and fall to a discount, this could not happen to the National Currency, which would be uniform and receivable everywhere, including payments to the government. Instead of curtailing the note issue because of specie drain, the board could rectify any deficiency of currency caused by such a drain.

It is doubtful if Law was actually concerned to have limits on excess currency, because to Law such excess was mainly hypothetical. He was actually concerned with providing "sufficiency" of currency. One of the features of his plan was that the board could never call in the currency, and, therefore, could never diminish the circulating medium. This contrasts to the banking system where banks may call in their notes at any time. The board could always increase the circulating medium if it desired, by lending more, or by buying stock (the latter proposal being a rudimentary forerunner of open-market operations). The fact that this was considered an important advantage by Law demonstrates his eagerness to increase the money supply. The sufficiency of circulation would promote all industry, and the "nation" rather than the banks would reap the profits from the loans. Furthermore, the interest rate (5 percent) would be lower than the existing rate, which Law estimated at about 6½ percent. In 1820, Law estimated the minimum currency needed at $100 million. Such an amount would more than double the circulating medium and approximately return the money supply to boom levels.[13]

With a lower rate of interest assumed to be an advantage for stimulating industry, Law did not discuss whether any limits needed to be set in lowering the interest rate. Indeed, he admitted that a 5 percent rate was chosen only for the purposes of expedience; that a 4 percent rate would be far better.[14] To Law, it was self-evident that the rate of interest could be lowered by an increase in the quantity of money; for when the supply of any commodity increased, this decreased its "value." [15]

To advance his plan,[16] Law attributed the depression mainly to a deficiency of currency, which caused shopkeepers to lose their markets and mechanics to lose employment.[17] Law also declared that his monetary expansion plan, not protective tariffs, was the proper cure for the distress of the manufacturers. To Law, domestic manufactures were distressed from

> the want of money, for the home manufacturers cannot afford to sell on long credits. They must have quick returns to pay workmen. I know of manufactures which have stopped, not because they were undersold by foreign goods, but solely because they could not get money. Money is the means to pay workmen, to set up machinery. . . .[18]

Protectionists had pointed out that small handicraft manufacturers were suffering less from the depression than the large manufacturers. To the protectionists, this was clear evidence that the more heavily capitalized manufactures suffered the most, and that therefore a protective tariff was needed for larger capital. To Law, on the other hand, the lesson was different:

When specie diminished, the banks curtail, and the large masses of money are . . . diminished; those therefore who have to purchase raw materials and to pay two or three hundred workmen every week, and who rely upon collecting large sums—first feel the want of money.[19]

Elaborating on the benefits from increased money, Law pointed to the great amount of internal improvements that could be effected with the new money. He decried the slow process of accumulating money for investment out of profits. After all, the benefit was derived simply from the money, so what difference would the origin of the money make? And it would be easy for the government to provide money, because the government "gives internal exchangeable value to anything it prefers." All it need do, concluded Law, was spend five millions of newly issued currency per year on public works, and, in a pump-priming effect, "the money thrown into circulating would, in the course of a year, enable individuals to make a number of improvements also."

Other advantages for his plan cited by Law: that national paper could not be affected by an external drain, that specie would be used to buy goods from abroad instead of "being locked up at home," and that America would be insulated from the fluctuating fortunes of foreign gold and silver mines. Law also cited Hume to support the advantages for production of increases in the circulating medium.[20]

Law admitted, in answer to critics of inconvertible paper, that his paper might depreciate, but he asserted that this was of minor importance compared to the beneficial lowering of the interest rate and the activation of industry. To those who maintained that a nation could satisfy its monetary needs by importing specie, Law retorted that this could only happen through a favorable balance of trade, which "rarely happens" in any country, particularly a new country, which had "so many wants" that it could not develop a large favorable balance. Merchants, furthermore, always preferred importing goods, upon which they could make a profit, to importing specie.

Law's preference for his plan over the existing banking system did not prevent him from preferring bank paper to specie. The imperative was to reverse the contraction of the money supply. Thus, he commended the various state legislatures for permitting banks to continue in operation without paying in specie.[21] In fact, Law proposed as an alternative that the Bank of the United States convert its existing assets of seven million dollars of 5 percent government bonds into new non-interest bearing Treasury notes. The bank would then use these notes, with the advantage of not being acceptable abroad, as a base for a two or threefold expansion of credits.[22] Law, however, far preferred his national paper plan to the existing system or to loan offices in the separate states.[23]

One of Law's most interesting contributions was his attempt to grapple with the embarrassing fact that, toward the end of 1820, New York City experienced an abundance of money for lending, and had low interest rates. This phenomenon presented two difficulties for Law: it seemed to eliminate the need for Law's planned reduction of the rate of interest, while, on the other hand, the fact that the depression still remained seemed to indicate that low interest was not the sovereign remedy. Law countered that the low interest rates in New York were purely temporary and the result of sudden remittances by foreigners—particularly from Spain, Portugal, and Naples—to take advantage of the high interest rates here, and especially, to obtain security for their funds during their domestic political convulsions, "which they may withdraw when quiet is restored." This is an early example of a "hot money" analysis.[24]

Law upheld his plan against an alternative scheme put forward by Littleton Dennis Teackle of Queen Annes County, Maryland. Teackle wished to base his proposed national currency on the "solid and immovable value" of the nation's real estate—the valuation to be made by a tribunal of lawyers, financiers, and commissioners.[25] Law countered with the shrewd objection that it would be impossible to evaluate accurately all of the nation's real estate. His major complaint was that Teackle envisioned the retirement of the notes in ten years, which would again cause severe monetary scarcity. The only remedy was a note issue maintained in perpetuity.[26]

A Boston writer attacked Law's plan, chiefly basing his argument on a distinction between "fictitious currency" and "legitimate currency." The latter consisted of idle capital of intrinsic value, or its representative. Thus, specie or bank notes backed by actual specie deposits or redeemable in specie were legitimate currency. Artificial currency was any currency not backed by specie.[27]

Another plan for a national note issue based on land was presented by an anonymous writer in *Niles' Register*.[28] He advocated a maximum note issue of $30 million. Notes would be redeemable in gold or silver after sixteen years. They would be loaned at 6 percent interest and preferably applied to the development of internal improvements. The notes would, of course, be receivable in all dues to the government. Bank notes would be redeemable in this new government paper, although the bank would also have the option of paying in specie. The writer did not advocate that the notes be made legal tender. These notes could not depreciate because they would be redeemable in public land, possessing "certain" and intrinsic value, while gold and silver would revert to their "true character" as articles of commerce. Under an inconvertible currency, the writer proclaimed, there would be an automatic balancing of foreign trade. If imports exceeded exports, then merchants could not obtain specie for export as they could under redeemable currency. Therefore, foreign exchange would rise above par, prices of imports would rise, and imports would diminish in favor of domestic purchases, while conversely, exports would be promoted by the relative fall in their prices. The burden on imports would spur the development of domestic manufactures. The writer was not content to assert a new equilibrium exchange rate—and a depreciated one at that—as his final conclusion; instead, he maintained that the balance of trade would swing to becoming favorable again and the exchange rate would revert back to par. He failed to realize, of course, that with the currency inconvertible, there would be no mechanism to assure a maintenance of the original par.

One monetary expansionist, "Agricola," is interesting for his denunciation of state debtors' relief laws, such as stay and appraisement, which he denounced as pure "quackery." [29] All that we really needed was money, he said. Let Congress, therefore, give the people a circulating medium for internal purposes. Although he signed himself "Agricola" from Ontario, New York, the writer conceded that he was also a merchant and manufacturer and claimed that the lack of circulating medium was oppressing the industrious and the middle classes.

One North Carolinian advocated inconvertible government paper while also proposing the abolition of incorporated state banking.[30] Gold and silver were foreign commodities, he declared. Paper was the best medium, precisely because no intrinsic property was being employed as money. The writer estimated that the total United States revenue was $25 million, and that the first issue of government paper should also be $25 million. This limitation on issue would insure against depreciation of the paper. The issue of notes could be stopped by the government whenever they depreciated in relation to specie. Also, the government could call on holders of its bills to fund them by purchasing interest-bearing government bonds. The writer urged that the notes be first used to acquire mortgages on real estate. The goverment's debt would then be offset by its mortgage assets. He envisioned a maximum issue of $50 million.

Another leading promoter of a national paper plan was the fabulous merchant and financier James Swan.[31] Swan accepted all the arguments of the critics of banks against bank paper. Indeed, he went further than Law, asserting that banks should be forced to pay their obligations in the same way as private individuals, so that the over-speculative banks might pay the penalty for their errors. He believed the remedy to be a new type of paper money that would not only eliminate the deficiency of specie, but also "give new life to our sunken trade, nourish the agricultural industry, create commercial wealth, and even render gold and silver altogether useless." The basis of this paper would be the approximately 800 million acres of public land owned by the United States government. Valued at its legal minimum sale price of two dollars per acre, the government owned the unalterable and undepreciable capital sum of $1.6 billions. On this capital, the government could certainly issue $150 million in notes, bearing a 3 percent interest. The government would lend its notes in individuals, to merchants on their inventories, and to proprietors on real estate mortgages. Since the loans were to be at 6 percent, and the notes would pay 3 percent to their holders, the effect was to charge a rate of 3 percent. The notes would be distributed to each state, in proportion to its population, and would be receivable at the Treasury and for state land sales and taxes. Based on a far greater amount of land capital than on scanty specie capital, they could not depreciate; indeed, asserted Swan, they would command a premium over specie, since they would bear a 3 percent interest, and since the Treasury would no longer receive specie. According to Swan, this unique interest-bearing feature of the new currency was its principal superiority to bank paper, which was not interest-bearing and "consequently [there was] no benefit in keeping it. Hence everyone sought to employ it, which caused a great rapidity in its circulation." Swan did not even think that a legal tender provision would be necessary, since the public would eagerly welcome an interest-bearing currency.

Some plans for a national inconvertible paper were more modest than any of the aforementioned, and simply involved the issuance of a few million dollars in new Treasury notes, which would be loaned to the banks at 5 to 6 percent interest to ward off specie runs.[32]

Proposals for an inconvertible federal paper money only fleetingly reached the stage of Congressional consideration. One instance was the resolution, in late 1819, by Representative Charles C. Pinckney of South Carolina, for the establishment of a government paper money system. The New York *American* was outraged.[33] Surely, it warned, Congress could not entertain such a proposition for a moment. It would inevitably banish specie from the country, depreciate the currency, greatly increase the cost of living, and defraud the honest debtor. The country, asserted the *American*, had sufficient specie in circulation and had succeeded in bringing prices down again "to their just level," injuring in the deflationary process only the speculators on credit. Naturally, these speculators would like to return to the "system of fictitious values" built upon immense paper issues.

Although no direct action was taken on Pinckney's proposals, more support was given in the House for a serious inquiry into the possibility of a government paper plan, and the House passed a resolution in July, 1819, requesting the Secretary of the Treasury to report measures "to procure and retain a sufficient quantity of gold and silver coin in the United States, or to supply a circulating medium, in place of specie." The conservative press was shocked at this resolution, which formed the basis for Secretary Crawford's famous Report on the Currency of the following year.[34] One of the most bitter attacks was leveled by the fiery William Duane, publisher of the Jeffersonian Philadelphia *Aurora*, and a powerful figure in Pennsylvania politics. In an open letter to Langdon Cheves, president of the Bank of the United States, Duane, in his typically vitriolic style, charged that Congress was about to set up a new Continental currency, the object of which was to ensure the supremacy of the villainous Bank of the United States.[35] Hezekiah Niles went so far as to suspect Crawford of secretly plotting the establishment of a paper system.[36]

Crawford's Report was sent to the House the following February.[37] It is true that he concluded against an inconvertible paper plan and that this ended any Congressional action on the subject. However, he did present a plan which he considered the best of any possible paper currency scheme. This plan has been unduly neglected by historians, for it presented many interesting facets and aroused considerable controversy in the contemporary press. Crawford, far from being a straightforward enemy of paper expansion, throughout his report found himself in a quandary on the paper money issue. He first stressed the disadvantages, and then the advantages, of a national inconvertible currency.[38] On the one hand, he recognized that paper issues would drive specie out of the country and lead to a rapid depreciation in the value of the currency. On the other hand, he maintained that an increase of paper issues increased monetary demand for goods, and "hence" caused production to rise beyond the level it would attain under a purely specie currency. Therefore, the current sudden contraction of paper money not only sharply lowered prices and injured debtors but also hampered enterprise and production. He acknowledged that falling prices benefited the export market, but pointed out that they also depressed the prices of all non-exportable goods, such as land and houses. Crawford, in fact, far more sophisticated than Law or the other national currency advocates, recognized that *falling* prices were far worse for enterprise than simply *low* prices. Stated Crawford:

> A manufacturer will not hazard his capital in producing articles, the price of which is rapidly declining. The merchant will abstain from purchases, under the apprehension of a further reduction in price, and of the difficulty of revending at a profit.

The advantage of paper money, then, was to stimulate production and enterprise, particularly in contrast to the wringer that the specie system was currently imposing on the economy.

The paper money plan outlined by Crawford was as follows: The government would issue Treasury notes and put them into circulation in exchange for specie or for government bonds ("stock") at par. The holder would have the option of converting the notes into *government bonds* ("stock") at any time. These bonds would be yielding a low rate of interest. The banks would be completely relieved of any obligation to pay their notes in specie; instead they would be obliged to redeem them in Treasury notes. As a check on banks, only the national currency would be receivable in payments to government. Furthermore, the banks would be required to buy government bonds on the latter's request.

Now, suggested Crawford, suppose the demand for money in the economy rose. This would push the market rate of interest above the rather low rate of interest set on government bonds. Individuals and banks would then exchange their government bonds for the national currency at government offices, and relend the money at the higher market value rate of interest. In this way, by issuing more currency as the demand increased, the market rate of interest would be driven down to the official rate on government bonds. Conversely, suppose that the demand for money fell. Then, the market rate of interest would fall below the rate of government bonds; holders of the paper currency would exchange it for government bonds in order to reap the higher interest return on bonds. The government would retire the currency handed in, the supply of money in circulation would fall, and the market rate of interest would rise to that on government bonds.

Crawford, by postulating a paper currency convertible into government bonds, expected that in this way the supply of currency would be automatically regulated so as to set the market rate of interest equal to the rate paid on government bonds. Further, the supply of currency would be regulated by the demand for it. Under this plan, Crawford believed that there could be no excessive issue of the money supply. If the issue of paper became excessive, the rate of interest on the market would fall, and, as we have seen, holders of paper would exchange it for government bonds, reducing the supply of paper in circulation. Thus, both the supply of currency and the rate of interest would be automatically regulated.

Crawford finally rejected his own plan, with considerable reluctance. He did it primarily because the record of governments showed that they could not be trusted with paper money, that they would inevitably abuse this power through excessive issues, and burden the economy with all the consequent evils of inflation and depreciation. His second reason was the location of the major monetary troubles in the South and West, which contributed a large part of the federal revenue through public land purchases, while the government spent most of its revenue in the East. As a result, there was a permanent drain of the currency from the West and South, a drain unjustly ascribed in those regions to the Bank of the United States, and this would continue whether the currency was specie or paper. So the regions with the greatest deficiency of currency could not be helped by a national paper. There was no alternative but to conclude that the national suffering must continue until property values and wages had fallen to where the banks would be able generally to resume specie payments.[39]

Crawford's final rejection of a national paper scheme was no great inspiration to the hard money stalwarts, who resented his doctrinal concessions to inconvertible paper, and his proferred, if finally rejected, plan for a national currency. Thus, William Duane, of the Philadelphia *Aurora*, simply dismissed the plan as a "tissue of absurdities."[40] More interesting was the reaction of Thomas Ritchie, publisher of the important Richmond *Enquirer*, fountainhead of Virginia Jeffersonianism, laissez-faire, and hard money doctrine. Ritchie penned a very intelligent critique of the Crawford Report, including its sections on the causes of the crisis, in three articles in the *Enquirer*.[41] Crawford admitted, began Ritchie, that no paper money could succeed unless protected from excessive issue to the same extent as specie, with the latter's universality of use throughout the world. Ritchie maintained that only specie or paper convertible into specie could avoid depreciation. Specie-convertible paper was protected from excess issue because an external drain would "restore the equilibrium." Crawford, on the other hand, suggested substituting for this specie convertibility a new type of convertibility—into funded government bonds. But in contrast to the relative stability of the value of specie, the universal medium, the value of government bonds fluctuated very rapidly. Their value, continued Ritchie, was affected by numerous factors: the prospects for profit; the quantity of bonds on the market; the status of the government debt; and the prospects of war or peace. Crawford, for example, admitted that in times of war or emergency, his proposed currency would collapse completely, whereas specie always rose in public esteem under crisis conditions.

Ritchie then turned to the automatic regulatory feature of the plan that had so recommended it to Crawford. First, Crawford had contended that an excessive paper issue would cause interest rates on the market to fall below the interest rates on government bonds, and thus impel holders of currency to convert their holding into bonds. But this argument assumed that the "rate of interest necessarily depends on the quantity and value of money in circulation." This, asserted Ritchie, was clearly incorrect. In Ricardian fashion, he declared that the value of money and the rate of interest depended on different principles. The former was determined by the proportion between the "circulating medium and the quantum of exchanges." The latter depended on the "real or supposed profit of capital; the profit of capital depends on the proportion between the quantity of capital and the demand for its profitable enjoyment." A fourfold increase in the money supply, said Ritchie, would raise prices by four and reduce the value of money by one-fourth, but it would not affect the *rate* of interest. The *amount* of interest and the amount of principal on any transaction might increase fourfold, but this need not change the rate.

To the contention that the rate of interest depended upon, and moved inversely to, the quantity of money in circulation, Ritchie thus countered with a "real" theory of interest, and movements in the quantity of money affecting only prices; if they affected all prices equally, then it was clear that a *ratio*, such as the rate of interest, would not be altered. He deduced, therefore, that it was possible to have excessive currency in circulation, without an increase in the profits of capital, and hence without effecting a change in the rate of interest. On the other hand, the supply of currency might be deficient, while the interest rate was low, because a poor prospect for profit had diminished the demand for capital. Ritchie concluded that interest need not be low when money was excessive; in fact, it was possible for excessive currency and boom conditions to be accompanied by a quickening of the spirit of enterprise and an increase in the prospects for profit. In that case, the bonds "would be converted into currency to be employed in active enterprises." Thus, Crawford's scheme was likely to have an *aggravating*, rather than a stabilizing, effect on excessive currency, and to propel the currency to a great stage of depreciation. Indeed, Ritchie declared, this was exactly what had happened in the recent boom before the depression. People had borrowed at high interest from the banks in order to acquire depreciated bank notes. This foregoing of fixed interest return to obtain money was certainly likely to occur under the Crawford national currency plan.

Similar perversity, added Ritchie, would occur in bad times. When the currency was deficient and the prospects for profit low, market interest rates would also be low, and people would tend to convert their currency into government bonds, thus aggravating the deficiency of currency.

Ritchie was not content to stop at this point in his penetrating analysis of the Crawford paper plan. He added that advocates of the scheme might reply that the government could always keep watch on the fluctuations in the prices of government bonds, and that, instead of maintaining convertibility into bonds at par, it could continually change the rates of convertibility in accordance with the rates of interest. To this early version of a "compensated dollar," Ritchie replied that the scheme was illusory. "A thing so variable as the real or supposed profits of capital, as variable as the value of funded stock (government bonds); things—dependent upon such a variety of causes, can never be defined with sufficient accuracy to answer the purposes of a standard." This "standard" was always changing in value, being affected by changes in many factors; especially the supply of government bonds, and the supply of and the demand for capital. These changes would be too numerous and subtle to be detectable by the government. The best course was to leave gold and silver alone; they would have infinitely fewer fluctuations than these "paper thermometers." Crawford's plan was no better than all the other paper schemes and we must return to the use of specie, the universal medium, which ebbed and flowed from one country to another according to its excess or deficiency.

If Crawford's doctrinal concessions to the inflationists angered the pure hard money advocates, his conclusion against paper and in favor of continuing deflation until convertibility was restored galled the inflationists. Thomas Law was moved to write a pamphlet specifically devoted to a critique of the Crawford Report.[42] Law attacked the widespread phobia against depreciation of currency; admittedly paper issues had a tendency to depreciate, but they also activated industry. He praised the many state legislatures for permitting banks to operate without having to redeem in specie. Law did not actually attack Crawford's paper proposal at length, but he took the occasions to present his own paper plan in detail.

James Madison, Ritchie's fellow Virginian, was willing to concede the theoretical possibility of a regime of paper money rigidly limited by the government. He added, however, that in practice, when money depended on the discretion of government, it would be bound to depreciate. Madison declared:

It cannot be doubted that a paper currency rigidly limited in its quantity to purposes absolutely necessary, may be made equal and even superior in value to specie. But experience does not favor a reliance on such experiments. Whenever the paper has not been convertible into specie, and its quantity has depended on the policy of the government, a depreciation has been produced by an undue increase, or an apprehension of it.[43]

A general attack on paper money schemes was leveled by Hezekiah Niles. Niles hailed the opportunity brought by the depression to purge the country of speculation and excess bank paper, provided that paper money schemes did not interfere. Money would then rise to its legitimate value.[44] As to the debt-burdened farmers, they deserve to reap the consequence of their imprudence.[45] Niles further pointed out that widespread complaints of "scarcity of money" always arose after the country had been flooded with paper, and the result was a scarcity of *genuine* money.[46] Hard-money pamphleteer "Seventy-Six" attacked the thesis of scarcity of money at length and added that anyone could purchase currency by selling his labor or his property. He also pointed out that "Whatever quantity of money exists . . . is used to the full; a greater or less quantity will simply lower or raise in exchange." [47]

Monetary proposals did not loom large in the Congressional arena during the depression. In the spring of 1819, proposals for suspension of payment by the Bank of the United States developed into scattered demands for a special session of Congress, to compel the Bank of the United States to suspend payment. The *National Intelligencer* scoffed at these demands as holding up false hope for a remedy—a remedy which would only aggravate the monetary disease.[48] The demands for a special session came to naught.

Another simple remedy was advanced to end the external specie drain: the prohibition of specie exports. A prominent advocate of this measure was Mordecai Manuel Noah, editor of the New York *National Advocate.* At the beginning of the panic, he stated simply that 1818 had seen a specie drain abroad of over $6 million, and that prohibition would end the drain and restore confidence in the banking system. Since almost all of the specie flowed to the East Indies, Noah proposed that each vessel to the East Indies be limited to a certain quota of trade, and that imports of East India goods be limited to the amount "required for general consumption." [49] Another writer, "Solon," coupled prohibition with the suggestion that the banks end their haphazard clearing operations and cooperate by not calling on each other daily for specie. This would permit expansion of the circulating medium.[50] The call for prohibition of specie exports was promptly challenged. "H," writing in the *National Intelligencer* and reprinted and specifically endorsed by the New York *Gazette*,[51] a very staid organ usually devoid of politics, charged that the proposal to prohibit export of specie was a "stale experiment . . . universally discredited by . . . every standard writer on political economy." It would aggravate the evil of depression by spreading uneasiness among merchants. Furthermore, such a law would cause the "moneyed men to hoard every bit of gold and silver that they could obtain." Stopping the East India trade would be quite harmful. The India trade provided "an immense advantage," supplying us necessaries such as tea and sugar, and goods which we exported to Europe at a profit.[52]

"Virginian" compared the proposal for prohibiting the export of specie to Spain's prohibition in the era when specie was its main article of wealth, after the mining discoveries in the new world.[53] Specie would always be exchanged for "more essential articles" needed for use and would seek out those countries which furnished the best and cheapest supply. If the United States could compete, it would have no deficiency of specie, as "Piano E. Sano" expressed it. Specie, like every commodity, contains a self-regulating principle.[54] A superfluity in one region sought a better exchange elsewhere. The specie drain was clearly caused by an excess of bank paper, which made part of the specie superfluous. He advocated as a remedy the strict enforcement of specie payments by the banks.

One writer relied primarily on Adam Smith for his attack on export prohibition.[55] "Hamilton" quoted verbatim from Smith's attack on the concept of scarcity of money, in which Smith had asserted that the so-called scarcity was simply a difficulty of borrowing or selling goods for money and the results of previous misjudgments and overtrading.[56]

The export of specie held no terrors also for those who were ready to establish an inconvertible paper system. Thus, "Anti-Bullionist" stated that with specie demonetized, there would be no reason at all to prohibit the profitable specie trade with the West Indies, since specie would simply be another commodity.[57]

A curious and unique argument against prohibition of specie export was delivered by "N.O." in the New York *Evening Post.*[58] He went to the opposite extreme and declared that the cause of the depression was an *excess* amount of specie, and therefore the remedy was to *encourage* the export of specie rather than prohibit. The author, however, failed to develop the reasoning behind his position.

In Congress there was considerable interest in the possibility of prohibiting the export of specie. Senator Talbot of Kentucky, chairman of the Senate Finance Committee, reported negatively on the question of prohibiting the export of coin. He cited history to demonstrate the impotence of all such legislative prohibitions, even under the most despotic governments. Talbot took this position despite the advocacy of export prohibition by Senator John Forsyth of Georgia, another member of the committee. Talbot declared that an unfavorable balance of trade would always cause a drain of specie. The best course, he concluded, was not to impose any such regulation but to let trade work itself without legislative restrictions.[59] The cue had been given to the finance committee a month earlier by Secretary of the Treasury Crawford, in response to a House request for his opinion on this problem. Crawford contrasted such practices of the dark ages to the "progress of reason" and "the advancement of the science of political economy in the seventeenth and eighteenth centuries, and its immutable laws."[60] The flow of specie, stated Crawford, depends upon the general balance of trade, which had become unfavorable due to the expansion of bank notes and bank credit. No legislative interference was necessary, except to enforce the obligation of the banks to redeem their notes in specie on demand.

Apart from the specie drain, another problem confronted the nation in this period—the disappearance of gold coin. This drain of gold resulted from the official American exchange rate between gold and silver undervaluing gold on the world market. Secretary Crawford and House committees, in 1819 and 1821, recommended a revaluation of gold to a ratio of approximately 15½ to 1 of silver, instead of 15 to 1. A House committee in 1821 reported that the United States had minted $6 million in gold but that practically none was being retained in this country.[61]

On March 3, 1819, Congress passed an act ending the legal tender quality for foreign gold coins. In November of that year, it failed to extend the legal tender quality as it had in the past. French and Spanish silver coins, however, continued to be legal tender. The act injured the Southwest, the major point of import for foreign gold coin. The General Assembly of Louisiana, led by David C. Ker, Speaker of the House, and Julien Pryches, President of the Senate, sent a resolution to the Senate in April, 1820, attacking the action for blocking a large flow of specie imports. The Assembly estimated that elimination of the legal tender provision, added to cutbacks in Mexican mining output due to the current revolution against Spain, had diminished the influx of specie into New Orleans by a half million dollars per year, which "flowing into circulation would have . . . diminished the general embarrassments under which our commerce labors." [62]

One fleeting proposal was that Congress devalue the dollar to ninety-six cents. It was mentioned, though not identified further, by the astute New York writer "Senex," who attacked such a proposal as injuring fixed income groups. Said "Senex": "The stockholders, landowners and annuitants and all persons having fixed income, would suffer a diminution of income to the extent of 4 percent, while merchants, manufacturers, and traders would increase the prices of the articles in which they deal." [63]

Surveying the state and national proposals, the expansionist argument ran as follows: the nation is suffering from a "scarcity of money"; the banks unaided are in no position to stop contracting or to expand currency; therefore the government should free the monetary system from the limitations of specie payment and permit expansion of inconvertible paper. The nation needed more currency, and government was the agency best able to provide it. Debtors would be relieved as the new notes were loaned to them and would be aided by the consequent price increases.

The expansionists also maintained that an increase in the money supply would bring about a low rate of interest—one of the essentials of prosperity. This view was grounded, of course, on an assumed inverse relation between the quantity of money and the rate of interest. In keeping with this view, some writers elaborated plans to stabilize simultaneously the interest rate and the quantity of money.

Restrictionists replied that the quantity of money determines its value, or purchasing power, and not the rate of interest. Interest rates were determined by prospects for profit on investments.

Restrictionists, on the other hand, averred that any increase in paper money would aggravate rather than cure the depression. Most of this group laid the basic cause of the depression to a monetary cycle of expansion and contraction. Not only would a present expansion renew the process but the inconvertible notes were bound to depreciate, wreaking further havoc and postponing recovery. The emission of inconvertible paper, therefore, would not really increase the *effective* money supply. The only cure for the depression from the monetary side was rigid enforcement of specie payment, permitting a return to thrift and a liquidation of unsound bank notes and business positions. This point of view was common to practically all the opponents of inconvertible paper. Some restrictionists added that bank notes were also excessive because they kept the price of American export staples too high for competition in world markets. Enforcement of specie payments and ensuing contraction were necessary to reduce export prices and revive the export trade. To this argument, some inflationists offered two ingenious objections. One was that higher domestic prices might indeed reduce exports in *physical* terms, that they would still increase the *monetary* value of exports. Another was that contraction would also cause a fall in the prices of *non-exportable* goods such as land and houses, and that a fall in such prices would not stimulate exports.

Confidence was another key point in dispute. The inflationists urged the equivalent of pump-priming, stressing that note emissions would restore confidence, thereby inducing money out of idle hoards and into credits and investments. As debtors were relieved, creditors would gain confidence, lend their money again, and recovery would ensue. To the restrictionists, on the other hand, confidence depended upon strict maintenance of specie payment. Strict specie payment would restore industry and economy and bring back confidence, drawing hoarded specie back into circulation. To the inflationist's contention that new loans to debtors would bolster general confidence, some hard money writers countered that lack of confidence and hoarding were *not* caused by purely psychological factors, but rather by the objective lack of good security available. This could only be remedied by enforcing specie payment and liquidating unsound banking and credit positions. They also replied to advocates of an increased velocity of circulation that increased velocity of money would only further depreciate the paper currency.

The *depreciation* issue was, indeed, the main problem for the expansionists; it was the main burden of the opposition attack and the most difficult to answer. Some expansionists conceded that the notes might depreciate and that this would be troublesome, but upheld the far superior advantages of an increased money supply. Other advocates were much bolder and frankly hailed depreciation as a desirable development. Within each state, expansionists proclaimed the advantages accruing to that state from building up a state-wide "home" market. Money would be retained to circulate at home, increasing the rapidity of circulation of the notes. Interstate debtors would be paid in farm produce instead of money, and this would help develop the home market for the state's farm produce.

Other expansionists, conversely, upheld as their ultimate goal the maintenance of a stable value of money. Instead of a vague policy of endless expansion, they hoped for a stabilization of money and prices after the current contraction had been offset. These writers reminded the specie advocates that specie also fluctuated in value. A truly stable money could only be obtained by a limited, regulated issue of inconvertible paper by the government. Some pursued the old will-o'-the-wisp of a money based in some way on the land values of the country. The notes, they alleged, would not depreciate because they would be backed by appraised public land holdings. The hard money writers countered this criticism of specie by admitting that while theoretically the government could issue and maintain a currency more stable than specie, in practice governments always tended to overissue paper.

Against the protectionist emphasis on higher tariffs as a cure for the depression, the inflationists argued that manufacturing was depressed, not from lack of markets but from lack of money. It was lack of money that prevented the manufacturer from buying raw materials, hiring workers and constructing plant.

In a sense, this clash of emphasis was a forerunner of the "Austrian" vs. the underconsumptionist theory of the crisis, both of which were to come to the fore in the depression of the 1930s. For the underconsumptionists stressed the cause of the crisis to be lack of consumer markets for products, while the Mises-Hayek theory blamed the crisis on a shortage of saved capital. In the panic of 1819, the protectionists stressed the lack of consumer markets abroad and the necessity for building up a market at home. The inflationists, on the other hand, stressed the shortage of money capital available to manufacturers as a cause of the crisis. Curiously, the policy prescriptions of the two groups were diametrically opposed rather than parallel. For the underconsumptionist of 1819 believed that consumption would be stimulated by tariffs, while the underconsumptionist of a later day urged monetary expansion as the remedy. On the other hand, the remedy proposed for the shortage of money capital was monetary inflation in 1819, encouragement of savings and thrift in the 1930s. The crucial difference seems to be that the inflationists of the early period saw monetary expansion primarily as a way of providing capital, whereas the inflationists of the twentieth century saw it as a means of stimulating consumption, increased investment following as a consequence.

The hard money forces denied that a scarcity of money existed. After all, money could always be purchased on the market. And if a scarcity of money did exist, it was a scarcity of *genuine* money—of specie—and this scarcity would continue until specie payments were fully restored.

With the economic argument conducted so often on so high a level, one might wonder why there were virtually no proposals for devaluating the dollar to account for the higher price levels in relation to specie. It must be remembered, however, that there were scarcely any advocates of such a course in Great Britain at this time—or even a hundred years later.

The debates over proposals for nationwide monetary expansion strengthen our previous conclusions on the absence of rigid geographical or class lines in the inflation controversies. Certainly the leading inflationist, Thomas Law, one of the most influential citizens of Washington, was the opposite of a poor agrarian.

V

RESTRICTING BANK CREDIT: PROPOSALS AND ACTIONS

Contrasting to proposals for expanding the money supply were suggestions for restricting bank credit such as placing curbs on the issue of bank notes or requiring banks to redeem in specie. They grew out of the grave problem of the defaulting and suspending banks, and of the widespread depreciation of their notes. The impetus came from both a belief that sounder banking would cure the panic by placing monetary and banking affairs on a firmer basis and the desire to prevent unsound bank credit expansion, and subsequent depression, in the future.

Secretary of Treasury Crawford, despite his toying with the idea of inconvertible paper, typified the opinion of those who wished to restrict banks and bank credit. In his Currency Report,[1] he declared that in order to return to a specie convertible basis, superfluous banks must be eliminated. Banks should only exist in the principal commercial cities of each state. Small denomination note issues should be prohibited and banks should discount "nothing but transaction [commercial] paper payable at short date." [2] The maximum amount of these discounts should equal the total of savings and deposit accounts and half the paid-in capital. Then the banks would always be able to maintain convertibility. The present system of banking, Crawford declared, had banished specie by issuing paper in excess of the demand for transmitting funds and had fostered extravagance, idleness, and the spirit of gambling. Crawford stated that restraints on the banks were a responsibility of the state legislatures, although he conceded that the federal government had contributed to the spirit of speculation by granting credit on public land sales and through the extension of credit by the Bank of the United States.

Banks were largely state responsibilities. And so the problem of the banks was thrashed out largely on the state level. In Georgia, the legislature voted in late 1818 to penalize any incorporated bank refusing to pay specie on demand, and imposing a 2¼ percent per month interest penalty. This followed the defeat of a 3 percent per month interest penalty proviso in a bill to incorporate the new Bank of Darien. Another important measure passed in the same session—prohibition of the circulation of notes of unchartered private banks and of the issue of small denomination notes.[3] In 1820, Georgia passed an act requiring annual reports from the banks, but it proved ineffectual.[4]

One of the methods of restraining bank credit expansion was to reject incorporations of new banks or to insert compulsory specie payment clauses in their charters. An indication of popular opinion was the presentment of a grand jury of Jasper County, a rural county southeast of Atlanta. The presentment asked for no further additions to bank charters.[5] The Georgia legislature turned down several applications for new banks. It rejected a charter of a proposed Agricultural Bank of the State of Georgia by a two-to-one vote. This bank would have had an authorized capitalization of $1 million. The bank was rejected even after the charter was amended to include an absolute specie paying clause.

The Georgia legislature also rejected by a similar majority a bill to authorize the Marine and Fire Insurance Company of Savannah to issue its own notes and discount promissory notes. On the other hand, it passed the charter of a new bank at Augusta, over opposition, and enacted a charter for the Bank of Darien without penalizing failure to pay in specie.[6]

Virginia was a leading stronghold of hard-money opinion. Its leading statesmen, such as Thomas Jefferson, attacked any issue of bank paper beyond the supply of specie. As we have seen in the case of the Crawford Report, Thomas Ritchie, editor of the Richmond *Enquirer*, used sophisticated economic arguments to attack any suggestion of inconvertible paper schemes.[7] Typical of Virginia opinion was an *Enquirer* editorial laying the blame for the crisis squarely at the doors of the banks. The only remedy was for the parasitic banks to be eliminated, with industry and economy allowed to effect a cure.[8] Ritchie also urged that if bank paper be permitted to continue in existence, there at least be vigorous restrictions on all banks, whether state or national, private or incorporated. Small denomination notes must be prohibited and paper must always be convertible into specie. The least reluctance to do so should forfeit the bank's charter.[9]

A writer from Petersburg, in southeastern Virginia, blamed the current plight on paper money and cited the French economist, Destutt de Tracey (whose work was being translated under the supervision of Thomas Jefferson), to the effect that when a merchant could not pay his debts, the best he could do was liquidate and to become bankrupt quickly.[10]

Another point of view was expressed by "A Virginian." He suggested the abolition of all *incorporated* banking, instead placing reliance on private banks, the owners of which would be fully liable for their debts. Such banks, he declared, "cannot overtrade, that is, issue more paper than the market requires; their credit will not exceed its just limits." [11]

Some writers, however, sounded a note of caution, stressing that bank note contraction should take place slowly, so as not to disrupt the economy unduly.[12]

A unique monetary plan was offered by Spencer Roane, the great Chief Justice of the Virginia Court of Appeals and the leading foe, on behalf of states' rights, of Justice John Marshall's loose constructionist decisions.[13] Roane began by asserting that "banking is an evil of the first magnitude," and in this sentiment he claimed the support of prevailing opinion throughout the United States. However, bank paper could not be eradicated and a return made to pure specie without causing "widespread ruin and distress." How, then, to reform the banks? As long as they remained in existence, they must be controlled. The Bank of the United States was not the proper instrument for this control, for it possessed the nationwide power of increasing or diminishing the circulating medium at will. The United States Bank had a far greater potential for harm than did the state banks. On the other hand, the state banks needed a general central control, to produce uniformity of action and confidence in their issues and to see that they redeemed their notes. As a substitute for the present unsatisfactory system, then, Roane proposed "Banks which shall be local as to the extent of their patronage and power, but national as to their responsibility." Roane—champion of states' rights—suggested a Constitutional Amendment to prohibit the states from creating any bank corporations and to authorize the federal government to establish an "independent bank" in every state, with the assent of that state. Of the capital stock of each such bank, one-fifth was to be subscribed by the United States government, one-fifth by the state, and the remainder by the citizens of the particular state. Each bank was to have fifteen directors, all citizens of the state—three to be appointed by the federal government, three by the state government, and the remainder by the other stockholders. "The objection to the United States Bank, as at present organized, would not apply to [these] bank[s]. . . . The patronage of the directory and its power over the circulating medium, would be confined to the state where it should be located." The Bank of the United States had compelled some branches suddenly to curtail their note issue, because of the independent and lax management of other branches. "An independent bank would be enabled to pursue a course regulated only by its own business and the balance of trade for or against the state where it should be located." On the other hand, the independent banks would be incorporated by the federal government and would therefore be uniform throughout the country, and all compelled to redeem in specie.

> It cannot be doubted that institutions that are relied on to afford a national currency, should be under national control. It would be as unwise to depend on state institutions for a medium of exchange, in which to receive the national dues, as it would be to depend on state authorities for the payment of those dues. [i.e., the system of the Articles of Confederation].

The Constitution, Roane asserted, gave Congress the authority to regulate the currency of the country and prohibit such regulation to the states. This should apply to paper currency as well as to specie.

Virginia's hard money contingent, in its distrust of banks, recognized that the Bank of the United States had inflated proportionately less than did the bulk of the state banks. However, like Roane, they feared the bank as having greater potentialities for evil. As Ritchie asked: state banks were certainly evil, but "what is there to control the power of the national bank?" [14]

The most famous and one of the most thoroughgoing opponents of bank credit was Thomas Jefferson. Jefferson reacted to the panic of 1819 as a confirmation of his pessimistic views on banks.[15] He elaborated a remedial proposal for the depression in a "Plan for Reducing the Circulating Medium," which he asked his friend William C. Rives to introduce in the Virginia legislature without disclosing authorship.[16] The goal of the plan was bluntly stated as "the eternal suppression of bank paper." The method was to reduce the circulating medium gradually to that "standard level" which pure specie would find for itself equally in the several nations. For this purpose, the state government should compel the complete and utter withdrawal of bank notes in five years, one-fifth of the notes to be called and redeemed in specie each year. Further, the state should make it a high offense to pass or receive any other state's bank notes. Those banks who balked at such a plan should have their charters forfeited or be forced to redeem their notes. In conclusion, Jefferson declared that no government, state or federal, should have the power of establishing a bank. He envisioned a circulation consisting solely of specie.[17]

Governor Thomas Randolph, son-in-law and close friend of Jefferson, in his inaugural address in December, 1820, summed up the predominant Virginia attitude toward banks.[18] Randolph stated that only specie, never paper, could be a measure of value. Specie, in universal demand, had a relatively stable value, while banks caused great fluctuations in the supply and value of money, with attendant distress. Randolph looked forward to the day when eventually the whole revenue of the government would be collected in specie only. He was willing to see the state print paper money, provided that it be absolutely convertible in specie and guaranteed to be equal in value to the specie owned by the state—in short, a 100 percent reserve program.

In Delaware, the restrictionist forces kept up a running fight with the expansionists and advocates of relief legislation during the 1819 and 1820 sessions. The restrictionists made their first move in the

House upon submission of the report of the Brinckle Committee to consider the state of the paper currency. Representative Martin W. Bates of Kent County moved to reject that part of the committee's report which declared it inexpedient to compel the banks to resume specie payment. Bates's motion carried the House by one vote and had the support of Representative Henry Brinckle, himself, but of no one else on the committee.[19] The House had not yet passed a compulsory resumption bill, however. In the next session, Brinckle introduced a resolution to establish a committee to introduce the required bill.[20] Brinckle's bill passed numerous tests in the House, albeit by one vote, but the Speaker of the House took the unusual step, on final passage, of personally voting nay, and thus blocking the resolution by a nine-to-nine tie.

In Maryland a leading expression of hard money sentiment was a citizens' meeting at Elkton, in the extreme northeastern end of the state, referred to previously. Not only did the "farmers and mechanics" of Cecil County pledge themselves to refuse to take the notes of nonspecie-paying banks but they proceeded to denounce the banks and call for strict laws to compel specie payment.[21] They "viewed with abhorrence" the alarming increase of "fictitious capital" furnished by banks, they assigned the principal causes of the "decline of agricultural, mercantile, and mechanical interests" to the banks, and they pledged themselves not to vote for any candidate that would not pledge to vote to compel specie payment by the banks. The meeting also passed resolutions of gratitude to Hezekiah Niles, editor of *Niles' Weekly Register*, and to the late State Representative Matthew Pearce, for their staunch anti-bank leadership.[22] The resolutions were widely reprinted throughout Maryland and also in the *Niles' Weekly Register*. They were denounced in the Baltimore *Federal Gazette* by its editor, William Gwynn, as slanderous; Gwynn charged that the citizens had been duped by Niles. Niles quickly retorted that Gwynn was himself a bank director.[23]

Niles by no means advocated complete abolition of bank paper, however. His suggested remedies for the financial troubles: (a) cease granting corporate charters to banks; (b) make bank stockholders fully liable; and (c) enforce payment of all specie demands.[24]

The Maryland hard money advocates did not succeed in tightening the laws against banks not redeeming in specie, but they succeeded in blocking any action for monetary expansion by the legislature.

One of the leading bank restrictionists of the period was Daniel Raymond, a Baltimore lawyer, who in 1820 wrote *Thoughts on Political Economy*, the first systematic treatise on economics published in the United States.[25] Raymond set forth a virtual 100 percent specie-reserve position on banking. Bank notes, he maintained, should be confined to bank capital. Raymond criticized the assertion of Adam Smith and Alexander Hamilton (whom he otherwise greatly revered) that bank notes added to the national capital in so far as they substituted for, and economized on, specie.[26] In reply, he cited David Hume that "in proportion as money is increased in quantity, it must be depreciated in value." An issue of paper money therefore had the same effect as debasing the coinage. The increase in price raised the prices of domestic goods in export markets and caused an unfavorable balance of trade. Bank credit also promoted extravagant speculation. Ideally, Raymond believed that the federal government should eliminate bank paper entirely and supply the country with a national paper fully (100 percent) representative of specie.[27] If this could not be accomplished, then Raymond suggested that banks be subjected to government control. Government would have a monopoly on the manufacture of paper, which it would give to banks, while regulating the maximum amount that they could lend in proportion to their capital. If this plan were not adopted, Raymond's third choice was government's taxing bank profits above the going rate of interest, thus eliminating the motive for increasing bank paper.

Another advocate of 100 percent reserve, signing himself "A Farmer," was asked, in the course of a debate in the pages of the *National Intelligencer*, by a "Brother Farmer": What would become of the farmers if the banks were annihilated? "Farmer" answered that they would no longer have debts or bankruptcies and that their income would then be in undepreciated specie.[28] Joining in the anti-bank sentiments, "A Stockholder" hailed the current credit liquidation and hoped that the purification process would continue until all banks were eliminated.[29]

In the District of Columbia there were proposals to consolidate the three banks of the district into one bank. These proposals were not adopted, however. Typical of the attacks upon it was one by "Nicholas Dumbfish," who assailed the consolidation as assisting "in perpetuating this wretched system of paper, which, if left to itself, will expire, whether by its own limitation or by the total and irretrievable loss of public confidence." Better to let these institutions die a natural death.[30]

New York was one of the main centers of monetary restrictionist sentiment. Typical was the famous *Address of the Society of Tammany to its Absent Members,* which circulated throughout the country. The report was written by John Woodward, and among its signers were the Grand Sachem of Tammany (then as now in political rule of New York County), Clarkson Crolius, and secretary James S. Martin.[31] The *Address* frankly lambasted banks as being "poisonous." In particular, it attacked bank loans to agriculture. Banks might be useful in rapidly liquidating commercial transactions, but could only bring ruin to agriculture. The *Address* recommended total abolition of bank loans to agriculture, as well as the forfeiting of the charters of any banks refusing specie payment. The Society of Tammany itself, however, when passing recommendations for remedies of the depression a week later, omitted banking from the list.[32]

The Tammany *Address* was widely circulated and considered, and drew comments and letters from many famous statesmen. James Madison, for example, wrote to Crolius praising the report. He declared that even when banks restricted their operations to temporary loans to persons in active business, promising quick returns, they were likely to be harmful. There was no doubt of the mischief involved in banks' lending indiscriminately and at long term.[33]

One of the leading figures of New York State, Judge William Peter Van Ness, pseudonymously published a pamphlet advancing two restrictions on banks: first, they may discount no "accommodation paper," i.e., simple loans that were not self-liquidating in the course of active trade; and second, that they grant no renewals of loans.[34] Van Ness reasoned that failure to follow this rule had caused the depression; for when a bank loaned so as to *constitute*, rather than merely *supplement*, the capital of a merchant, it thereby sponsored "adventurers" rather than sober businessmen. Accommodation paper, furthermore, was created for the sole purpose of being discounted, whereas "business paper" arose from the actual sale of a good.[35] Van Ness believed that the Bank of the United States could aid greatly in furthering such a program.

The New York City press had largely restrictionist views. The New York *American* concluded that the true remedies for the depression were: "The gradual . . . but flexible reduction of bank discounts, refusing to incorporate any new institutions, compelling those which exist . . . to redeem their notes in specie . . . or forfeit their charter." [36]

One unique approach to the monetary problem appeared as an anonymous pamphlet on currency and credit.[37] "Seventy-Six" attacked paper and bank credit. He was unique in advocating a *grain* standard instead of a specie standard. He argued that grain must really be the best money since people resorted to barter in grain as a last ditch measure.

A significant report on the New York situation was delivered by Assemblyman Michael Ulshoeffer, from New York City, of the Committee on Currency.[38] Ulshoeffer's task was to investigate remedies for the disordered currency. As he explained, "the great object in view is that the various banks should redeem their notes promptly in specie, and that such notes should pass at their par value in every part of the state." The enormous banking capital in the state should be reduced, he demanded, and only a vast retrenchment in the paper money supply, and its prompt redemption, would effectively restore paper to par throughout the state. It was true, he conceded, that public opinion governed the value of all paper money, and that the public must be trusted to distinguish between good and unsound banks. Yet, laws might aid public opinion and restore public confidence. The state banks, he charged, had refused to redeem their notes, had kept their offices closed, and had placed all manner of obstacles in the path of redemption, while continuing to lend and circulate their notes. Therefore, Ulshoeffer recommended that the state treasurer not receive notes of any bank not promptly redeeming in specie, or not passing at par in the principal cities.

Governor De Witt Clinton, in his message opening the 1819 session of the legislature, implicitly called for an end to new bank charters for the present, indicating that the multiplication of banks was one of the main causes of the current depression, and stating that he had always been opposed to this expansion.[39] Clinton charged that investing banks with the power to coin money instead of issuing paper would be less pernicious, since at least the coins would have intrinsic value. Taking this section of the Governor's speech as a point of departure, the Senate and Assembly appointed a Joint Committee on the part of the Governor's speech dealing with currency. The report of Chairman David Allen, of the Eastern district, concluded it inexpedient to grant any more bank charters.[40] The Allen Report particularly attacked overextension of banking as one of the major causes of the depression. The banks were all right when confined to commercial centers, where they invigorated trade. But banks overextended when they began to establish themselves in remote agricultural areas, emitting "excessive issues of bank notes without the means of redeeming them," and the depreciation of their notes.[41]

One of the most astute writers in the press of the period was "Senex," who had his own solution for the problem of the country banks in New York.[42] He explained that pernicious effects of country banks' overissue stemmed from their having opened accounts with sound city banks, the latter thus assuming the liabilities of the former. After accepting country bank notes on deposit, the city banks felt bound to redeem the country notes in specie, both from want of foresight and out of the desire to please their customers. If they had not done so, the country notes would have circulated only in their local areas. The remedy was simple: the city banks should refuse to support these worthless notes. This would "reduce the amount of floating paper money by substituting metallic currency in their place."

There was no great need in New York for legislative action to enforce specie payment, since it had been largely taken care of in the

1818 session, before the panic had started. New York had then passed a bill compelling any bank to pay its notes in specie or Bank of United States notes, or suffer a payment of penalty interest to the noteholder. The strength of the proponents was seen in their defeating, by a two-to-one margin, Senator Martin Van Buren's attempt to vitiate the bill almost completely by exempting notes already in existence from its provisions. The legislature, in the same session, also prohibited any private, unchartered banking whatsoever, whether for purpose of note issue, deposit, or discount.

The most dramatic bank crisis in New York City during the depression was the failure of Jacob Barker's Exchange Bank, a private bank of unorthodox principles which had been established in New York City, a stronghold of financial conservatism. Barker had secured an exemption for three years from the legislative ban on private banking, but he went insolvent as soon as the panic arrived.[43] He was moved to pen a rather remarkable apologia for his actions.[44] Barker's pamphlet depicted a virtual morality play. His bank was begun after the war as a humanitarian gesture, doing its business mainly "with mechanics and residents of the neighboring counties, who were unable to obtain accommodations from other banks." Barker's rivals, the corporate banks, were angry because of this benevolence and conspired to wreck the bank. Barker was able to withstand all the wicked maneuvers, until pressure for redemption somehow built up from various sources, and he was forced to suspend specie operations, which in New York meant to go out of business.

A rebuttal pamphlet, printed anonymously, put its finger on a common point of restrictionist attack: small denomination notes.[45] "Plain Sense" pointed out that Barker's notes were overissued and, consequently, were now exchanging at a 45 percent discount. Particularly evil was small note circulation, and Barker's Bank was especially active in issuing small notes, which circulated among the poorer classes and "increase the change in favor of the banker" through destruction, accidents, etc. Furthermore, such people accepted the notes, even when depreciated, out of ignorance or necessity. The author advocated that banks be prohibited from issuing notes under $20. Such prohibition would restrict the area of their circulation; "notes would constantly be flowing into the hands of men having large capitals, and engaged in extensive transactions, who would return them into the bank for payment when they came into their hands." The public would then be safe, and the banker would have to confine himself to fair profits "arising from the employment of his real capital."

Another writer, using the signature "A Merchant," pointed out a second major argument against small note issue: that it leads to rapid disappearance of specie from circulation. He urged that the New York legislature follow the lead of Pennsylvania, Maryland, and Virginia and prohibit all notes under $5 denomination.[46]

Anti-bank sentiment was strong in Pennsylvania, which, as seen, was a battleground for expansionist proposals. As the panic arrived, alongside petitions for monetary expansion came petitions for coerced specie payment. Requests bombarded the legislature for liquidation of the charters of all the banks that had suspended specie payments, and for rendering the property of individual stockholders fully liable. Some of the petitions went so far as to urge revocation of all bank charters in the state. Conspicuous in sending such petitions were Mifflin County in central Pennsylvania, neighboring Union County, and Bucks County in the extreme eastern part of the state.[47] In far west Pittsburgh, the Republicans of the district (and the Republicians were the only effective political party in the state), and all Republican candidates for office, favored a compulsory specie payment law.[48] These Republicans also favored a tax against the Bank of the United States. In both of these demands, they were endorsed by the *Pittsburgh Statesman*.[49] State Senator Condy Raguet, in the course of his very extensive inquiry into the extent of the depression in Pennsylvania, sent a questionnaire to leading citizens as well as legislators in each county, sampling opinion on the depression. One of his questions was, "Do you consider that the advantages of the banking system have outweighed its evils?" [50] Of the nineteen counties sampled, sixteen answered in the negative, and these covered all areas of the state.

Raguet, who concluded that the depression was caused by bank credit expansion in the boom and subsequent contraction when specie drained from bank vaults, urged that every new or renewed bank charter have the following restrictive provisions:

(1) a penalty of 12 percent interest per annum and forfeiture of the charter, should any notes or deposits not be redeemed in specie on demand. (This was the most important provision.[51] The inclusion of deposits with notes was characteristic of Raguet, who pioneered in emphasizing their simultaneity in constituting the money supply.)

(2) loans to be limited to 150 percent of paid-in capital.

(3) all profits over 6 percent to be divided equally between stockholders and the state.

(4) prohibition on borrowing from a bank by one of its directors, also ban on a bank director's holding legislative office.

(5) annual inspection of bank accounts.

(6) prohibition of small notes under $5 denomination.

(7) no bank should be permitted to buy its own notes, or notes of any other bank, for less than par. (This was to check the speculative practice of country banks' buying their own notes in the city at a discount, instead of having to redeem them at par.)

(8) no bank should be able to own any securities of the United State government, or its own stock, or the stock of any other corporation. (The purpose of banks, as gleaned from their charters, wrote Raguet, was to accommodate merchants, farmers, mechanics, and manufacturers, and not to lend to stock speculators. Investing in government securities was a particular spur to speculation, since the greater marketability of government bonds caused government to issue more notes than it would otherwise.)

(9) no loans on security of bank's own stock.

(10) a required contingency fund for redemption of 10 percent of the bank's capital.

Although Raguet was decidedly unsympathetic to the existence of any banks aside from those with 100 percent reserve for their demand liabilities,[52] he doubted whether repeal of existing charters was expedient. Instead, he advocated inserting the provisions listed, before any charters were renewed. For existing banks in suspension, Raguet recommended that the charters not be renewed, that they be prohibited from making any new loans or note issue, and that they be given three to five years to collect their debts and wind up their affairs.

Similar calls for restrictions on banks, particularly for the forcing of specie payment, were made in William Duane's Philadelphia *Aurora*.[53] Duane advocated compulsory specie payments and full individual liability for banks' stockholders. Similar provisions had unfortunately been turned down in 1814, when forty-two new banks were incorporated. And now, as then Governor Simon Snyder and other critics had predicted, those rural counties which had been the most enthusiastic supporters of bank expansion were "the most distressed and impoverished," and the same areas were petitioning the legislature to confine all banks to cities.

"A Pennsylvanian," in an article in the Philadelphia *Union*, in the course of an open letter to the Raguet Committee, recommended the following provisions in bank charters:

(1) no bank may refuse to redeem its paper when it has specie in its vaults (a milder provision than recommended by Raguet).

(2) no bank suspending payments should be allowed to issue paper or declare dividends.

(3) directors of suspending banks must call on stockholders not yet paid in full, and sue defaulting stockholders.

(4) every director to be individually liable for the paper.

The writer asserted that these measures, in addition to ending fraudulent practices, would prevent future depreciation of bank paper, reduce bank paper outstanding, and increase its value.[54]

The Pennsylvania legislature began restricting bank expansion in late 1818, at the urging of former Governor Snyder, now a State Senator. It passed resolutions compelling suspended banks to make public statements of their affairs and prohibiting them from declaring dividends during the period of suspension.[55] In the spring of 1819, Pennsylvania annulled the charter of any bank refusing to redeem its notes in specie, except for the very important case of brokers who had bought the notes at a discount.[56]

In 1819, the Pennsylvania legislature passed a law forfeiting the charter of any bank established under the mass incorporation act of March, 1814, which, after August of 1819, should refuse to redeem its notes in specie. Stockholders and directors would be individually liable and there would be a 6 percent interest penalty on the bank.[57] In 1820, the Pennsylvania General Assembly suggested a constitutional amendment prohibiting the United States Bank from having branches within the states.

In Rhode Island, the panic quickly led to abolition of the state's peculiar system of debt collection—particularly speedy in the case of a bank collecting from its borrowers, as compared to creditors trying to collect from the bank. Another step taken by Rhode Island, in June, 1820, was to prohibit banks from circulating notes in excess of their paid-up capital. This was not really necessary in a state with conservative banking.[58]

Vermont had passed a stringent law, in 1817, prohibiting the circulation of non-specie paying bank notes, so that the hard money forces needed mainly to repulse expansionist programs, which in Vermont consisted largely of appeals for chartering new banks. One intense dispute took place over a phenomenon peculiar to Vermont—the fact that there were many private Canadian bills in use in the state as money. A bill was presented in the legislature to prohibit the circulation of Canadian private notes; this bill almost passed, but was finally rejected. In the meanwhile, the opposition attempted to pass a law compelling the state to receive Canadian notes for taxes and debts due, but this was summarily diminished.[59]

In New Hampshire, hard money forces, led by former Governor William Plumer, caused a great stir in the 1820 session, by petitioning the legislature against any charter renewals for banks. The suggestion was tabled by the legislature.[60]

A New England writer, "O.," brought up an acute point: one cause of excess bank credit expansion was the banks' agreement between themselves to accept and exchange each others notes. In effect, they borrowed from each other without paying interest. "O." saw perceptively that competition between numerous banks could restrict the total supply of bank notes, for each bank could only issue its notes to a narrow, limited clientele, beyond which the notes would be returned to the bank quickly for redemption. Interbank agreements could suspend this force. Therefore, "O." recommended that legislatures consider such agreements to be violations of bank charters.[61]

Thomas Jefferson's thoroughgoing opposition to paper money was heartily concurred in by his old enemy and current friend, Massachusetts elder statesman John Adams. Adams, writing to his old Jeffersonian opponent, John Taylor of Caroline, denounced banks roundly and placed the blame for the depression on their shoulders. Paper money beyond the value of specie he considered to be "theft" and bound to depreciate as in the case of debased coins.[62] He cited a similar abysmal failure of paper money in Massachusetts in 1775, which was quickly and efficiently replaced in circulation by silver.

John Adams' son, Secretary of State John Quincy Adams, had similar views on bank paper at that time.[63] A plan for government paper money had been sent to him by a Frenchman, Peter Paul De Grand. Adams wrote De Grand that he would send the plan on to Secretary of Treasury Crawford, but that he himself felt that it would create fictitious capital. He commended to De Grand the Amsterdam bank system, where paper was "always a representative and nothing more"—a 100 percent equivalent of the specie in the bank's vaults.

In Indiana, a bill in 1821 to prohibit issue of irredeemable bank curency failed in the legislature,[64] although a citizens' meeting in Washington County, across the river from Louisville, denounced the entire banking system as a destructive and fraudulent monopoly.[65] Missouri outlawed private unchartered bank notes in 1819.[66] In Ohio, Governor Ethan Allen Brown laid the blame for the depression on excessive bank credit and declared the only remedy to be the gradual reduction of bank paper, which would revive the credit of the banks.[67] As early as the beginning of 1819, a Committee on the State of the Currency and Banks of the Ohio House recommended that the law against private unchartered banks be enforced, and that inquiries be made into the conditions of banks not reporting their accounts.[68]

The depth of sentiment throughout the West against banks in general and the Bank of the United States in particular, for their excessive expansionist and contractionist activities, was revealed by incidents in rural Ohio. In the fall of 1819, General William Henry Harrison, later President of the United States, was a successful candidate for the Ohio State Senate. A citizens' meeting before the elections criticized him for being a director of a local branch of the Bank of the United States. Harrison, in a lengthy reply, insisted he was a sworn enemy of all banks and especially the Bank of the United States.[69] He declared that he was unalterably opposed to the establishment and continuance of the United States Bank.

The major energies of Ohio during this period, in fact, were occupied by its famous war against the Bank of the United States. This war was not depression-born, having begun in late 1817 with a proposal to tax the business of the bank's Ohio branches, in order to drive them out of the state. The tax was defeated in this session, but carried overwhelmingly in February, 1819, after the anti-bank forces had triumphed in the fall elections of 1818. Leader in the fight was Representative Charles Hammond, from Belmont County.[70] Anger at the bank was compounded of three elements: inflationists' irritation at the bank's contractions and calling on state banks for redemption; hard money resentment at the bank's expansionist activities during the boom; and general political anger at a privileged "money power." The law that levied a tax on the bank also imposed the same tax on all unincorporated banking in the state, thus revealing the predominance of general anti-bank opinion in Ohio. Attempts to tax or penalize the bank were struck down in famous United States Supreme Court decisions—Maryland's in *McCulloch vs. Maryland* (1819) and Ohio's in *Osborn vs. Bank of United States* (1824).[71]

In the frontier town of Detroit, in Michigan Territory, the citizens became aroused about the depreciated state of their circulating medium, which consisted principally of Ohio bank notes. In early 1819, they organized a meeting to deal with the depreciated small-change notes which individuals were issuing and circulating. The meeting pledged the members not to accept any individual change notes that were not redeemable within three days after demand for redemption.[72] In December of the same year, the leading citizens of Detroit held a meeting over the depreciated state of Ohio bank notes. They noted in alarm that the recent suspension of specie payment by these banks opened the door to a much greater depreciation. Therefore, the citizens resolved that those banks not redeeming their notes in specie were unworthy of confidence. The meeting appointed a committee of five to inquire into the condition of all the banks whose notes were circulating in Michigan, and to publish their results periodically in the Detroit *Gazette*. The committee was also directed to inquire into the status of individuals issuing small notes.[73]

The citizens of Detroit also took action against clipped, or "cut," silver, which made its appearance in force during the panic. The Detroit *Gazette* urged its readers to accept cut silver only by *weight*, and not at face value. A year later, in August, 1821, a large meeting of Detroit citizens resolved to refuse to accept cut silver coins, and to do all they could to discourage their circulation. This voluntary action effectively ended cut coin in Detroit.[74]

The state of Tennessee saw a concerted drive by hard money forces at the same time that expansionists were pushing their proposals. A petition from Warren County, a rural county in mid-Tennessee, demanded bluntly that banks be placed on a plane of "constitutional equality with the citizens," by compelling them to redeem their notes in specie. Refusal should entail a penalty interest on the bank, and stockholders should be personally liable. Similar petitions were received from Smith and Giles Counties, in mid-Tennessee.[75] A bill to compel specie payment or suffer an interest penalty was introduced in the House in the late 1819 session, by the hard money leader, Representative Pleasants M. Miller of Knoxville. The bill passed the House by a 20-to-14 vote, but was rejected in the Senate.[76] Representative J. C. Mitchell, of Rhea County in East Tennessee, proposed instead to make all real and personal property of bank stockholders liable for bank debts, but the House spurned this for the stronger Miller bill.[77] After assuming office in 1821, Governor William Carroll turned the tide of the state's expansionist legislation and called for coerced resumption of specie payments, a step which was eventually adopted. One point of interest for the later postdepression years was that the young future President James K. Polk, a wealthy cotton planter, began his political career with a staunch advocacy of return to specie payments. Polk maintained that specie payments were essential for confidence and in order to end depreciation.[78] Polk also proposed a measure to speed up execution against the property of any bank that might refuse to pay specie. Joining young Polk at this time was the frontier representative from western Tennessee, Davy Crockett, who "considered the whole Banking system a species of swindling on a large scale." [79]

A great deal of anti-bank sentiment was expressed in Kentucky during the controversy over inconvertible paper schemes. State Senator Jesse Bledsoe, from Bourbon County, delivered a speech which was later reprinted in pamphlet form. The speech was essentially a denunciation of the banking system as the cause of the depression through granting credit, thereby generating debt burdens and bankruptcies. Bledsoe called for the abolition of incorporated banking and compulsory redemption in specie by the banks.[80]

Amos Kendall, influential editor of the Frankfort (Ky.) *Argus*, and a future Jacksonian advisor, became a bitter opponent of the entire banking system as a result of the depression.[81] The very thought of banks he found "disgusting." The best method of rendering them harmless, he felt, was simply to prohibit them by constitutional amendment. If, as seemed likely, such a step was not politically feasible, then the next best step was to require every bank to give a security fund to the courts to provide for payment for their paper. This requirement, he believed, would insure that all liabilities could be redeemed (in effect, a 100 percent reserve plan) and would be more effective than to require individual stockholder liability.

As soon as the panic struck, Governor Gabriel Slaughter quickly called for action to restrict the banks.[82] He advocated making stockholders and directors individually liable for bank notes. Ideally, Slaughter sought a federal constitutional amendment to outlaw all incorporated banks.[83]

In the Kentucky legislature, Representative John Logan from Shelby County, near Frankfort, proposed a set of resolutions to investigate the mass chartered "independent" banks with a view to repeal the charters of those found violating their requirement to pay specie on demand. These banks, forty in number, had opened in the spring of 1818, expanded their notes rapidly, and were now refusing to redeem. They had an aggregate capital of $89 million.[84] Representative Thomas C. Howard, of Madison County, south of Lexington, attempted to amend the resolution to repeal immediately the charters of *all* the independent banks. The resolution for investigation passed overwhelmingly, but the repeal measure was beaten by a three-to-one margin.[85]

Kentucky moved swiftly against the banks. In early 1819, the bank committee reported to the House a rather mild bill along the lines of Slaughter's message. It required that banks pay a tax of ½ percent per month on their capital, that the directors be individually liable for the notes of their bank, and that there be "double liability" for stockholders. When the bill reached the floor, there was a flurry of atempts both to weaken and strengthen the measure. The pro-bank forces succeeded in including an amendment requiring the state treasury to receive the notes of all banks complying with the bill. They failed by a two-to-one vote to require the state to receive the notes of all banks incorporated in Kentucky, regardless of what provisions they followed.

The restrictionists passed far stronger amendments. One was a proviso requiring the state to refuse any notes in taxes unless the bank, each year, bonded with an auditor security in pledge that the banks pay all demands in specie. This passed by a two-to-one vote. An amendment to extend the provisions from the "independent" banks to all banks in the state failed by two to one. Finally, the legislature passed the bill restricting the action of the independent banks.

In January, 1819, there was also introduced into the legislature a very vigorous series of anti-bank resolutions. They charged that banks were a moneyed monopoly and substituted speculation for production. They concluded that banks should be abolished by the federal government and the states. No action was taken on this proposal.[86] Early in the 1820 session, the legislature finally repealed the charters of the independent banks, ending also their mass of depreciated notes. Almost all these banks had suspended payments by mid-1819.[87] The bill, commended heartily by Niles, passed by a two-to-one vote in the House and by a narrow three-vote margin in the Senate.[88]

Restrictionist proposals in the federal arena concentrated, of course, on the activities of the one federally chartered bank, the Bank of the United States. Representative John Spencer, from upstate New York near Onondaga, and chairman of the famous committee that had revealed some of the malpractice of the bank, introduced a resolution to forfeit the bank's charter unless it accepted restrictions on its activities.[89] These included provisions against fraud in the purchase of bank stock, reduction of its capital, and a maximum limitation of $5 million of bank holdings in United States bonds. Spencer withdrew his proposal after he saw that there was no chance for adoption. Representatives David Trimble from the vicinity of Lexington, Kentucky, and Joseph Johnson from northwest Virginia, went further to propose outright repeal of the bank charter. Trimble declared that the bank had failed in two of its original purposes—equalizing exchanges within the country, and checking the paper issues of local banks. On the contrary, it had contributed to excessive credit expansion by waiving the collection of stock installments in specie. He predicted that if the bank continued in operation the currency would only be further depreciated and deranged. Representative James Pindall, from northwest Virginia, denounced the bank for expanding its issues, as well as for withdrawing needed specie capital from other banks.

The Trimble Bill failed by an overwhelming margin. Indeed, the only restriction on the bank that passed was a bill by Representative Burwell Bassett from eastern Virginia, to prohibit any director of the bank from dealing in its own stock.[90]

Except for these proposed restrictions or abolition of the Bank of the United States, Congress had little chance to consider the banking problem. One interesting pronouncement, however, was a report in February, 1820, by Representative Joseph Kent, of Maryland, from the outskirts of Washington. Kent, Chairman of the District of Columbia Committee, reported on a proposal to consolidate the banks in the Capital territory.[91] Kent opposed compulsory consolidation. He stated that competition in banking was salutary, and that while banks were injurious, there would be no remedy in suddenly prostrating them. Instead, the evil excesses of banking were currently being corrected through failures and lowered profits.

One of the few leading citizens opposing severe restrictions on banking from a point of view not simply expansionist, was the influential New York merchant, Churchill C. Cambreleng.[92] He declared banks only secondarily responsible for the economic evils, since they were not the only creators of "fictitious capital." If bank credit were suppressed, other forms of credit would replace it. "Legislatures might as well attempt to confine the wind—as to encircle credit with legal restrictions." Cambreleng, however, was by no means in favor of unrestrained banking action. On the contrary, he believed that unincorporated private banks injured trade and property and should be eliminated. Incorporated banks were beneficial, but they must be rigidly regulated by the government, namely: there should be a maximum limit on the amount of paper issued; annual statements and reports by banks should be required; and banks should be compelled to pay specie on penalty of a 12 percent interest payment. Such regulations, asserted Cambreleng, were particularly needed in the southern and western states.

Thus, monetary restrictionists did not all limit themselves to opposing inflationist schemes and calling for enforcement of specie payment by the banks. Many went further to suggest regulations of banks to facilitate the maintenance of specie payment. Quite a few wanted to confine banks to the principal commercial cities, to prohibit notes of small denominations, or to confine bank loans to short-term commercial discounts. Some believed that vigorous competition between banks would suffice to restrict the note issue of each. They saw that interbank agreements would thwart such restriction and concluded that such agreements should be outlawed. Many leading restrictionists proceeded onward to condemn all banks, and either recommended outright repeal of all bank charters or an enforced 100 percent specie reserve. This position is particularly interesting, as it predated the enunciation of the similar Currency Principle in Great Britain.

It is clear, once again, that hard money opinion was not stratified along geographical or occupational lines. Restrictionist sentiment ranged from such eminent and disparate leaders as Thomas Jefferson and John Quincy Adams to obscure western farmers. Hard money opinion was particularly strong in Virginia, New York City, and New England, but it permeated every state and territory in the Union. Party lines meant little, for ultra-hard money sentiments were echoed by arch-Republicans and Federalists alike. In New York State, the two bitterly disputing Republican factions (De Witt

Clinton, and Van Buren-Tammany) both upheld a sound money position. Hard money leadership was abundant and influential in the West as well, although wealthy and influential leaders of opinion were also ranged on the other side of the fence. Furthermore, it cannot be said that commercial towns favored one or the other of the monetary positions—expansionist and restrictionist—while rural areas favored another. Each subdivision of each geographic region engaged each other vigorously in the press, and disputants often came from the same county. Taken all in all, it is fair to say that the majority of leading opinion was on the hard money side, at least to the extent of supporting specie payment and opposing inflationist plans. Only a minority of restrictionists pressed further for more drastic measures against bank paper.

The Panic of 1819 intensified hostility against the Bank of the United States, and enmity toward the bank grew throughout the country. Aside from long-standing hostility on general political or constitutional grounds, opponents of the bank consisted of the uncompromising wings of two diametrically opposed camps: the inflationists who wanted inconvertible government paper, and the hard money forces who criticized the bank for acting as a national force for monetary expansion. Historians portraying the struggle over the Bank of the United States have often overlooked, or slurred over, this critical distinction.[93] The Jacksonian war against the bank has often been depicted as an inflationist battle against central bank restrictions on credit. Yet the opposite viewpoint, which realized that the bank's nationalizing force was a powerful engine of credit expansion, was also important, as evidenced by hard money attacks on the bank during the 1818–21 period.

Another major area of controversy generated by the depression presented far more clear-cut sectional and occupational features than the monetary debates; this was the tariff question.

VI
THE MOVEMENT FOR A PROTECTIVE TARIFF

The depression of 1819 was a great tonic to the movement for a protective tariff for American industry. Domestic industry, particularly in textiles, had expanded greatly under the impetus of the War of 1812, which virtually blocked foreign trade and imports of manufactured goods. The textile industry, in particular, was hit by the impact of foreign and especially British competition in the postwar period. Leading the complainants were the cotton manufacturers, and they were joined, among others, by the woolen manufacturers, the paper manufacturers of New England, the bar iron manufacturers, and the Louisiana sugar planters.[1] Many protectionists charged that there was a British conspiracy afoot to dump their goods in the United States and crush infant American competitors.[2]

The tariff of 1816, adjusting American rates after the abnormal restrictions of the war period, established a moderate tariff, largely for revenue, averaging about 20 percent of value. Duties on cotton and woolen goods were set at 25 percent, but were supposed to fall in 1819. Thus, the higher rates were conceived as a temporary measure to ease the adjustment of domestic manufactures to the new competitive conditions. Probably the most protective feature of the new tariff was the adoption of a specific duty on cheap cottons.[3] The effect was to exclude cheap cottons from India, and thus remove the major threat to the mass market of new plants such as the factory at Waltham, Massachusetts. The first advocate of this duty, in fact, was the Massachusetts cotton manufacturer, F. C. Lowell.

The other major victory achieved by the protectionists before the depression was an increase in the duty of bar iron in 1818, and the indefinite extension of the 25 percent duty on cotton goods in the same year.

To further their cause, the protectionists established at the end of 1816 an American Society for the Encouragement of American Manufactures.[4] This was soon followed by affiliated subsidiary societies: the Delaware Society for Promoting United States Manufactures; the Pennsylvania Society; the Philadelphia Society for the Promotion of National Industry; and others in Washington, D.C., Baltimore, New York and New England. Head of the American Society was Vice-President of the United States, Daniel D. Tompkins; many leading political figures joined, including Madison, Jefferson and John Adams.

The society set its aims at making the temporarily high cotton and woolen duties permanent; the absolute prohibition of the import of cotton from India; a proviso that all government officials clothe themselves in domestic fabrics, and any other necessary protection. The first objective was soon attained; the second objective had been achieved *de facto* though not *de jure* by the minimum provisions of the Tariff of 1816. By the spring of 1818, under the impact of the boom, as well as the attainment of their goals, the protectionist movement had become more or less dormant.[5]

The advent of the depression in late 1818 came, therefore, as a particular boon to the protectionist cause. Societies for the Promotion of Industry blossomed with renewed vigor, expanded, and flourished throughout New England and the Middle Atlantic states—the relatively industrialized areas—and deluged Congress and the press with protectionist petitions and manifestos. The unquestioned leader in this drive was the energetic Matthew Carey, Philadelphia printer and leader of the Philadelphia Society.[6] Carey and his associates were ever ready to emphasize and maximize the extent of the distress, as a prelude to the call for a protectionist remedy.[7]

Carey organized, in the winter of 1819, a Convention of the Friends of National Industry, which included protectionist leaders from nine states—Massachusetts, Rhode Island, Connecticut, New York, New Jersey, Pennsylvania, Delaware, Maryland and Ohio.[8] The delegates met in New York on November 29, with Carey as secretary and William Few, president of the New York Society, as president. The memorial that the convention sent to Congress, written by Carey, set the protectionist "line," which they were to repeat in countless monographs, letters, and petitions.[9] Its main proposal was an increase in duties on imported goods to protect American manufactures; two subsidiary proposals were a tax on auction sales, and the abolition of time payments on import duties. The memorial began by pointing to the nation's great economic difficulties; in addition to the depression of manufactures, commerce and shipping were prostrated, real estate depreciated in value, and "a great portion of our mechanics and artists are unemployed." Agricultural staples were reduced in price, and Americans were deeply indebted to foreign nations. In the midst of this distress, the cities were being filled with foreign manufactured products. Excessive importation of manufactured goods was the cause of the depression, particularly the pernicious China and East India trade in cheap cottons, which drained American specie in exchange for "worthless fabrics." The solution to the depression was, therefore, sharply increased protective duties.

Carey's theory of prosperity and depression was simple: free trade caused depression, protection would bring prosperity.[10] Summing up his position in a comparative "table," he asserted that the results of free trade were, in turn: immense imports; bargain purchases of foreign goods; a drain of specie abroad; decay of national industry; discharge of workmen; growth in unemployment and poor relief; bankruptcy of manufactures; failure of merchants; agricultural distress and decline in prices of staples; stoppage of specie payments by banks; sacrifice sales of property. Full protection, on the other hand, would lead to: imports in moderation only; a prosperous industry; full employment for every person able and willing to work; disappearance of bankruptcies; rising property values; a secure home market for such agricultural products as cotton and wool; and prosperity to merchants. Carey contended that the distress among the merchants was due to their excess number, caused by free trade. Lack of protection deprived many young men of employment opportunities in manufactures, forcing them into overemployment in the merchants' field. Protection would shift the excessive number of merchants into manufacturing, thereby benefiting manufacturing as well as the remaining merchants who would face less competition.[11]

To Carey, the condition of the United States was empirical evidence of the evils of nonprotection and the alleged adoption of the pernicious maxims of Adam Smith, while France and other European countries exemplified the benefits of protection. Carey brusquely dismissed arguments of critics that many fully protected countries of Europe were at that moment suffering also from depression. Their depression, he asserted, followed from wartime exhaustion of resources. Carey did not explain why this "exhaustion" required several years after the war to bring about a depression.[12]

Carey's chief associate, Dr. Samuel Jackson, developed a particularly significant facet of the protectionist argument. Jackson stressed that protection was necessary to bring about full employment. During the Napoleonic wars, he declared, American commerce was active enough so that "the labor-power of the country . . . was employed to the full." Now this source no longer existed, and a growing portion of the population was unemployed. The development of domestic manufactures was necessary to absorb the growing class of now surplus producers. Not only idle labor but also idle capital could become employed.[13] Similarly, a leading Pennsylvania protectionist, Peter S. Du Ponceau, countered the opposition argument that subsidized manufacturing would withdraw capital from the more profitable field of farming. He declared that idle capital, as well as unemployed textile workers, would enter manufacturing.[14]

To the contention of free traders that free trade would not cause unemployment, since labor would shift from the inefficient to the efficient industries, Carey replied that people were generally idle and lax, hence immobile in their occupations. Therefore, they required protection wherever they were situated. Carey did not see that this concession shifted much of the blame for unemployment from the free trade system to the unemployed themselves.[15]

To the free trade assertion that unemployed workers in manufacturing should return to the soil, Carey countered with an interesting argument: that manufacturing employees were largely women and children, who were unsuitable for farm work and would thus remain unemployed. Another Carey argument held that low agricultural prices demonstrated an agricultural overproduction, just as failures of merchants proved an oversupply in trade.[16]

An interesting argument was developed by the protectionist journal, *Patron of Industry*, in commenting on inflationist proposals to increase the quantity of money.[17] The proponents assumed, declared the *Patron*, that the root difficulty was scarcity of money. There was, however, a much more significant problem: the impossibility of *employing* money in a safe and profitable manner. The very fact that people were in such straits as to clamor for governmental loans indicated that they could not employ the money to advantage. In other words, there was an absence of productive employment, for money as well as labor. Protection was the remedy to bolster industry and give confidence to the economy. An article with a similar point of view, by "Plain Truth," printed in the Pittsburgh *Gazette*, stated that there was an abundance of idle money capital which would be available for lending, except that no profitable employment could be found.[18]

An influential voice for protection was raised by the prominent New England Presbyterian clergyman, the Reverend Lyman Beecher. In a Thanksgiving sermon in 1819, later reprinted in pamphlet form, Beecher called for protection as the chief "means to national prosperity" and recovery.[19] Beecher was one of the most lucid of the protectionists. He included the general arguments: that protection would provide employment for the idle and a steady home market for depressed agriculture. He laid particular stress on the monetary drain caused by an adverse balance of trade and the use of protection in ending this drain. Beecher also stressed, far more than Carey and his groups, that American manufactures as *infant* industries specifically needed protection. Beecher was one of the few protectionists to take cognizance of the charge that tariffs might promote domestic monopoly and tyrannize over consumers. His answers to the argument were thoughtful. In the first place, consumers could repeal the tariff if this result ensued. Furthermore, Beecher declared, tariffs would not insure an entire domestic monopoly for all products—just partial protection for some products. Finally, Beecher asserted that any rise in the prices of manufactured goods would only be temporary, that new firms would be attracted to the industry and old firms would expand, until the prices fell.

Protectionists, of course, had little use for laissez-faire theories. A particularly clear example was presented by "A Manufacturer" of

Philadelphia. Lamenting over the depressed conditions, he asserted that the government had the duty as well as the power under the "general welfare" clause of the Constitution to regulate trade and commerce. For the "government is the national physician." Furthermore, since the welfare of the manufacturer was clearly identical with the nation's welfare, permanent and full protection was required in the interest of the nation as a whole. And "if our manufacturers shall become wealthy, they will circulate and retain the precious metals in this country."[20]

Congress was of course the focal center for protectionist agitation, since the state legislatures were constitutionally prohibited from erecting tariffs. All that a state government could do, in fact, was to join in the agitation. There was little controversy on the state level since it was not an issue there.

The outstanding protectionist leader in Congress was Representative Henry Baldwin, from Pittsburgh. It was Baldwin who headed the newly formed House Committee on Manufactures, which the protectionists were able to split off from the traditional Committee on Agriculture and Manufactures, during the 1819–20 session. This new committee became the fountainhead of future protectionist measures. In the 1820 session, Baldwin promptly introduced the Baldwin Bill for a protective tariff. The bill passed the House by a substantial margin and lost in the Senate by only one vote.

Baldwin came from one of the very strongest points of the new protectionism—western Pennsylvania, centering in Pittsburgh. This was one of the leading industrial areas, not only in textiles but also in iron and glass production. Pittsburgh was now an area of heavy unemployment. For his efforts on behalf of protection from 1819 to 1821, Baldwin was feted by a citizens' meeting in Pittsburgh, and later affectionately dubbed Father of the American System.[21] Baldwin himself was an important iron manufacturer, who owned three large rolling mills, including the largest one in the Pittsburgh area. His interest in a protective tariff was quite immediate, and he did not neglect iron in his proposed tariff increases.[22] He also admitted that the cut glass industry and others centering in Pittsburgh received very large relative increases of protection in his bill.[23]

As might be expected, Pittsburgh was one of the first areas to memorialize Congress for protection. Typical was the memorial written by a committee of manufacturers in October, 1818, and again at the end of December. Further petitions were sent by the newly formed Allegheny County Society for Protecting Agriculture and Domestic Manufactures. Pittsburgh, in fact, went further than other communities by attempting to establish a cooperative marketing association for the whole town—this was the Pittsburgh Manufacturing Association, founded in 1819.[24] Not only manufacturers but also farmers from the area were seemingly impressed by the arguments and anxious to secure a home market in the face of falling foreign markets; they petitioned Congress for tariff protection for industry.[25] Many of the petitions signed "practical farmers" or "impartial farmers," however, were written by industrialists, like Alexander McClurg, an associate of Baldwin, and secretary of the new Society for Promotion of Agriculture and Domestic Manufactures of Allegheny County.[26]

Pennsylvania support for protection was indicated by the pleas for Congressional relief issued simultaneously by Representative Richard Povall of Philadelphia, head of the Pennsylvania House Committee on Domestic Manufactures, and by Senator Charles Shoemaker from Berks and Schuylkill Counties, of the Senate Committee on Agriculture and Manufactures.[27] In addition to the standard tariff arguments, Povall asserted that free trade favored the rich at the expense of the poor, since it brought about depression and sacrifice sales to the rich. Shoemaker stressed the importance of a tariff on iron. Representative William Duane's report as head of the select Committee on Domestic Economy stated that adequate national protection to all branches of industry was indispensable to recovery.[28]

Pennsylvania contributed its mite to the protection battle by levying a special duty on retailers of foreign merchandise and by requiring new licenses from retailers of foreign goods.[29]

Other states in the West joined in the protectionist movement. In Ohio, Governor Thomas Worthington called for a tariff to promote a shift in resources from overproduced agriculture to manufactures and to stop the specie drain. He advocated self-sufficiency and stressed a very popular exhortatory theme: calling on all good citizens to patronize domestic products. One of his major addresses for protection was delivered before the Scioto Agricultural Society, in 1819, perhaps an indication that many Ohio farmers were convinced by the home market argument.[30] In his 1819–20 message to the legislature, Governor Worthington recommended the encouragement of woolen manufactures. A joint committee of the legislature was established in the next session to inquire into possible aid to Ohio manufactures by the state government. The report of Representative Joseph Vance (from Champaign County) recommended a state loan to a Steubenville woolen factory.[31]

General William Henry Harrison ran for the Ohio State Senate in 1819 on a pro-tariff as well as an anti-bank platform. As chairman of the Board of Supervisors of Tioga County, General Harrison spurred a series of resolutions to alleviate the hard times. The sponsors agreed to abstain from the use of any imported goods, and to give preference to domestic articles.[32] Successfully elected, Harrison moved a resolution in the state legislature to support increased tariffs to bring about recovery of domestic manufactures.[33]

Kentucky was also enthusiastically protectionist, as typified by the Speaker of the House in Washington, Henry Clay, and this sentiment was accompanied by a widespread campaign for voluntary preference for domestic products. Ladies' hats made of local grass were recommended as being as good as the finest wool, while roasted barley was used in many cases as a substitute for imported coffee.[34]

Many Missourians were eager for protection for Missouri's lead, iron, and salt industries. The protectionist cause was particularly taken up by the St. Louis *Enquirer* and the St. Charles *Missourian*.[35]

Delaware is an interesting example of the swell of protectionist sentiment. At the beginning of the crisis, in 1819, the Delaware Senate passed a resolution declaring that manufactures were a great national concern, in the public interest, and hence required protection. The resolution passed the Senate, but lost in the House by a vote of 7 to 10.[36]

Delaware, however, became one of the prime centers of the protectionist movement. E. I. Du Pont, from Wilmington, the nation's leading powder manufacturer, was one of that movement's original sponsors.[37] By the next session, sentiment had changed. Representative Whitely reported from the House Committee on Agriculture and Manufacturing of Delaware that the origin of the distress was the present commercial system, aiding as it did foreign manufactures at the expense of domestic manufactures. The distress of domestic manufactures had thrown agriculture into depression for lack of a home market. Whitely's concluding resolution asking Congress for protection was adopted unanimously.[38] By a slim margin, and after a sharp battle, the Delaware legislature took supplemental measures to aid their manufactures, exempting all owners of cotton and woolen machinery from either taxes or the debt-paying execution process.[39] A proposed blow at imports was defeated, however, when a bill narrowly failed to pass which provided that peddlers must acquire a license under the condition that they sell no foreign goods.[40] Supposedly "free-trade" North Carolina, however, doubled its tax on peddlers who sold goods imported into the state. Kentucky debated a similar measure.[41]

Neighboring Maryland boasted two of the nation's leading protectionists: Hezekiah Niles, who worked tirelessly for protection in his *Weekly Register;* and Daniel Raymond, whose *Thoughts on Political Economy* strongly backed a protective tariff and was a treatise particularly designed to be a counterweight to the free trade position of the classical economists.

New York was the site of one of the main organs of the protectionist movement, the New York *Columbian*, a paper reflecting De Witt Clinton's views.[42] The *Columbian* pursued the cause through letters and editorials and reprinted Carey's Addresses of the Philadelphia Society. The emphasis in New York was on the cotton manufacture. One letter stressed that protection to cottons would be particularly useful to the state. Further, protection would inspire confidence and thus "would produce capital" and remedy the depression.[43]

One of the most interesting protectionist writings was an article in the *Columbian* stressing that protection would furnish "constant employment." As a remedy the writer, "H. B.", further suggested that the state establish a woolen and cotton factory, state owned, to teach the youth of New York City the "useful art of spinning and weaving–the state to furnish the raw material and receive the proceeds as it is finished for the consumer." He also suggested a state owned cotton and woolen warehouse to sell the cloth wholesale and retail.[44] Everyone was urged to wear only domestic clothing, and the clergy were particularly requested to set the proper example.

One of the most ambitious efforts of the protectionists in this period was the establishment of a semi-weekly newspaper in New York, *The Patron of Industry*, to serve as the bellwether of the movement. It ran a brief course in 1820 and 1821, at the height of this wave of tariff agitation. The *Patron* was published by the National Institute for the Promotion of Industry.[45, 46]

The two major groups in New York State politics were the followers of Governor Clinton and the bitterly opposed Tammany faction of the Democratic-Republican party. That the two groups were not very far apart on the tariff as well as on monetary questions may be seen in the famous *Tammany Address* of John Woodward. One of Woodward's many proposed remedies for the crisis was the absolute prohibition against importing any article that could be manufactured domestically "on tolerable terms." To supplement these legal measures, all citizens and governments were expected to give preference to American products.[47]

New England was a more difficult field for protectionists to plow. New manufacturers in New England were largely in the cotton industry, and tariff agitation from this area centered on this commodity. An interesting development was the use of the Washington Insurance Company of Providence, insurer for most of the Rhode Island cotton mills, as lobbyist for protection of the cotton industry. The protectionists also established a *Manufacturers' and Farmers' Journal* in Rhode Island during 1819.

By May, 1820 (when the Baldwin Bill came to a vote in Congress), seven state legislatures had passed resolutions urging Congress to pass the bill. These states were Rhode Island, Connecticut, New York, New Jersey, Pennsylvania, Delaware, and Ohio.[48] The heavy investments in cottons and woolens were stressed in the Pennsylvania declarations, and the textiles were stressed by New York Governor De Witt Clinton, in his advocacy of protection.[49] Under Clinton's leadership, New York extended subsidies to woolen manufactures in the state.

Many minor industries, in addition to the major ones of cotton, wool, and iron, asked for protection. Typical was the petition of the Society of Paper Makers of Pennsylvania and Delaware. They pointed to the extent of paper manufacture and the number employed in the industry, and advocated protection to remedy its distress and to keep the profit of its manufacture in the country.[50] Even the book printers demanded protection, headed by Matthew Carey, a leading Philadelphia printer.[51] The protectionists, while concentrating on the major industries, were generally quite willing to include numerous industries under the protection umbrella. "An Agriculturist" advocated absolute prohibition of all imports of foreign industry, in order to build up a home market for American grain produce.[52] Hezekiah Niles, though a staunch protectionist leader, balked at this trend. He stated emphatically:

> most of these manufacturers are prostrated not for want of protecting duties, but in consequence of general impoverishment of the country arising principally from want of protection to the great leading branches of cotton, wool, and iron.[53]

Emphasis on cotton and wool and the lure of a home market for agriculture were, in fact, the features of a typical "grass roots" tariff petition. Thus, some citizens of Middletown, Connecticut, in a petition to Congress, stressed the advantage to agriculture of domestic manufactures.[54] Using an "infant industry argument," they declared that

> adequate protective duties . . . would soon create or revive such a number of manufacturing establishments, that ere long their rivalry would probably reduce the price of their fabrics below the present standard of those imported.

On the other hand, if we now permitted American manufactures to die of neglect, we would have to buy only European goods at an exorbitant advance and reimburse manufacturers for their present losses. In essence, this was a forerunner of the classic argument that a firm undercuts prices in order to crush its rival and later extract a monopoly price.

Protection reached a peak in Congress late in the 1819–20 session, with the battle over the Baldwin Bill.

The heart of the Baldwin Bill was a rise in tariffs on cottons and woolens from 25 percent to 33 percent duty, plus a minimum for cheap cottons, the total increase in cotton duty being 50 to 70 percent. Tariffs were also to be increased on a variety of manufactured goods.

Mr. Baldwin began the debate on the bill in the House, stressing the depression, the decline in property values, and unemployment.[55] Debate in the Senate was led by Senator Mahlon Dickerson of New Jersey, chairman of the Committee of Manufactures which reported the bill. He stressed the dominant theme of the protectionists—the great distress of the country and protection as the remedy. Protection would provide a home commerce and a home market for agriculture, raise property values, cure unemployment, eliminate the unfavorable balance of trade and the specie drain. Also speaking for protection was Senator James J. Burrill, Jr., of Rhode Island. The Baldwin Bill passed the House by a considerable majority, 90 to 69. It failed in the Senate by only two votes, 20 to 22.[56] Geographically, taking both Houses into consideration, the pattern of the voting was as follows:

Voting on the Baldwin Tariff Bill

	For	*Against*
New England	24	18
Middle Atlantic	64	7
West	19	12
South (including Southwest)	3	54
	110	91

In the Middle Atlantic states, Maryland supplied almost the entire anti-tariff vote. The bulk of the protectionist majority was supplied by four states (House figures only): New York (25–0); Pennsylvania (22–1); New Jersey (6–0); Ohio (6–0).

The Baldwin Bill was reintroduced in January, 1821, but with little success. The beginnings of business recovery were becoming apparent, and protectionist ardor cooled considerably. It was finally able to succeed three years later.[57]

Not all protectionists confined their doctrines to the national level. Every once in a while, a protectionist writer would accept the challenge of his opponents and push protection doctrine near to its logically absurd limit. Thus, Matthew Lyon of Eddyville, Kentucky, advocated a state law prohibiting imports into Kentucky of all "foreign" cotton goods and other foreign manufactured products.[58] "Plain Truth" in the Pittsburgh *Gazette* suggested a western tariff to prevent a continued specie drain from the West, and to develop its own manufactures to provide a home market for western expenditures. He advocated western secession if necessary for this purpose.[59] "Mechanic of Detroit" went even further. He attributed the economic difficulties of the Detroit artisans to the merchants of the town importing large quantities of goods that could have been made in Detroit. Merchants, he asserted, should only purchase the product of local, rather than of "foreign," mechanics.[60] One Pennsylvanian evolved an ingenious scheme reminiscent of later American development, to exclude imported manufacture by using the state power of quarantining commerce ruinous to morals, industry, and "political" health.[61] "A Pennsylvanian" suggested that every retailer in the state be forced to take out a state license, and that the condition of the license be the retailers' agreement not to sell any imported goods on credit to anyone, except tools for manufacturers or mechanics.[62] This would prevent people from running into excessive debt and help out domestic manufactures.

The protectionist movement encountered formidable opposition that was able to defeat its proposals, although four years later protection was to triumph in the Tariff of 1824. Effective opposition came from the Monroe administration. The Washington *National Intelligencer*, known as reflecting administration views, strongly opposed higher tariffs. Ardent opposition came, as is well known, from the South. Strongly agricultural and relying on export markets for their staples of cotton and tobacco, the South opposed the protectionist measures vigorously. Southern opposition in the Congressional tariff vote was virtually unanimous.

Particularly active opposition to the tariff came from John Taylor of Caroline, who wrote many memorials for Agricultural Societies of Virginia, attacking the tariff. The focal point of opposition in Congress was the House Committee on Agriculture, which prepared comprehensive anti-tariff reports based primarily on the Taylor memorials. Also actively opposed to an increased tariff were merchant groups in the North—particularly Salem, Massachusetts—and the Chamber of Commerce of Philadelphia, which sent opposition memorials to Congress.[63] Whereas the protectionists devoted a great deal of attention to the depression, the "free traders" in opposition devoted little space to the depression, since they could not counter with a simple remedy of their own. Free traders generally concentrated on general political or economic questions such as, the benefits of international trade and the division of labor, the danger of monopoly, the injustice of special privilege, and the morals of factory life.

Some free traders undertook, however, to rebut the depression argument. Counters took two general forms: (a) denying the depression was caused by lack of protection and that the tariff could provide a remedy, and (b) asserting a tariff would aggravate rather than relieve the hard times. On the first point, the free traders argued that the depression was universal and strong in the leading European countries. Yet, they were heavily protected; therefore, a protective tariff in the United States could offer no cure. This was a leading argument of the House Agriculture Committee.[64]

Condy Raguet, only of late a protectionist himself,[65] in his 1820 report on the depression to the Pennsylvania Senate, brought up the point that if the protectionists were right, the manufacturing towns should have been the hardest hit by the depression, whereas hard times were universal throughout the nation.[66]

The positive argument against the new tariff was that it would worsen the depression rather than improve it. It would largely do so by increasing the depression of agriculture and commerce, which would be taxed for the benefit of possible new industries. Thus, the merchants of Portland (Maine) warned that higher tariffs would destroy their maritime commerce and also the nation's agricultural markets abroad.[67] The Portland petition was endorsed by the Portland *Gazette*, the Boston *Gazette*, and by a convention of Maine merchants and agriculturists at Portland.

Merchants of Salem, Massachusetts, in a petition written by the famous Supreme Court Justice Joseph Story, turned the tables on the protectionists by accusing them of being visionary theorists, heedless of the practical effects tariffs would have in destroying the capital and profits of commerce. Tariffs, they declared, would worsen the depression by increasing unemployment in commerce.[68] Many critics pointed out that agricultural exports would be damaged because lower imports would supply less dollars abroad with which to buy American products.[69] A New England writer, "Public Good," asked his readers to suppose that all imports into the country were prohibited. American mechanics and farmers would then have *fewer* means with which to purchase domestic manufactures than before. Importers would earn less and exporters' markets abroad would suffer.[70]

A group of Boston merchants charged that a protective tariff would cause widespread starvation among the mechanics and merchants of the seaports.[71] More specifically, merchants and distillers of Boston objected to a proposed import duty on molasses. They pointed to their investment of $11 million in buildings, protesting that a tariff would lead to the unemployment of thousands of people in the molasses and rum trade.[72]

A more general argument held that protective tariffs would necessarily cause unprofitable business. An interesting presentation of this view appeared in a memorial by citizens of Charleston, written by the wealthy South Carolina banker and landowner Stephen Elliott.[73] Elliott pointed out that a tariff would penalize labor and capital employed in commerce and agriculture, and would divert factors from the latter to manufacturing. But if labor and capital employed in manufacturing produced as much profit as that employed in the other occupations, a tariff would be unnecessary, since labor and capital would then shift to manufacturing without government help. If manufacturing were *not* as profitable then tariffs would be forcing labor and capital into unprofitable employments.[74]

One of the most sophisticated expositions of the doctrine that increased tariffs would only aggravate the depression was delivered by John Taylor of Caroline. Thus, in his memorial of the farmers and merchants of Fredericksburg, Virginia,[75] Taylor established this chain of causation: tariffs cause diminished imports, that would in turn bring about restriction of exports, which would cause a fall in the prices of domestic products. The depression had already brought about great price declines, declared Taylor, which were equivalent to an increased value of the money unit. The result was an increase in the *real* burden of tariff duties. The further price fall following higher tariffs would add still more to the real burden.

Taylor regarded tariffs as a burden because he saw them as taxes on consumption; a tariff was a tax which diminishes consumption, hence diminishes production and prosperity. Taylor wrote:

> The tariff . . . is a tax upon the national ability . . . since it was imposed, one half the national ability to pay taxes has been destroyed by the doubled value of money, and a reduction to the same amount in the value of products and property. Therefore the burden of taxation has been doubled by circumstances without the agency of legislation . . . if the whole duty is continued, it will compel the payers to retrench their consumption. . . . The enjoyments of consumption are the food of industry; diminish them, and it flags; leave them free, and it is invigorated.[76]

Taylor also pursued this reasoning to advocate *reducing* tariffs in order to reduce the real tax burden on consumption—a surprisingly modern position. The House Committee on Agriculture, in its anti-tariff report, echoed this position.[77] Others also advocated reduction in existing tariff as a method of remedying the depression. For example, the *National Intelligencer* early in the depression declared that a depression needed a *reduction* in tariffs instead of an increase, to benefit the harassed merchants.[78]

An interesting counter on the unemployment problem was delivered by one of the most influential of the anti-protectionists, the leading New York merchant and politician, Churchill C. Cambreleng.[79] The United States, he declared, was underpopulated, so unemployment could not be a permanent problem. Present unemployment was merely temporary, and even natural. "Every nation experiences a want of employment at intervals, amidst the natural fluctuations of industry."

There was, of course, a good deal of deprecating of the manufacturers asking for protection. Cambreleng denounced the protectionists as idlers and malcontents, or as wartime speculators in manufacturing stock who wanted a government subsidy. John Taylor laid the plight of the manufacturers at the door of the banks; these were speculative manufacturers who had invested with "fictitious capital" supplied by the banks, and now were left without funds as a result of credit contraction.[80]

The New Orleans *Louisiana Gazette* spoke for many anti-tariff readers when it stated: "In these times of extraordinary embarrassment, we ought particularly beware how we prune the wing of honest industry" and concluded, "*laissez-nous faire*." [81] An amusing attack on the tariff from the laissez-faire point of view, by "The Friends of Natural Rights," attacked "Professor Matthew Carey" and "Professor Hezekiah Niles" for implicitly advocating government ownership and management of all property, with the government guaranteeing full employment (no moments of idleness) for all capital and labor.[82] The writers thus described the "Careyan Scheme of Government":

> The people of the United States being in a very unenlightened condition, very indolent and much disposed to waste their labor and their capital . . . the welfare of the community requires that all goods, wares, merchandise, and estates . . . should be granted to the government in fee simple, forever . . . and should be placed under the management of a Board of Trustees, to be styled the Patrons of Industry. The said Board should thereupon guarante [sic] to the people of the United States that thenceforth neither the capital nor labor of this nation should remain for a moment idle.

Among the maxims that such a Board would try to inculcate in the people:

> It is a vulgar notion that the property which a citizen possesses, actually belongs to him: for he is a mere tenant, laborer, or agent of the government, to whom all the property in the nation legitimately belongs. The government may therefore manage this property according to its own fancy, and shift capitalists and laborers from one employment to another.

These writers thus saw in the tariff position a logic implicitly leading to a wholly government-planned economy.

In Congress, the leading speeches opposed to the Baldwin Bill were delivered by future president John Tyler, Representative from Charles City County in eastern Virginia, and by Representative Nathaniel Silsbee, from the great shipping center of Salem, Massachusetts.[83] Tyler, like Story, denounced the protectionists as hasty theorists, willing to destroy commerce and agriculture to put their experiment into practice. Tyler also brought up the interesting and important point that, in the long run, even manufacturers would not benefit from the subsidy, since competition would flow into the protected industries until their rates of profit were no higher than in any other industry.[84] Silsbee also stressed the aggravating effect the tariff would have on the existing depression in the seaports.[85]

The protectionists offered two subsidiary measures as part of their political program. Both were designed to supplement tariffs in restricting imports. One proposed that the government cease granting time to importers for payment of duties. The particular criticism of this system was that the debt induced excessive imports. Some merchants joined the protectionists in this proposal in order to limit the competition of those fellow-importers who had meager capital, and were therefore dependent on credit.[86] The Convention of Friends of National Industry began the drive to abolish credits on duties. It pointed out that since the war many foreign merchants had been induced by the credits to import heavily, thereby depressing domestic manufactures and injuring American mercantile stability.[87]

Conversely, other merchants fought back in defense of the credits system. The Chambers of Commerce of Philadelphia and New York City defended the system. They charged that abolition would repress enterprise, credit, and commerce. The New York *Daily Advertiser* pointed out that abolition would help the large capitalists at the expense of the small, since it was the young and enterprising merchants who would be forced to abandon trade for lack of capital.[88] John Pintard—leading merchant, founder of the New York Historical Society, and Secretary of the New York City Chamber of Commerce—taking a position similar to John Taylor on the tariff, charged that imposition of a cash duty would increase the tax burden on commerce. He estimated that cash duties would double the real value of taxes on imports.[89]

A group of Baltimore merchants headed by Isaac McKim, adopted this ingenious reasoning: "all duties on imports are taxes on consumption." An importer had to have time to convey the goods to consumers. In every government grant of credit to the importers, the time period of the credit fell short of the period before which the capital of the merchants could be realized.[90] The Baltimore merchants struck a similar note as did Cambreleng—cycles of trade were inevitable in business affairs:

Commerce always tends to extremes and excesses of trading occur under all systems and in the finest periods of commercial prosperity. But if importation does sometimes swell until business stagnates, commerce has a power of self-correction and the resource of self-recovery, and reverses soon allay the intemperate ambition of gain.

One proponent of credit on duties went to the extent of proposing a *lengthening* of the credit period as a remedy for the depression.[91] He reasoned as follows: A particular depressant in the commercial situation was the large amount of custom house bonds owed by merchants for payment of import duties. They could not sell the goods they imported because of the "scarcity of money and the stagnation of business." Therefore, to acquire the money to pay the bonds, the merchants had to discount their bills at the banks. After the merchants paid the bank notes into the Treasury in payment of their debts, the Treasury deposited the notes in the Bank of the United States, thereby adding to the pressure on state banks to redeem their notes in specie. This exerted deflationist pressure, obliging banks to curtail greatly their loans and discounts. Thus, the author demonstrated how taxes exerted a deflationary effect on the money supply and economy.

Senator William A. Trimble (Ohio), an ardent protectionist, introduced a bill to suspend credits on duties, but the bill failed to come to a vote in Congress, as the failure of other protectionist measures doomed this one as well.

The other subsidiary measure was a prohibitory tax on sales at auction. Protectionists charged that auction sales, which had become a prominent form of wholesale import sales after the war, spurred cheap foreign competition with American products.[92] Thus, a group of Merchants and Citizens of Philadelphia, in a memorial to Congress, pointed to the pernicious effects of auction sales during the previous few years.[93] Auction sales provided a means for agents of foreign exporters to dispose of their goods easily. These channels had been deluged with every sort of imported goods, fostered by the "extreme elevation of the market at the close of the war, owing to the few foreign productions in the country at the time." Auction sales of imported goods had wrecked domestic manufactures, by underselling the established merchants. Here again the leading role in attacking auctions was taken by merchant competitors of the auction system.[94] Critics also charged that auction prices fluctuated more rapidly than regular prices, since they were not regulated by cost. A prohibitory tax had first been proposed by a group of New York City merchants and traders as early as 1817.[95] Merchants were, however, by no means unanimous in advocating a prohibitory tax on auction sales. Baltimore merchants split on the issue, and the Chamber of Commerce of New York City opposed a tax on auctions.[96] The drive for a 10 percent tax on auction sales was launched in earnest by the protectionist Convention of Friends of National Industry.[97] It pointed out that large quantities of imported clothes were sold at auction. Even domestic goods sold at auction were frowned on, because auctions generally promoted goods of "inferior quality." The proposed 10 percent tax was to apply to both foreign and domestic goods at auction.

Congress, however, rejected a bill, submitted by Representative Baldwin at the same time as his tariff proposal, to levy a 10 percent tax on auction sales.[98] Baldwin charged that the auction system was ruining the fair traders by "inundating the country with worthless goods at reduced prices, benefiting foreigners and bankrupting American merchants." On the other hand, Representative Albert H. Tracy of Buffalo defended traders who sold at lower prices and advocated consumer freedom to buy from whatever source they desired. Representative Johnson of Virginia asserted that the measure would ruin one part of the country for the benefit of another, and that free choice was still the best system of trade. Middle-of-the-roaders, such as the influential Representative Samuel Smith of Baltimore, advocated a very small duty of 1 to 2 percent. The auction bill was closely fought. It was first rejected in the House by a vote of 77 to 72, and then was modified to a 5 percent tax on dry goods and 1 percent on minor items, and passed by an 89-to-61 vote. After the defeat of the Baldwin Tariff Bill, however, the bill never came to a vote in the Senate.

Failing to obtain legislative action, merchants of New York and other cities decided to combat the competition of auction sales of imported goods by banding together to refuse to buy goods at auction. Thus, the United Dry Goods Association of New York, representing nearly all the wholesale and retail dry goods merchants of the city, met on May 21, 1821 and resolved not to purchase any dry goods at auction, in order to combat the "price fixing" of the "auction monopoly."[99] Protectionists had high hopes for this measure, and Niles hailed the action as a check on the British menace to American employment and injury to the merchant and retailer.[100] Shortly thereafter, similar boycott action was taken by organizations of Philadelphia, Boston, and Baltimore merchants, in the dry goods and hardware fields.[101] The New York Association took the lead in appointing a Vigilance Committee to keep watch over the membership in carrying out the pledge. Not only did they agree not to buy at auction but they also agreed not to sell any goods at auction, except at sheriffs' sales for bankruptcy. All these boycott efforts soon came to naught, and the report of the Vigilance Committee in September of that year provides insight into the reasons for its complete failure and into the difficulties faced by any such "cartel" arrangement.[102] First, there was a lack of "complete uniformity of views upon the subject." A few merchants, mainly small dealers, were opposed to the suppression of auction sales. Second, several large merchants, though opposed to auctions on principle, indulged in their self-interested advantage and continued to purchase—more cheaply—at auction. Third, New York, the auction center of the country, was filled with merchants from other cities who did not participate in the agreement and continued to buy at auction. And fourth, even the most "patriotic" (i.e. anti-auction) merchants were chafing at the restriction because, unfortunately, American importers did not import a sufficient variety of goods as demanded by consumers. Therefore, many merchants were "in a measure compelled" to buy at auction "for the sake of an assortment of goods" provided by auctions from foreign exporting houses. The Association, followed by the merchants of other cities, had to repeal its boycott. The repeal in New York carried by only two votes, 64 to 62.

In addition to the failure to obtain federal legislation, a proposal to tax auctions in Maryland was rejected by only two votes, after a struggle in the Maryland House.[103]

Thus, the depression rejuvenated a protectionist movement that had arisen after the war and become dormant. The postwar movement resulting in the Tariff of 1816, however, had been a general patriotic expression connected with the war and its aftermath, and meant to provide temporary relief to the industry spawned by war. Adherents comprised most Americans, including such later vigorous free traders as Thomas Jefferson and John Calhoun. With the passing of the war, the tariff issue had more or less disappeared. The character of the new depression-born movement would become more familiar to later generations. The movement was led by the new manufacturers, most of whom had begun during the war of 1812 when foreign trade was virtually suspended. Cotton textiles led the clamor for greater protection from imports, followed closely by woolen, iron, glass, and paper manufacturers. The battle over an increased tariff, which reached its peak in 1820 over the Baldwin Bill, was far more of a sectional controversy than the monetary issues. Protectionist sentiment flourished in the states where the manufactures were located—especially in the Middle Atlantic states, and adjacent states such as Ohio. The South, on the other hand, dependent on the export of its staples, almost solidly opposed the higher tariff, while the West and commercial New England split on the issue.

VII
CONCLUSION

Confronted with the nation's first great panic, Americans searched widely for the causes of and remedies for their plight. Their search led them to a wide variety of suggestions and controversies, many of which showed keen insight and economic sophistication. Discussion was carried on in the newspapers, in monographs, and in the halls of legislatures. Particularly striking is the high caliber economic thinking of the influential journalists of the day and of many leading political figures. The absence of specialized economists was in a way compensated by the economic knowledge and intelligence of the articulate members of the community, including the leading statesmen.

One of the chief centers of attention was the monetary system. The nation's monetary system was highly imperfect; banking on a nationwide scale was new, and the nation suffered from inconvertibility and varying rates of depreciation during the War of 1812 and elimination and then renewal of a Bank of the United States. There had always been men who favored inconvertible paper for purposes of national development and men who opposed it, but lately little attention had been paid to such schemes. The panic caused monetary troubles to intensify and take on a new urgency. Groups of monetary expansionists arose, many of them respectable pillars of their communities, who wished to stop contraction of the money supply and expand the circulating medium instead. Various types of plan were developed and advanced, on both a federal and state level. Most discussion was on the state level, where all banks except the Bank of the United States were chartered. The most moderate wished to bolster the failing banks by permitting them to suspend specie payment temporarily while continuing in operation. Others turned to the creation of wholly state owned banks or loan offices to issue inconvertible currency. Many states adopted measures to bolster or expand the money supply, including attempts to outlaw depreciation of bank notes. Four western states—Illinois, Missouri, Kentucky, and Tennessee—went to the length of establishing state owned inconvertible paper. The measures were only adopted after keen controversy.

Many writers advocated more ambitious schemes of a federal inconvertible paper money. None came to a vote in Congress, but the House asked Secretary of Treasury Crawford to report on the desirability of such a plan. Crawford's rather reluctant rejection buried the idea. His own paper scheme, though finally rejected by him, drew sharp comment, which incidentally provided some keen analysis of monetary problems and businesss fluctuations.

The basic argument of the monetary expansionists was a need to relieve an alleged scarcity of money, thereby eliminating the depression by aiding debtors and raising prices. The more sophisticated inflationists added their contention that the rate of interest depended inversely on the quantity of money, and that expansion would therefore lead to a beneficial lowering of the rate of interest, and hence to restored prosperity.

The "sound money" opponents of such schemes formed a majority of leading opinion. Their major argument was that depreciation would ensue from any inconvertible paper schemes. But in the process of forming their opposition, much higher level analysis was elaborated. Many hard money writers formulated a monetary explanation of the business cycle—seeing the cause of depression in an expansion of bank credit and money supply, a subsequent rise in prices, specie drain abroad, and finally contraction and depression. Monetary expansion would only renew this process and prolong the contraction necessary to liquidate unsound banks and reverse the specie drain. The only cure for the depression, they concluded, was a rigid enforcement of specie payment. Sound money writers conceded that monetary contraction would bring temporary disturbances, but declared that any legislative intervention would only aggravate the situation.

Much of the discussion concerned the procedure to best maintain *confidence*. The inflationists urged that new money would bolster confidence and induce money to leave idle hoards, thereby restoring prosperity. Their opponents, on the other hand, maintained that confidence could only be achieved by strict adherence to specie payment.

Believing that excessive bank credit was primarily responsible for the depression, restrictionists generally advocated various controls over credit as a method of relieving the present depression and preventing future ones. Various plans were offered (in addition to insistence on strict adherence to specie payments): for example, banks should be allowed only in cities; prohibition of small denomination notes; and the prohibition of interbank borrowing. Hostility to banks was widespread throughout the nation, and many influential figures went so far as to advocate abolition of banking, or virtual abolition through imposing 100 percent reserves. In practice, however, they were often willing to accept more immediately attainable proposals for restricting bank credit. Leading Virginia statesmen were particularly prominent in the hard money ranks.

Thus, America had quite a few exponents of the "Currency principle"—100 percent reserve banking and the idea that fiduciary bank credit causes a business cycle—several years before Thomas Joplin first gave it prominence in England. Perhaps one reason for this precedence was that Americans, while benefiting from the famous English bullionist discussions on problems of an inconvertible currency, were forced to grapple with inflation under a mostly convertible currency several years before the English—who did not complete their return to specie payments until 1821.

Hostility was also engendered toward the Second Bank of the United States, which had touched off the monetary contraction at the onset of the panic. Legislatures passed resolutions urging the elimination of the bank, and some states levied taxes on it or sanctioned suspension of specie payment to the bank only. Little was done in Congress to curb the bank, however. The depression intensified a long standing political controversy concerning the power of the bank. It is often overlooked, however, that hostility to the bank on economic grounds came from two opposing directions: from those who attacked it as too restrictive, and from the hard money *ultras* who considered it a nationwide engine of monetary expansion. Such ultra hard money leaders as the Virginia group had little use for either state or federal banking.

Much of the discussion between the hard and soft money forces was on a highly sophisticated level. Some inflationists welcomed the prospect of a limitless flood of money and even advocated depreciation as helping to build up a home market, but wiser ones countered the opposition with the thesis that an inconvertible currency could be more stable in value than specie. Specie was subject to fluctuations of supply and demand, but paper could be regulated by the government so as to provide a stable value of the dollar. Hard money men were generally content to grant this in theory but to deny its practicality, asserting that the government would always tend to inflate the currency. Some added the subtle theoretical argument that the value of money could not be measured, and denied that such stabilization was either possible or desirable.

The twin planks of the relief platform in the states were inconvertible state paper and debtors' relief. Debtors' relief took the form of stay laws and minimum appraisal laws. These measures had been used before in America, but not on such a widespread or intensified scale. In some cases they were adopted by themselves; in others they were used as means to bolster the circulation of the new inconvertible notes. Controversy over debtors' relief proposals raged in states throughout the Union. Minimum appraisal laws were enacted in four western states—Indiana, Missouri, Ohio, and Tennessee—while stay laws were enacted in eight, two of them in the East (Maryland and Vermont). Some other eastern states (e.g., New York, Rhode Island, Pennsylvania) modified their procedures to ease the strain on insolvent debtors.

The reasoning of the relief forces was generally simple and straightforward: the debtors were in a bad plight, and it was the duty of the legislature to come to their relief. Stress was often laid on the burden placed on debtors by the rise in the purchasing power of the dollar during the depression, with debtors being forced to repay in money of far greater value than they had borrowed. The opponents of relief could not deny the plight of the debtors. Their economic argument emphasized that alleviation of the debtors' problems would only intensify the depression in the long run, for creditors would lose confidence, and this would aggravate the depression and delay recovery. The only lasting help for debtors was to let the economy take its course and await the resumption of confidence. Furthermore, the debtors would thereby be forced to hew to the virtues of thrift and hard work, the only long run basis for prosperity.

One debt problem was a federal one: the public land debt, a mass of which was owed to the government. Granting more liberal terms of credit clearly constituted no interference with private contract. Congress moved to permit debtors to relinquish the unpaid portion of their land, to forgive much of the outstanding debt and keep title to the rest, and to grant extended time for payment. The impetus for this relief came from the West, but it was generally supported in all sections and passed overwhelmingly. Leading opposition, in fact, came from westerners who wanted aid confined to the actual settlers. President Monroe's inaction in the face of the depression has been often stressed, but it should not be forgotten that he took the lead in sponsoring public land debt relief. Monroe did not overlook the depression in that case when he believed federal action appropriate.

The tariff question was another issue that sprang into prominence during the depression. After the War of 1812, the tariff of 1816 had been enacted with general approval in the national spirit carried over from wartime, and in the wish to aid the manufactures developed during the war. Since then, the tariff issue had been dormant, only to revive in the depression in its more modern form as an active, almost evangelical, movement. The movement centered in the Middle Atlantic states and was led by cotton and woolen manufacturers. A determined drive for a high tariff was narrowly defeated in the Senate in 1820, along with two subsidiary measures designed to hamper imports: a prohibitory tax on auction sales—the major sales outlet for imported textiles—and a suspension of the federal government's practice of granting time for the payment of import duties.

The protectionists seized every opportunity to stress the severity of the depression, to press their claim that the tariff would furnish a cure. Manufactures would be bolstered and agriculture assured a steady home market. The phenomenon of widespread unemployment was heavily stressed by the protectionists, and they asserted that a protective tariff would bring about full employment for labor. The existence of unemployment was particularly used to rebut standard free trade objections that a higher tariff would withdraw needed resources from agriculture and commerce.

The free trade opposition centered in the South, where agriculture depended on exports, and in New England shipping centers. Free traders, when they answered the depression argument, maintained that the tariff would aggravate the depression in commerce and agriculture by blocking foreign trade. Some sophisticated free traders also charged that a higher tariff would aggravate the depression by imposing a tax burden on consumption, demonstrating also that falling prices had already increased the real burden of the tariff on the nation's consumers. Thus, they arrived at the position that burdens on consumption should be abated during a depression.

The depression gave rise to suggestions for internal improvements as a partial remedy, in arguments reminiscent of the public works proposals of a later day. These projects would alleviate the depression by giving work to the unemployed, invigorating enterprise in the community, and quickening the circulation of money.

Many citizens objected to all these legislative remedies on the grounds of laissez-faire principle. Their arguments had two facets: (a) the government could not remedy the situation, and (b) a remedy could only come from the market processes themselves: via liquidation of unsound conditions and a return to the fundamental virtues of "industry and economy." Even many of those with other proposals to offer felt that they must pay lip service to the pervasive belief in the importance of these twin virtues. Stress on the moral virtues often took the form of attack on luxurious consumption and other extravagances of the day. Embryonic Veblenians called upon the rich to set an example in thrifty living to the lower classes, who tended to imitate the former.[1]

The laissez-faire partisans opposed higher tariffs and debtors' relief legislation. Most of them were hard money stalwarts as well. Controls over banks were not considered interference in the market but rather an exercise of the government's sovereign rights over the money supply and a prevention of bank interference with the market. The most cogent upholders of this view were the leading Virginians. Some ardent states-rights Virginians, in fact, were willing to grant federal control over banking. A few free traders, in contrast, favored an inflationist monetary policy. Some advocates of laissez-faire were uneasy about stringent regulation of banks, and a few evolved a rudimentary self-generating theory of business cycles, in which cycles were depicted as inevitably recurring business processes, always furnishing their own corrective countermovements. Protection and easy money, conversely, did not necessarily go hand in hand, as some leading protectionists remained staunch hard money men.

The struggles over remedial proposals took their place in the context of nineteenth century struggles over monetary and debt relief proposals. Many historians orient their discussion of such struggles in America along class or sectional lines. The image is often conjured up of poor western farmer-debtors favoring inflation, battling rich eastern merchant-creditors favoring sound money. The results of this study cast strong doubt on this common ideal-type.[2] In the widespread monetary struggles during the depression of 1819–21, at least, the battle of inflation vs. hard money cut sharply across regional, geographic, wealth, and occupational boundaries. The fact that two wealthy cotton planters from Nashville were the leaders of the opposing sides of the raging controversies typified the monetary and debtors' relief debates. Furthermore, several western governors and inflationist leaders completely changed their position after viewing the results of the inconvertible paper schemes. These shifts could scarcely have occurred so swiftly if their opinions had been determined by their class, occupation, or region. Caution should be exercised in employing the much used term "agrarian," for often an agrarian turns out to be a wealthy land speculator rather than an impoverished settler. Sectional and occupational differences were far more clear cut in the tariff controversy, however, with manufacturers in the Middle Atlantic states ranged against southern farmers and planters and New England merchants.

The controversies inspired by the Panic of 1819 continued to make their imprint on later years in America. The protective movement, denied its victory at the time, triumphed in 1824. Inflation of inconvertible notes by states was generally discredited as an anti-depression weapon by the rapid depreciation of the notes. Many of the anti-bank, ultra hard money leaders of the Jackson-Van Buren period first came to a hard money position during this depression. Andrew Jackson himself foreshadowed his later opposition to banking by making himself the fervent leader of the opposition to inconvertible paper in Tennessee. Thomas Hart ("Old Bullion") Benton, later Jackson's hard money arm in the Senate, was converted to hard money by his experience with banking in Missouri during the panic. Future President James K. Polk of Tennessee, who was to be Jackson's leader in the House and later to establish the ultra hard money Independent Treasury system, began his political career in Tennessee in this period by urging return to specie payment. Amos Kendall, later Jackson's top adviser and confidant in the bank war, became an implacable enemy of banks during this period. Condy Raguet, though not a Jacksonian politically, did favor the Independent Treasury plan. He was converted to hard money during the Panic of 1819, after having been a leading inflationist since the end of the War. (The depression also converted Raguet from a protectionist to one of the leading champions of free trade.) Raguet's depression-born search for stricter controls over bank credit expansion led him to be one of the leaders in the free banking movement of the late 1820s.

One of the most impressive aspects of the discussions about the depression was the high intellectual level of the debate, as carried on in newspapers and elsewhere. Participants showed familiarity with English and Continental economists, and with the English reviews, and attempted to relate their practical proposals to a framework of theory to a degree that seems remarkable today.[3]

There is a strong possibility that the panic gave a great impetus toward the launching of a class of economists in this country—in both the academic and journalistic fields.[4] The first treatise on economics published in this country was Daniel Raymond's *Thoughts on Political Economy* in 1820 (expanded into *Elements of Political Economy* in 1823). It was written very much under the impact of the monetary and tariff controversies of the depression, in which Raymond was embroiled. John McVickar, the nation's first academic economist, began teaching economics at Columbia College around this period, and later in the 1820s evolved the "free banking" plan, with bank notes to be secured by government bonds and land mortgages. In fact, many began teaching and writing economics during the 1820s, such as Thomas Cooper, Henry Vethake, William Beach Lawrence, Willard Phillips, Alexander Everett, George Tucker, William Jennison, Jacob N. Cardozo, the Reverend Samuel P. Newman, the Reverend Francis Wayland. Certainly much of this flowering of economics in the United States can be attributed to the impetus given to economic thought by Ricardo, Say, and other European economists. Part of the credit, however, may well be assigned to the controversies over economic policy that the Panic of 1819 had brought into sharp focus.

The Panic of 1819 exerted a profound effect on American economic thought. As the first great financial depression, similar to a modern expansion-depression pattern, the panic heightened interest in economic problems, and particularly those problems related to the causes and cures of depressed conditions. Such important unsolved economic problems as monetary and banking policy, tariff protection, debt collection, internal improvements, all existed before the depression and all continued after it was gone. But the panic gave them new dimensions and aroused new speculations which were not to disappear with the return of prosperity.

APPENDIX A
MINOR REMEDIES PROPOSED

Aside from major controversies already discussed, other scattered proposals and discussions appeared during the depression. Internal improvements financed by the states, for example, were suggested in many quarters as remedial measures for the depression, thus anticipating modern public works proposals. These suggestions were reflections of the growing interest in internal improvements since the end of the War of 1812. An internal improvement drive was particularly strong in Pennsylvania, an early leader in improvement sentiment.[1] Philadelphia's Representative William Lehman, head of the Committee on Public Roads of the Pennsylvania House, sponsored a bill, early in 1820, for the appropriation of over $660 thousand on thirty projects throughout the state. One million dollars was envisioned as the final goal of the plan.[2] Lehman avowed that the measure was necessary for the immediate relief of the portion of people without employment. The bill, he said, was as much to relieve the unemployed as it was to lessen the cost of transport. Passage of the bill would relieve many citizens by giving them employment and would also call a large sum of money into "active circulation." A supporter, Philadelphia's Representative Josiah Randall, stressed the widespread depression and unemployment and claimed as one of the bill's most important effects "the relief it will give to the laboring classes of the community."

In the course of his remarks, Lehman used currently familiar arguments in justifying the increased public debt his policy would entail. For how could the whole society be at a loss, when the debt "would still circulate among the members of the same body?"

Stormy Representative William Duane, in his report on the depression, offered internal improvements as his only suggestion on the state level for relieving the depression. The expenditures would pay labor and go into active circulation. He also suggested that the low prices of labor offered the government a good opportunity to launch construction projects.

The only vocal opponent of the bill was Representative Jarrett, who asked why the Philadelphians who wanted the bill and were so eager for internal improvements did not invest their own ample capital in private improvement projects? [3]

Pennsylvania's Governor Joseph Hiester, opposed, as was Duane, to inconvertible paper money, suggested public improvements as a remedy to the "stagnation of trade and business," and, in his message at the end of 1821, attributed part of the recovery to employment furnished by the public improvements that the state had recently carried out.[4] George Mifflin, a leading Pennsylvania politician, wrote that internal improvement was the only lever that could lift the state to recovery.[5]

The New Jersey legislature adopted, in January, 1820, a resolution favoring the construction of a Delaware and Raritan Canal. The sponsors, supported by the *Times* (New Brunswick), urged that dormant capital would be put to work, and agricultural depression as well as unemployment would be relieved. The project never began because of insufficient subscription of funds.[6]

A leading proponent of public works as a remedy for the depression was the prominent North Carolinian, Archibald D. Murphey. Murphey asserted that the cause of the depression was the lack of a home market for American agriculture. The remedy, then, was to build up the home market, particularly the soil and commercial facilities. To this end, Murphey proposed an extensive plan of internal improvements, including the building of canals, the deepening of rivers, and the construction of highways. Murphey, also an inflationist, favored keeping the state's money at home. He urged using the new paper money to build public works projects.[7]

Much western sentiment was reflected in a resolution introduced in the Ohio Senate by General William Henry Harrison, the future President—a foe of banks and a proponent of tariffs. Harrison argued that it was unwise to pay off the public debt too rapidly. Any surplus revenue that might accumulate, he urged, should be used to aid roads, canals, and other internal improvements.[8] And in eastern Tennessee, the anti-relief *Patriot* urged governmental clearing of eastern Tennessee rivers, *in lieu* of debtors' relief, to permit the shipment of surplus produce to market.[9]

There was also considerable discussion over the various state usury laws, which generally restricted interest to a 6 percent maximum. Some advocated further tightening and stricter enforcement of the usury laws as a means of relieving debtors. In 1820, New Jersey tightened its usury laws.[10] In the following session, citizens of populous Essex County, following the lead of Salem County, petitioned for a reduction in the legal maximum interest, but this was rejected by the Assembly's Committee of

Finance (Pennington) on the grounds that such a reduction would operate *against* debtors by inducing creditors to call their loans.[11]

Tennessee also tightened its usury law in 1819 by setting a legal maximum of 6 percent. A lone figure in the Tennessee House, J. C. Mitchell of Rhea County, urged defeat of the bill and the repeal of all laws on usury. Mitchell argued that a creditor had as much right to get the best price for his money as a farmer to get the best price for his horse. Tennessee's relief leader, Representative Felix Grundy, countered with the argument that property value was determind by use, whereas the value of money was the same everywhere, thus presumably harking back to the Aristotelian concept of the barrenness of money as an argument against interest. Grundy concluded that if no limit were placed on interest, the lenders would grow rich at the expense of the borrowers.[12]

Advocates of repeal or of great easing of the usury laws appeared in other states. One Kentuckian, for example, urged that the only way to relieve the depressed conditions would be to let interest rates *rise* to 10 percent.[13] Such a high interest rate, he argued, would bring money in from outside Kentucky, and spur out-state investment in Kentucky bank stock. There was no sanctity, after all, about the number "six" as a legal maximum. "Mercator" pointed out in the Richmond *Enquirer* that usury laws restricted credit rather than promoted it.[14] When the market rate of interest rose above the legal maximum, many creditors felt bound to obey the law and were therefore deterred from lending, while the other lenders had to be indemnified for the extra risk of evading the law. "A Citizen" reasoned that the very fact of credit-exchange signified that the borrower as well as the creditor believed that he benefited from the transaction.[15] The "Citizen" sprinkled his discussion liberally with quotations from Jeremy Bentham's *Defense of Usury*. He attributed the attack on creditors to envy of those who preferred future goods by those who more strongly preferred the present.

Generally, states did little about the problem. An example was Virginia, when in 1818–19 two opposing bills were introduced: one to strengthen usury laws and another to repeal them. Both attempts were defeated in the House by three-to-one margins. The Vermont legislature received numerous petitions for a usury law, but two House committees rejected them in the fall of 1821.[16]

Inevitably, poor relief increased during the depression. Governor Thomas Worthington of Ohio responded by urging the expansion of poor houses in the state.[17] On the other hand, some opinion urged that the debilitating poor laws be eliminated. Governor De Witt Clinton of New York, in his 1818 message, advocated repeal of the poor laws, because they subsidized pauperism. It was necessary, he maintained, to make living by charity a greater evil than living by industry. The pro-Tammany New York *American* agreed, quoting Jacob N. Cardozo's (Charleston) *Southern Patriot* with approval for criticizing the poor laws as placing a premium upon idleness.[18]

John Woodward, in his famous *Tammany Address*, had two minor remedies to offer for the depression: first, that money brokers be licensed and drastically limited in number, and that they be prohibited from making loans or functioning outside large cities.[19] This was a reflection of popular and bank attacks on brokers for allegedly depreciating the value of bank notes. Second, he deplored the excessively high prices of hotels, inns, and the like, and advocated maximum price controls on the rates of inns and hotels. This would spur business by lessening the cost of travel.

There were some who adopted the protectionist theory of the cause of the depression without adopting the remedy. Thus, one writer believed that domestic industry should be built up and fewer manufactured goods imported from abroad; but instead of protection, he advocated a return to family manufactures. In Delaware, in fact, there was a fleeting movement for subsidization of household manufactures. Small premiums for household manufacture in fields where prices were depressed were recommended by Governor Jacob Stout, but rejected by a House committee.[20]

Another reaction to the depression, if not precisely a remedy suggested for it, was agitation for government to reduce tolls on its toll bridges and turnpikes. Thus, in Virginia, the citizens of Frederick and Shenandoah Counties asked for reduction of their bridge tolls in view of the depression and the great reduction in the prices of produce. The proposal was accepted by the Virginia legislature.[21]

During the depression, savings banks were begun in many communities as a method of helping the poor by making saving easier as well as relieving the community to that extent of the burden of poor relief. Savings banks had only first begun in America at Philadelphia in December, 1816. Four arose in Connecticut during the depression. In Boston, a unique variant of a savings bank was born in the depression. It was the Boston Fuel Savings Institution, organized to help the poor save money in the summer so that they could buy their own fuel in the winter. For their small deposits of money, they received non-negotiable certificates, to be redeemed in the winter in wood, that the institution bought in the summer and stored for the cold weather.[22]

One of the most distinctive proposed remedies for the depression was offered by "George Le Fiscal," in the New York *National Advocate*. He suggested that local communities aid businessmen and workers by making careful estimates of the state of demand of each trade, and in each community keep detailed accounts on which occupations and trades were under, and which were oversupplied.[23]

In those pockets of skilled urban crafts where at least informal unions had developed, some difficulties arose regarding falling wage rates. Thus, an attempt to lower wage rates brought on a strike of Philadelphia carpenters in 1821.[24] Perhaps most tightly organized of workers were the journeymen cordwainers of Philadelphia, who succeeded in compelling their employers to raise their wages in the latter part of 1820, a fact perhaps not entirely unrelated to the heavy unemployment of cordwainers during the same period. The master shoemakers retaliated by continuing to try to push cordwainer wages back to the previous level, an action which the journeymen unsuccessfully tried to prevent by judicial process.[25] In New York City, in 1819, the masons combined to try to prevent a reduction of their daily wage rates, and this action suspended construction activity in New York for a short time. John Pintard, one of New York City's leading merchants and founder of the New York Historical Society, wrote at the time: "We have been retarded in consequence of a conspiracy on the part of the masons, against reducing their wages one shilling from 16/ to 15/ per day, the former being the war price. All industry has been suspended for a fortnight in expectation of compelling builders to yield. But a steady perseverance on the part of the latter against shameful imposition has brought their appetite to, and work is once more resumed. . . . These combinations are very unjustifiable."[26]

APPENDIX B
CHRONOLOGY OF RELIEF LEGISLATION

Stay laws imposed moratoria on collections of debts; minimum appraisal laws set a fixed price below which the debtor's property could not be sold at auction; compulsory par laws prohibited anyone from exchanging bank notes of the state at a discount; the "summary process" was a particularly rapid procedure for collection of debts to banks.

1818

October	Vermont: House passed stay bill.
	Rhode Island: repeal of "summary process" on debts to banks.
December	Pennsylvania: stay and minimum appraisal bills proposed.

1819

January	Delaware: stay and minimum appraisal bills defeated in House of Representatives.
	Ohio: State Bank proposed.
February	Maryland: compulsory par law enacted.
	Ohio: compulsory par law enacted.
April	New York: stay and minimum appraisal bills defeated in Senate.
October	Tennessee: stay law passed.
November	Vermont: House passed stay bill.
December	Kentucky: stay law passed.

1820

January	Maryland: stay law passed.
	Indiana: minimum appraisal law passed.
	North Carolina: stay and minimum appraisal bills proposed.
	Ohio: compulsory par law repealed.
February	Kentucky: stay law passed.
	Delaware: compulsory par law enacted.

	Virginia: minimum appraisal bill defeated in House of Delegates.
March	Pennsylvania: easing of execution law. Loan office bill defeated in House of Representatives.
June	New Jersey: stay bill and loans to debtors defeated in General Assembly.
July	Tennessee: stay law passed. Bank of State of Tennessee enacted.
	Massachusetts: compulsory par bill proposed.
October	Vermont: stay bill defeated in House.
November	Kentucky: Bank of Commonwealth enacted.
December	Kentucky: stay law passed.
1821	
January	Illinois: stay law passed.
	Virginia: stay bill defeated in House of Delegates.
February	Illinois: State Bank enacted.
	Maryland: loan office proposal defeated in House of Delegates.
March	New York: easing of execution law.
	Pennsylvania: minimum appraisal-stay law passed.
June	Missouri: stay law passed.
	Georgia: specie payments suspended to Bank of United States.
July	Louisiana: stay law passed.
October	Tennessee: minimum appraisal bill defeated in Senate.
December	Kentucky: minimum appraisal law passed.
1822	
April	Vermont: stay law passed.
December	Missouri: stay and minimum appraisal laws, and loan office, repealed.
1823	Kentucky: stay laws modified.
	Maryland: compulsory par law repealed.
1824	Indiana: minimum appraisal law repealed.
	Kentucky: stay law repealed.
	Illinois: State Bank repealed.
	Georgia: resumption of specie payments.
1826	Tennessee: resumption of specie payments.

NOTES

PREFACE

1. W. R. Scott found that early business crises in England—in the sixteenth and seventeenth centuries—were attributable to specific acts of government rather than to the complex economic causes that marked modern depressions. W. R. Scott, *The Constitutions and Finance of English, Scottish, and Irish Joint-Stock Companies to 1720* (Cambridge: Cambridge University Press, 1912), pp. 465–67.

2. Very little work has been done on the Panic of 1819, either on its events or on contemporary opinion and policies. Samuel Rezneck's pioneering article dealt largely with *Niles' Register* and the protectionist controversy. William E. Folz's unpublished dissertation was devoted mainly to a description of the events of the pre-Panic period, especially in the West. Thomas H. Greer's useful article dealing with the Old Northwest overemphasized the traditional sectional and class version of debtors' relief controversies, in which the West was considered to be almost exclusively in favor of debtors' relief and the East opposed. Samuel Rezneck, "The Depression of 1819–1822, A Social History," *American Historical Review*, XXXIX (October, 1933), 28–47; William E. Folz, "The Financial Crisis of 1819; A Study in Post-War Economic Readjustment" (unpublished Ph.D. Thesis, University of Illinois, 1935); Thomas H. Greer, "Economic and Social Effects of the Depression of 1819 in the Old Northwest," *Indiana Magazine of History*, XLIV (September, 1948), 227–43.

I. THE PANIC AND ITS GENESIS: FLUCTUATIONS IN AMERICAN BUSINESS, 1815–21

1. For a general survey of the American economy of this period, see George Rogers Taylor, *The Transportation Revolution, 1815–60* (New York: Rinehart and Co., 1951).

2. Total United States population was 7.2 million in 1810, 9.6 million in 1820. U.S. Department of Commerce, *Historical Statistics of the United States, 1789–1945* (Washington, D.C., 1949), p. 25.

3. The banks were largely note-issue institutions. The big-city banks were already using deposits, but there is little or no information about them.

4. U.S. Congress, *American State Papers: Finance*, III, 559, January 26, 1819 (Washington, D.C., 1834), p. 398.

5. U.S. Department of Commerce, *Historical Statistics*, p. 245.

6. Clive Day, "The Early Development of the American Cotton Manufacture," *Quarterly Journal of Economics*, XXXIX (May, 1925), 452.

7. U.S. Congress, "Digest of Manufactures, Supplement," *American State Papers: Finance*, IV, 691 (Washington, D.C., 1834), p. 397 ff. Also George Heberton Evans, *Business Incorporations in the United States, 1800–1943* (New York: National Bureau of Economic Research, 1948), pp. 12–21.

8. Allan G. Gruchy, *Supervision and Control of Virginia State Banks* (New York: D. Appleton-Century and Co., 1937), pp. 14–18, 48–56; Davis R. Dewey, *State Banking Before the Civil War* (Washington, D.C.: Government Printing Office, 1910).

9. U.S., *Annual Report of the Comptroller of the Currency*, 1876, p. xxxix ff.; Albert Gallatin, *Considerations on the Currency and Banking Systems of the United States* (Philadelphia: Carey and Lea, 1831); and Boston *New England Palladium*, July 27, 1819.

10. Gallatin, *Considerations on the Currency*, p. 281; William M. Gouge, *A Short History of Paper Money and Banking* (New York: B. & S. Collins, 1835), pp. 61, 405 ff.; William H. Crawford, *Reports of the Secretary of the United States* (Washington, D.C., 1837), II, 481–525.

11. See also Dewey, *State Banking*, pp. 63–68; John Jay Knox, *History of Banking in the United States* (New York: B. Rhodes and Co., 1900), p. 445; for an account of small denomination paper, see J. T. Scharf and T. Westcott, *History of Philadelphia, 1669–1884* (Philadelphia: L. H. Everts and Co., 1884), I, 581; for an account of West Virginia bank expansion, see Charles H. Ambler, *Thomas Ritchie, A Study in Virginia Politics* (Richmond: Bell Book and Stationery Co., 1913), pp. 66–67.

12. Walter B. Smith and Arthur H. Cole, *Fluctuations in American Business, 1790–1860* (Cambridge: Harvard University Press, 1935), pp. 146, 185; Anne Bezanson *et al.*, *Wholesale Prices in Philadelphia, 1784–1861* (Philadelphia: University of Pennsylvania Press, 1936), II, 352–55, 409; Arthur H. Cole, *Wholesale Commodity Prices in the United States, 1700–1861* (Cambridge: Harvard University Press, 1938), I, 161.

13. These are Treasury estimates for fiscal years ending September 30. U.S. Treasury Department, Bureau of Statistics, *Monthly Summary of Imports and Exports for the Fiscal Year 1896* (Washington, D.C.,

1896), pp. 622–23. Official data on United States imports are not available before 1821.

14. Timothy Pitkin, *Statistical View of the Commerce of the United States of America*, 3d ed. (New York: Durne and Peck, 1835), p. 294; and Worthy P. Sterns, "The Beginning of American Financial Independence," *Journal of Political Economy*, VI (1897–98), 191.

15. Smith and Cole, *Fluctuations*, p. 147; Bezanson, *Wholesale Prices*, I, 353.

16. Ray B. Westerfield, "Early History of American Auctions: A Chapter in Commercial History," *Connecticut Academy of Arts, Sciences, Transactions*, XXIII (May, 1920), 164–70; "Observer," *Review of Trade and Commerce of New York, 1815 to Present* (New York, 1820); J. Leander Bishop, *A History of American Manufactures, 1608–1866* (Philadelphia: E. Young and Co., 1864), II, 256 ff.; New York State, *Assembly Documents*, 1843, No. 10 (Albany, 1843), p. 130 ff.; Victor S. Clark, *History of Manufactures in the United States, 1607–1860* (Washington, D.C.: Carnegie Institute, 1916), II, 241 ff.; Arthur H. Cole, *The American Wool Manufacture* (Cambridge: Harvard University Press, 1926), I, 156 ff., 217; Horace Secrist, "The Anti-Auction Movement and the New York Workingmen's Party of 1829," *Wisconsin Academy of Sciences, Arts, and Letters, Transactions*, Vol. XVII, Part 1 (1914), p. 166.

17. Bezanson, *Wholesale Prices*, I, 355.

18. For an account of the difficulties of the cotton and woolen industry after the war, see Caroline E. Ware, *The Early New England Cotton Manufacture* (Boston: Houghton Mifflin Co., 1931), pp. 66, 126 ff.; Bishop, *A History*, pp. 211 ff., 236; "Reports of House Committee on Commerce and Manufactures," U.S. Congress, *American State Papers: Finance*, III, 32–35, 82 ff., 103, 461; Cole, *American Wool Manufacture*, pp. 85, 144, 152 ff.; "Report of House Committee on Domestic Manufactures," Pennsylvania Legislature, *Journal of the House, 1819–20* (January 28, 1820), p. 413; and J. T. Scharf, *History of Delaware* (Philadelphia: L. J. Richards and Co., 1888), II, 304 ff.

19. Day, *Early Development*, p. 452; Norman S. Buck, *Development and Organization of Anglo-American Trade, 1800–1850* (New Haven: Yale University Press, 1925), pp. 134–47. See also Evans, *Business Incorporations*, pp. 12–30; Ware, *Early New England*, pp. 56 ff.

20. Trade restrictions, however, had already reduced re-exports to $16 million by 1811, the immediate prewar year. Pitkin, *Statistical View of Commerce*, p. 35; U.S. Treasury, *Monthly Summary*, and Emory R. Johnson, Thurman W. Van Metre, G. G. Heubner, and D. S. Hanchett, *History of Domestic and Foreign Commerce of the United States*

(Washington, D.C.: Carnegie Institute, 1915), II, 31 ff. On exports from the principal cities, see Robert G. Albion, *The Rise of the New York Port* (New York: C. Scribners' Sons, 1939), p. 390.

21. Pitkin, *Statistical View of Commerce*, pp. 95–144.

22. Cole, *Wholesale Commodity Prices*, p. 161; Pitkin, *Statistical View of Commerce*, pp. 108–15.

23. William M. Gouge, *Journal of Banking* (Philadelphia: J. Van Court, 1842), pp. 346, 355.

24. New note issue series by banks reached a heavy peak in 1815 and 1816 in New York and Pennsylvania. D. C. Wismer, *Pennsylvania Descriptive List of Obsolete State Bank Notes, 1782–1866* (Fredericksburg, Md.: J. W. Stovell Printing Co., 1933); and *ibid.*, *New York Descriptive List of Obsolete Paper Money* (Fredericksburg, Md.: J. W. Stovell Printing Co., 1931).

25. U.S. Congress, *American State Papers: Finance*, IV, 705 (March 22, 1824), 759.

26. Dewey, *State Banking*, pp. 6–21.

27. For data, see Walter B. Smith, *Economic Aspects of the Second Bank of the United States* (Cambridge: Harvard University Press, 1953), p. 49. Also U.S. Comptroller of the Currency, *Annual Report, 1876*, p. 261; R. C. H. Catterall, *The Second Bank of the United States* (Chicago: University of Chicago Press, 1903), p. 501. Other assets of the Bank were $9.5 million in government bonds, $2.7 million due from state banks. Capital totaled $35 million.

28. Folz, *Financial Crisis*, p. 164; Smith, *Economic Aspects*, pp. 105, 112; U.S. Congress, *American State Papers: Finance*, IV, 705 (March 22, 1824), 523.

29. A contemporary estimated the number of banks in 1818 at 500. "Philotheus," Baltimore *Federal Republican*, July 9, 1819. Also Gouge, *Journal*, pp. 223–26; New York Legislature, *Senate Journal*, 1819 (January 26, 1819), pp. 66–70.

30. N. S. B. Gras, *The Massachusetts First National Bank of Boston, 1784–1934* (Cambridge: Harvard University Press, 1937), pp. 710–11.

31. Knox, *History of Banking*, pp. 485–86.

32. Gouge, *Short History*, p. 166 ff.

33. Purchasers were only required to pay one-fourth of the total within forty days of purchase, and the penalty of forfeiture for failure to complete payment in five years was repeatedly postponed by Congress. U.S. Congress, *The Public and General Statutes Passed by the Congress of the United States of America* (Boston: Wells and Lilly, 1827), II and III, *passim.*

34. See the data compiled from the records of the General Land Office, in Smith and Cole, *Fluctuations*, p. 185; and in Arthur H. Cole,

"Cyclical and Seasonal Variations in Sale of Public Lands, 1816–60," *Review of Economic Statistics*, IX (January, 1927), 42 ff. Also Thomas P. Abernethy, *The Formative Period in Alabama, 1815–28* (Montgomery, Ala.: The Brown Printing Co., 1922), p. 50 ff.; C. F. Emerick, *The Credit System and the Public Domain* (Vanderbilt, Tenn.: Southern History Society Publication No. 3, 1898); U.S. Congress, *American State Papers: Finance*, III, 5, 10; *ibid.*, IV, 859–61.

35. On a building boom in New York City, see the comment by an influential merchant of the day, John Pintard, *Letters to His Daughter, 1816–20* (New York: New York Historical Society, 1940) I, November 16, 1818, 154. Also New York *Gazette*, February 4, 1818. On a rental and property value boom in other states, U.S. Congress, *Annals of Congress of the United States*, 17th Congress, 1st Session (1821–22), March 12, 1822, pp. 1281–97; Washington (D.C.) *National Intelligencer*, July 24, 1819; Thomas Cushing (ed.), *History of Allegheny County, Pennsylvania* (Chicago: A. Warner and Co., 1889), p. 547; William E. Connelley and E. M. Coulter, *History of Kentucky* (Chicago: American Historical Society, 1922) II, 593; Waldo F. Mitchell, "Indiana's Growth, 1812–20," *Indiana Magazine of History*, X (December, 1914), 385; Hattie M. Anderson, "Frontier Economic Problems in Missouri, 1815–28," *Missouri Historical Review*, XXXIV (October, 1939), 48 ff.; Dorothy B. Dorsey, "The Panic of 1819 in Missouri," *ibid.*, XXIX (January, 1935), 79–80; Report of J. H. Brown at 1st Annual Meeting of Kentucky Bar Association, in William Graham Sumner, *History of Banking in the United States* (New York: Henry Holt and Co., 1896), p. 89; Charles H. Garnett, *State Banks of Issue in Illinois* (University of Illinois, 1898), p. 7; Pennsylvania Legislature, *Journal of the Senate, 1819–20*, February 14, 1820, pp. 311–37. On the rise in the price of slaves during the boom, John L. Conger, "South Carolina and Early Tariffs," *Mississippi Valley Historical Review*, V (March, 1919), 415–25.

36. U.S. Department of Commerce, *Historical Statistics*, pp. 169, 219–20.

37. Taylor, *Transportation Revolution*, pp. 23, 336.

38. Thomas S. Berry, *Western Prices Before 1861* (Cambridge: Harvard University Press, 1943), pp. 32, 45 ff. On the heavy increase in costs of transporting convicts, see Pennsylvania Legislature, *Journal of the Senate, 1820–21* (April 3, 1821), p. 816.

39. U.S. Congress, House, *Annual Report of the Commissioner of Navigation, 1901*, 57th Congress, 1st Session, House Document No. 14, p. 585.

40. Joseph E. Hedges, *Commercial Banking and the Stock Market Before 1863* (Baltimore: Johns Hopkins University Studies, 1938).

41. U.S. Treasury, *Monthly Summary;* Cincinnati, *Cincinnati Directory, 1819* (Cincinnati, Ohio, 1819), p. 52.

42. Pitkin, *Statistical View of Commerce*, pp. 95–144; Smith, *Economic Aspects*, p. 280.

43. Cole, *Wholesale Prices*, p. 161; Bezanson, *Wholesale Prices*, II, 67–70. Also Smith, *Economic Aspects*, pp. 72–75; George R. Taylor, "Wholesale Commodity Prices at Charleston, South Carolina, 1796–1861," *Journal of Economic and Business History*, IV (August, 1932), 856–70.

44. Taylor, *Transportation Revolution*, pp. 200–202.

45. The order of magnitude of these earnings was approximately $3 million. See Pitkin, *Statistical View of Commerce*, p. 166.

46. On the general attitude of hostility by the public as well as the banks toward attempts to redeem notes in specie, see Crawford, *Report;* Dewey, *State Banks*, pp. 73–79 ff., 107 ff.; *Niles' Weekly Register*, XIII, (August 2, 1817), 357; *ibid.*, XIV (February 7, 1817), 32; *ibid.*, XIV (June 20, 1818), 281, 285; *ibid.*, XIV (May 30, 1818), 225; New York Legislature, "Report on Committee on Currency," *Journal of the Assembly*, 1818 (February 24), pp. 307–11; Knox, *History of Banking*, p. 576. On an agreement by the banks of Philadelphia not to redeem balances against each other without delay, see Harry E. Miller, *Banking Theories in the United States Before 1860* (Cambridge: Harvard University Press), p. 215.

47. Condy Raguet to David Ricardo, April 18, 1821, in David Ricardo, *Minor Papers on the Currency Question, 1809–23*, Jacob Hollander, ed. (Baltimore: The Johns Hopkins Press, 1932), pp. 199–201.

48. On the silver premium, see Raguet Report, pp. 223–31; Smith, *Economic Aspects*, pp. 106, 123–24, 283, 286; James Flint, *Letters from America* in Reuben G. Thwaites, ed., *Early Western Travels, 1748–1846* (Cleveland: A. H. Clark Co., 1904–07), IX, 136.

49. Smith, *Economic Aspects*, p. 49.

50. *Ibid.*, pp. 40, 119, 286. Also see Catterall, *Second Bank*, p. 503.

51. Gallatin, *Considerations*, pp. 45–51; Delaware General Assembly, *Journal of the House of Representatives, 1819* (January 28), pp. 104–6; New Hampshire *Gazette*, August 19, 1817; John J. Walsh, *Early Banks in the District of Columbia, 1792–1818* (Washington, D.C.: Catholic University of America Press, 1940), pp. 49, 80, 82, 123 ff., 168. Massachusetts banks, in contrast, were able to expand their note issues slightly from 1818–21; Gras, *Massachusetts First National Bank*, pp. 44–49. Also see Wismer, *New York Descriptive List* and *Pennsylvania Descriptive List*, *passim.*

52. Folz, *Financial Crisis*, pp. 170–86; and Louis R. Harlan, "Public Career of William Berkeley Lewis," *Tennessee Historical Quarterly*,

VII (March, 1948), 13; Sister M. Grace Madeleine, *Monetary and Banking Theories of Jacksonian Democracy* (Philadelphia: The Joeblen Press, 1943), p. 14.

53. On business failures and debt judgments, *Niles' Weekly Register*, XVI (May 8, June 7, 1819), 179–80, 258–62; Richmond *Enquirer*, April 23, May 25, June 4, September 3, 1819; Philadelphia *Poulson's American Daily Advertiser*, June 19, July 29, August 5, 1822. On the difficulties of domestic manufactures in the depression, Bishop, *A History*, II, 248–53, 256–63; Ware, *Early New England*, pp. 67–68; Cole, *Wholesale Prices*, I, 147 ff.; and Theodore G. Gronert, "Trade in the Blue-Grass Region, 1810–20," *Mississippi Valley Historical Review*, V (1918), 313–23. On the failure of lead mines in the crisis, Ruby J. Swartzlow, "The Early History of Lead Mining in Missouri," *Missouri Historical Review*, XXIX (January, 1935), 114.

54. Cole, *Wholesale Prices*, p. 161; Smith and Cole, *Economic Fluctuations*, p. 146; and Berry, *Western Prices*, pp. 71–74, 81–83; Arthur H. Cole, *Wholesale Commodity Prices in the United States, 1700–1861* (Cambridge: Harvard University Press, 1938), *Supplement*, pp. 182–91; Thomas S. Berry, "Wholesale Commodity Prices in the Ohio Valley, 1816–60," *Review of Economic Statistics*, XVII (August, 1935), 92; Taylor, "Wholesale Commodity Prices at Charleston; " Walter B. Smith, "Wholesale Commodity Prices in the United States, 1795–1824," *Review of Economic Statistics*, IX (October, 1927), 181–83; Swartzlow, "Early History," p. 201; Frederick W. Moore, "Fluctuations in Agricultural Prices and Wages in the South," *The South in the Building of the Nation* (Richmond: Southern Historical Publishing Society, 1909), V, 426–34. For the fall in the price of and return on slaves, Francis Corbin to James Madison, October 10, 1819, *Massachusetts Historical Society, Proceedings*, XLIII (January, 1910), 261; Smith, *Economic Aspects*, pp. 78–79, 280. On the fall in rental and property values, see Clark, *History*, pp. 378–86; Richmond *Enquirer*, August 5, 1820; Connelley and Coulter, *History*, p. 599; Malcolm R. Eiselen, *The Rise of Pennsylvania Protectionism* (Philadelphia, 1932), pp. 44 ff.

55. *Historical Statistics*, pp. 245–48; Pitkin, *Statistical View of Commerce*, pp. 95–144; and James W. Livingood, *The Philadelphia-Baltimore Trade Rivalry, 1780–1860* (Harrisburg: Pennsylvania Historical Society, 1947), pp. 18–20, 89, 142.

56. *Historical Statistics*, p. 248; Pitkin, *Statistical View of Commerce*, pp. 180–82.

57. *Historical Statistics*, pp. 239–40, 245.

58. Cole, *Wholesale Prices*, pp. 148, 165; Smith and Cole, *Economic Fluctuations*, p. 147; Bezanson, *Wholesale Prices*, p. 353.

59. Smith and Cole, *Economic Fluctuations*, p. 185.

60. One indication of the general decline in business activity was the considerable decline in total letters carried by the U.S. Post Office, a decline the more remarkable for interrupting a period of rapid secular growth, and despite continuing increase in the number of post offices and miles of post roads. Letters carried declined from a peak of 9.6 million in 1819 to 8.5 million in 1821. Wesley E. Rich, *The History of the U.S. Post Office to the Year 1829* (Cambridge: Harvard University Press, 1924), p. 183.

61. Smith, *Economic Aspects*, p. 124.

62. On whiskey as a medium of exchange in the crisis, see Alfred E. Lee, *History of the City of Columbus* (New York: Numsell and Co., 1892), I, 368–69; on grain as a principal medium, see Greer, "Economic and Social Effects," p. 232. On barter, see Charles F. Goss, *Cincinnati, the Queen City, 1788–1912* (Chicago: S. J. Clarke Co., 1912), I, 140 ff.; Dorsey, "The Panic of 1819," p. 85; J. Ray Cable, *The Bank of the State of Missouri* (New York: Columbia University Press, 1923), p. 24; James A. Kehl, *Ill Feeling in an Era of Good Feeling* (Pittsburgh: University of Pittsburgh Press, 1956), p. 188.

63. William Greene, "Thoughts on the Present Situation and Prospect of the Western Country, April 21, 1820," in "A New Englander's Impressions of Cincinnati in 1820–Letters by William Greene," Rosamund R. Wulsin, ed., *Bulletin of the Historical and Philosophical Society of Ohio*, VII (April, 1929), 116–22. Also *Annals of Cleveland, 1818–20* (Cleveland: WPA in Ohio, 1938), I, 398, 479, 539, 543, 569, 590, 629, 649; New York *American*, August 28, 1819; Harold E. Davis, "Economic Basis of Ohio Politics, 1820–40," *Ohio Archaeological and Historical Quarterly*, XLVII (October, 1938), 290, 309; Logan Esarey, *History of Indiana* (Indianapolis: B. F. Bowen and Co., 1918), I, 280 ff.

64. See the above sources on manufactures, including Ware, *Early New England*, pp. 65–72; Bishop, *History*, II, 253; Cole, *American Wool Manufacture*, I, 147 ff.; U.S. Congress, *American State Papers: Finance*, IV, 28 ff.; 290 ff.; 357 ff.

65. Massachusetts Department of Labor, "Historical Review of Wages and Prices, 1782–1860," *Sixteenth Annual Report* (Boston, 1885), Part III, pp. 317–28. Also see the index of wage rates based on these estimates, in Rufus S. Tucker, "Gold and the General Price Level," *Review of Economic Statistics*, XVI (February, 1934), 24; *ibid.*, "Real Wages Under Laissez-Faire," *Barron's*, Vol. XIII, No. 43 (October 23, 1933), p. 7.

66. William A. Sullivan, *The Industrial Worker in Pennsylvania* (Harrisburg: Pennsylvania Historical and Museum Commission, 1955), pp. 68, 72.

67. See the report of a Committee of Citizens of Philadelphia, headed by Condy Raguet, in *Niles' Weekly Register*, XVII (October 23, 1819), 116; also U.S. Congress, *American State Papers: Finance*, III, 641; Matthew Carey, *Essays in Political Economy* (Philadelphia: Carey and Lea, 1822), pp. 319–20; *Niles' Weekly Register*, XVI (August 7, 1819), 385; *ibid.*, XXI (September 1, 1821), 1; Flint, *Letters*, pp. 236, 248; Rezneck, "The Depression," pp. 29–32; New York, *Minutes of the Common Council of the City of New York*, IX (December 10, 1819), 663.

68. A report of the Female Hospitable Society of Philadelphia blamed the increase in pauperism during 1819–20 on unemployment there. Benjamin J. Klebaner, *Public Poor Relief in America, 1790–1860* (New York: Columbia University, microfilmed, 1952), pp. 9, 20.

69. See the message of Governor Joseph Hiester to the Pennsylvania Legislature, December 5, 1821, in Pennsylvania, *Pennsylvania Archives*, George E. Reed, ed., Fourth series, V (Harrisburg, 1900), 281.

70. Smith, *Economic Effects*, pp. 271–72.

71. See the aforementioned sources on prices.

72. On the revival of manufacturing activity, see *Niles' Weekly Register*, XX (March 17, 1821), 34–35; Ware, *Early New England*, p. 88; Philadelphia *Union*, September 4, 1821; Bishop, *History*, pp. 270, 294, 297; Gronert, "Trade," p. 323; Folz, *Financial Crisis*, pp. 234–35. On revival of trade, see Hattie M. Anderson, "Frontier Economic Problems in Missouri, Part II," *Missouri Historical Review*, XXXIV (January, 1940), 189.

73. W. C. Mitchell, *Business Cycles, I, The Problem and Its Setting* (New York: National Bureau of Economic Research, 1927), p. 75.

74. *Ibid.*, pp. 76–79.

75. *Historical Statistics*, p. 63.

76. Arthur F. Burns and Wesley C. Mitchell, *Measuring Business Cycles* (New York: National Bureau of Economic Research, 1946), pp. 97*n*, 408*n*., 503–5.

77. George K. Holmes, *Cotton Crop of the United States, 1790–1911* (U.S. Department of Agriculture, Bureau of Statistics) Circular No. 32, p. 6; *ibid.*, *Rice Crop of the United States, 1712–1911*, *ibid.*, Circular No. 34, pp. 7–8; Smith, *Economic Aspects*, pp. 24, 306.

78. The urban commerce engaged in handling farm products was bolstered by the high physical production.

79. Although the flow of manufactured imports after the war dealt a heavy blow to household manufactures, particularly in New England and the eastern urban areas, household woolen manufactures in the West and even upstate New York continued to flourish and expand undisturbed. Cole, *American Wool Manufacture*, I, 182 ff.

80. Mitchell, *Business Cycles*, p. 78.

81. Kathleen Bruce, *Virginia Iron Manufactures in the Slave Era* (New York: The Century Co., 1931), p. 127.

82. Burns and Mitchell, *Measuring Business Cycles*, pp. 78–79.

83. We shall see, however, that when a problem such as the land debt arose, which Monroe considered within the province of the federal government, the President was quick to take action.

84. James D. Richardson, ed., *A Compilation of the Messages and Papers of the Presidents* (New York: Bureau of National Literature, 1897), pp. 608–16.

85. *Ibid.*, pp. 623–31. Monroe, however, vaguely hinted to Congress that domestic manufactures should in some way be supported.

86. *Ibid.*, pp. 642–49.

87. *Ibid.*, pp. 655–63.

88. Detroit *Gazette*, December 17, 1819. For other attempts to minimize the depression, see the New York *Daily Advertiser*, June 14, 1819, June 25, 1819; Philadelphia *Union*, June 2, 1819; New York *Gazette*, December 9, 1818; Washington (D.C.) *Gazette*, reprinted in Raleigh *Star*, June 25, 1819.

89. Some of the proponents of laissez-faire were in favor of measures to restrict bank credit expansion. While these measures hardly preserved the status quo, they were not considered programs of government intervention, but rather policies to prevent bank inflation—*itself* considered an interference with market processes.

90. [Willard Phillips] "Seybert's Statistical Annals," *North American Review*, IX (September, 1819), 207–39.

91. New York *Daily Advertiser*, March 6, 1819, August 21, 1819, June 10, 1819, May 20, 1819, June 17, 1819. The only exception the *Advertiser* was willing to make was sumptuary laws, to enforce frugality and limit extravagance, but it saw no chance of a free people adopting such legislation.

92. New York *Evening Post*, June 15, 1819. For other expressions of laissez-faire views, see New York *Gazette*, December 9, 1818; Richmond Correspondent, in the Boston *New England Palladium*, May 28, 1819; the charge of Judge Ross to the grand jury, Montgomery County, Pa., *Niles' Weekly Register*, XVIII (July 1, 1820); Peter Force, *National Calendar, 1820* (Washington, 1820), pp. 214 ff.; Churchill C. Cambreleng ("One of the People"), *An Examination of the New Tariff* (New York: Gould & Banks, 1821), pp. 19–21.

93. Washington (D.C.) *National Intelligencer*, May 5, 1820.

94. See New York *National Advocate*, October 2, 16, November 7, 24, 1818; February 5, June 5, 18, 30, July 9, 16, 22, 31, August 6, September 3, October 2, 1819.

95. Philadelphia *Union*, August 10, 13, 1819.

96. See New York *Daily Advertiser*, June 15, 1819. For other expressions of the industry and economy theme, see address of Governor Franklin, North Carolina General Assembly, *Journal of the House*, 1821 (November 22), pp. 7–12; *Address of the Society of Tammany to Its Absent Members* (New York, 1819); "Homespun," in New York *Commercial Advertiser*, October 15, 1819; Jackson Memorial, *Niles' Weekly Register*, XIX (September 2, 1820), 9; address of Governor James P. Preston, Virginia Legislature, *Journal of the House of Delegates*, 1819–20 (December 6, 1819), pp. 6–9; charge of Judge Ross to grand jury, *Niles' Weekly Register*, XVIII (July 1, 1820), 321; "Senex," in New York *Columbian*, February 11, 1819; Baltimore *Federal Republican*, May 22, 1819; "Experience," in Richmond *Enquirer*, October 1, 1819; Detroit *Gazette*, January 29, 1819; New York *American*, October 13, 1819.

97. New York *Daily Advertiser*, August 21, 1819; New York *American*, July 1, 1820. Also see the New York *National Advocate*, June 8, 1819; "Z.," in Philadelphia *Union*, February 17, 1819; and Pintard, *Letters*, p. 197.

98. Annapolis *Maryland Gazette*, June 3, 1819.

99. *Extracts from the Minutes of the General Assembly of the Presbyterian Church of the United States of America, 1819* (Philadelphia, 1819), pp. 171–72. The Convention opened on May 20 in Philadelphia, and consisted mainly of delegates from the Middle Atlantic states, particularly upstate New York.

100. U.S. Congress, *American State Papers: Finance*, III, 589 (April 14, 1820), pp. 522–25. Actions to cut government salaries were put into effect by the Common Council of New York City, by a two-to-one majority of the Virginia House, and suggested by the House Finance Committee of the New Jersey legislature, and by Governor Joseph Hiester of Pennsylvania. Conservative papers urged retrenchment in national spending and the national debt, and Thomas Jefferson wrote letters to his friends denouncing the Federal deficit. Virginia General Assembly, *Journal of the House of Delegates*, 1821 (January 23), pp. 131 ff.; *ibid.* (December 11, 1820, January 11, 1821), pp. 30 ff., 110 ff.; New Jersey Legislature, *Proceedings of the General Assembly*, 1820 (November 1), p. 18; Pennsylvania Legislature, *Journal of the House*, 1820 (December 19), p. 246; *Minutes of the Common Council of New York City* (February 28, 1820), p. 756; New York *Daily Advertiser*, January 1, 1820; New York *American*, July 29, 1820; Thomas Jefferson to Thomas Ritchie, December 25, 1820; Jefferson to Judge Spencer Roane, March 9, 1821, in Thomas Jefferson, *Writings*, T. E. Bergh, ed. (Washington, D.C.: Thomas Jefferson Memorial Association of the United States, 1904), XV, 295, 325.

II. DIRECT RELIEF OF DEBTORS

1. United States, *Public Statutes at Large*, II, 73, 533.

2. *Ibid.*, III, 96, 433, 515, 555. Postponement of forfeiture laws were passed in 1810, 1812, 1813, 1814, and 1815.

3. U.S. Congress, *Annals of Congress*, 16th Congress, 2d Session, p. 15.

4. *Ibid.* The message was presented on November 14, 1820. The relief issue had been briefly raised late in the previous session in a resolution of the Louisiana legislature, but consideration was deferred until the 1820–21 session. *Ibid.*, 16th Congress, 1st Session, p. 467.

5. Johnson was later to become a key leader in the Jacksonian movement and Jackson's intimate agent. He became vice-president under Van Buren.

6. *Ibid.*, pp. 17, 22.

7. U.S. Congress, *American State Papers: Finance*, IV, 599 (December 5, 1820), pp. 547 ff.

8. Memorials came from Ohio, Illinois, Indiana, Alabama, Tennessee, and Kentucky. *Ibid.*, pp. 22, 36, 77, 99, 116, 126, 130, 131, 134, 141, 153, 212, 249, and 436.

9. Speech of Thomas, January 11, 1821, U.S. Congress, *Annals of Congress*, 16th Congress, 2d Session, p. 156. Thomas was an aristocratic lawyer, formerly a Representative from Tennessee, and Federal Judge in Ohio. He nominated his friend William Henry Harrison for President in 1840.

10. *Ibid.*, pp. 161–78. Edwards had been Chief Judge of the Kentucky Court of Appeals and Governor of Illinois Territory.

11. These were its "Mississippi stock," made receivable in the Southwest, and in claims to its lands in the Northwest.

12. On January 30, 1821. *Ibid.*, p. 251.

13. *Ibid.*, pp. 214–22.

14. Eaton was a lawyer, landowner, and land speculator, and an intimate associate of Andrew Jackson, his wife having been Jackson's ward. He was later to be Secretary of War under Jackson.

15. *Ibid.*, pp. 180, 214–36. The New Englander was Senator Morrill of New Hampshire. Other Senators attacking the amendment were Noble of Indiana, Johnson of Kentucky, Thomas, and King and Walker of Alabama.

16. Thus, arguing for the extra relief to settlers were Senators Johnson, King of Alabama, Ruggles of Ohio, while on the opposite side were Talbot of Kentucky, Edwards, and Noble.

17. *Ibid.*, p. 333. The bill passed on February 10, 1821. Senator Eaton voted for the final bill.

18. *Ibid.*, p. 441.

19. *Ibid.*, pp. 1187–89 and 1221 ff.

20. *Ibid.*, pp. 1221 ff., 1228 ff.

21. In this action, one of the leading advocates of the bill, Richard C. Anderson of Kentucky, head of the Committee on Public Lands, joined forces with the anti-reliefers to defeat the proposal by a narrow vote of 85 to 70. Henry Clay, of Kentucky, was leader of the extreme relief forces on this occasion.

22. Metcalf was later to become Governor and Senator from Kentucky, and to oppose state inconvertible paper plans.

23. For the text of this law, see U.S. Congress, *Public Statutes at Large*, III, 612–16.

24. *Niles' Weekly Register*, XV (January 31, 1819), 423; XIX (November 25, 1820), 194.

25. Abernethy, *Formative Period*, p. 56.

26. Madeleine, *Monetary and Banking Theories*, pp. 27 ff.; Greer, "Economic and Social Effects," pp. 228–29.

27. Although one of the supporting arguments for proposals for increased paper currency was the consequent relief of debtors, they will be considered separately, because of the many other issues that the monetary proposals presented. In many cases, stay laws were tied together with the monetary plans and were promulgated as attempts to bolster the general acceptability of the new paper, and so to benefit the debtor who could use it in payment.

28. Delaware General Assembly, *Journal of the House of Representatives*, 1819 (January 26), p. 91; (February 2), p. 139.

29. *Ibid.* (February 3), pp. 150 ff. Three of the dissenters, however, were from New Castle County.

30. The vote was 26 to 10. For the vote, see New Jersey Assembly, *Votes and Proceedings of the General Assembly*, 1819–20 (June 13, 1820). For the report of the Hopkinson Committee, see *ibid.* (June 2, 1820), pp. 202–5. Hopkinson had been a distinguished Federalist lawyer and Congressman from Philadelphia, and was soon to return there.

31. New York Legislature, *Journal of the Senate*, 1819 (April 5), pp. 251–52.

32. *Ibid.*, 1821 (March 13), p. 223.

33. Matthew P. Andrews, *Tercentenary History of Maryland* (Chicago: S. J. Clarke Co., 1925), p. 1741; Boston *New England Palladium*, February 1, 1820. Maryland also abolished imprisonment for debt in 1819. The movement for abolition, however, is only tangential to our study, since it was a continuing humanitarian movement rather than an economic measure.

34. Cleveland *Register*, July 6, 1819.

35. New York *Daily Advertiser*, June 17, 1819; January 11, 1820.

36. By a vote of 62 to 59, after repeated refusal to postpone the bill by fluctuating margins, as high as 97 to 56. Vermont General Assembly, *Journal of the House*, 1818–19 (October 10, 1818, November 6, 1818, November 10, 1818), pp. 143 ff., 167.

37. The bill passed by a vote of 87 to 47. *Ibid.*, 1819–20 (November 10, 1819), pp. 172 ff.

38. The vote was 115 to 38. *Ibid.*, 1820–21 (October 27, 1820), p. 101.

39. Walter Hill Crockett, *Vermont, the Green Mountain State* (New York: The Century History Co., 1921), III, 181.

40. Howard K. Stokes, "Public and Private Finance," in Edward Field, ed., *State of Rhode Island and Providence at the End of the Century; A History* (Boston, 1902), III, 264–71, 291 ff.; and Clarence S. Brigham, "The Period from 1820 to 1830," in *ibid.*, I, 304.

41. Throughout this paper, "conservative" will be used as a term connoting such views.

42. Richmond *Enquirer*, February 1, 1820.

43. *Ibid.* The debate took place in the House of Delegates on January 28.

44. *Ibid.*, February 5, 1820.

45. Rives was later to become one of the most prominent Virginia statesmen, a Jacksonian who favored state banking and balked at the subtreasury scheme. Also supporting the bill was Representative Joseph Lovell of Kanawha, in West Virginia, who pointed to the "unusual embarrassment" of the times. *Ibid.*, February 3, 1820.

46. *Ibid.*, February 1, 1820.

47. The danger of setting a precedent in impairment of contract was stressed by Representative Andrew Stevenson, of the city of Richmond. *Ibid.*

48. *Ibid.*, February 5, 1820.

49. One was rejected by a vote of 76 to 47, and the other by 95 to 84. The latter bill had previously been tentatively approved by a vote of 109 to 71. Virginia General Assembly, *Journal of the House of Delegates*, 1820–21 (January 19, January 25, February 17), pp. 126, 140, 131.

50. *Ibid.*, 1819–20 (December 6, 1819), pp. 6–9.

51. See below for arguments on industry and economy as the remedies for hard times.

52. North Carolina, Historical Research Project, *A Calendar of the Bartlett Yancey Papers* (Raleigh: North Carolina Historical Survey Project, 1940), p. 4.

53. Representative Noble was from Bedford County in far Western Pennsylvania, and Representative Reeder represented Luzerne and Susquehanna Counties in the North. For their proposal, see Pennsylvania Legislature, *Journal of the House*, 1818–19 (December 10, 1818), p. 113.

54. Findlay was later U.S. Senator and Treasurer of the U.S. Mint under Jackson.

55. For the text of the report, see *ibid.*, 1819–20 (January 28, 1820), pp. 476–88.

56. Duane's own remedies will be considered below.

57. State Senator Condy Raguet, of Philadelphia, headed a committee to investigate the extent, causes, and remedies of the distress. Its report will be considered further. Its text is in Pennsylvania Legislature, *Journal of the Senate*, 1819–20 (January 29, 1820), pp. 221–36, and the documentary appendix to the report is to be found in *ibid.* (February 14, 1820), pp. 311–37.

58. Kehl, *Ill Feeling*, pp. 12–13.

59. Pennsylvania Legislature, *Laws of Pennsylvania*, 1819–20 (March 28, 1820), p. 155.

60. "A Pennsylvanian" in Philadelphia *Union*, February 11, 1820.

61. Greer, "Economic and Social Effects," p. 238.

62. Charles C. Huntington, *A History of Banking and Currency in Ohio Before the Civil War* (Columbus: Ohio Archeological and Historical Society, 1915), pp. 300 ff.; comment of Philadelphia *Union*, August 27, 1821; Cleveland *Herald*, October 16, 1821.

63. Cleveland *Herald*, March 20, 1821. This attitude contrasts with the tone of the press before the laws were passed when it was angry at the rapacity of the creditors. Thus, see Cleveland *Register*, May 25, 1819, August 10, 1819.

64. On the pervasive insolvency in Ohio in this period, see William Greene, "Thoughts"; John J. Rowe, "Money and Banks in Cincinnati Before the Civil War," *Bulletin of the Historical and Philosophical Society of Ohio*, VI (July, 1948), 74–84; Goss, *Cincinnati*, pp. 139–41; Davis, "Economic Basis," pp. 289–90.

65. Jacob Piatt Dunn, *Indiana and Indianans* (Chicago: American Historical Society, 1919), p. 326.

66. Indiana General Assembly, *Laws*, 3rd General Assembly, p. 68; on debtors' relief laws in Indiana, see Waldo F. Mitchell, "Indiana's Growth," pp. 389–91.

67. Indiana General Assembly, *Journal of the Senate*, 1818–19, p. 36.

68. Indiana General Assembly, *Laws*, 4th General Assembly, pp. 113 ff.; Mitchell, "Indiana's Growth."

69. Garnett, *State Banks*, pp. 8–13. This law succeeded previous laws, enacted in 1813 and 1817, which had provided stays of one year for refusal of creditors to accept at par the notes of various Illinois banks. George W. Dowrie, *The Development of Banking in Illinois, 1817–63* (University of Illinois, 1913), p. 11; Knox, *A History of Banking*, p. 712.

70. Dowrie, *Development*, p. 32; and Alexander Davidson and Bernard

Stuvé, *A Complete History of Illinois* (Springfield: Rokkor Co., 1881), p. 307.

71. Illinois General Assembly, *Journal of the House*, 1820–21 (January 13, 1821), p. 157.

72. See the excellent articles by Dorsey and Anderson.

73. The existence of this special immigration boom helped to delay the crisis in Missouri to the end of 1819. Anderson, "Frontier Economic Problems," Part I.

74. On the controversy over debtors' relief legislation in Missouri, see the articles by Dorsey, Anderson, and Hamilton.

75. Primm states that the St. Charles *Missourian*, May 3, 1821, itself declared that "nine-tenths of the people were demanding economic relief." James Neal Primm, *Economic Policy in the Development of a Western State, Missouri, 1820–60* (Cambridge: Harvard University Press, 1954), p. 3. But see Anderson, "Frontier Economic Problems," Part I, p. 58*n*.

76. Only two members of the grand jury refused to sign this presentment, and they reasoned that discussing such legislation was none of the grand jury's business. See Anderson, "Frontier Economic Problems," I.

77. "A Citizen" in St. Louis *Enquirer*, March 3, 1821; Franklin *Missouri Intelligencer*, May 28, 1821.

78. Primm gives the impression that overwhelming sentiment in this period favored relief legislation. While mentioning letters favoring relief legislation and a rural citizens' meeting, however, Primm omits the opposition of the bulk of the press and of the rural citizens' meeting at Boonville. Primm, *Economic Policy*, pp. 2–5.

79. McNair was an influential merchant of St. Louis. Missouri General Assembly, *Laws*, 1st General Assembly, Special Session, 1821, pp. 32–34.

80. Missouri General Assembly, *Journal of the House*, 1st General Assembly, 2d Session, 1821, pp. 7–10.

81. Missouri General Assembly, *Laws*, 1st General Assembly, 2d Session, 1821, pp. 46–52.

82. Anderson, "Frontier Economic Problems," I, 65.

83. Green was a wealthy merchant, leading lawyer, and land speculator. He was brother-in-law of Ninian Edwards, of Illinois. Green's son later married Calhoun's daughter, and Green became Calhoun's chief editorial arm, as editor of the Washington *United States Telegraph*. Green later became President Tyler's unofficial representative to Europe.

84. Missouri General Assembly, *Laws*, 1st General Assembly, 2d Session, 1821, p. 74.

85. Hamilton, *Relief Movement*.

86. "Friend of Justice" in Franklin *Missouri Intelligencer*, September 4, 1821; Hamilton, *Relief Movement*, p. 78.

87. Anderson, "Frontier Economic Problems," p. 67.

88. St. Louis *Missouri Republican*, October 9, 1822. The charge that wealthy debtors rather than poor ones were responsible for the relief drive was common to the opposition in many states. Anderson, "Frontier Economic Problems," believes that this charge was correct, at least in Missouri. She states that the relief measures were largely for the benefit of the large land speculators, and that Representative Duff Green, the well-to-do relief leader, was himself heavily in debt at the time. Primm, *Economic Policy*, pp. 8–9, errs in asserting that the opposition to relief legislation based itself purely on a defense of wealth and on attacking the reliefers as poor and enemies of property.

89. Hamilton, *Relief Movement*.

90. On the 1821 election, see Primm, *Economic Policy*, pp. 10 ff. Primm, by failing to mention the hotly fought 1822 election, vastly underestimates the extent of popular opposition to the relief program. He also neglects to mention that Governor McNair, in urging repeal of the relief legislation, specifically mentioned its failure to have the desired effects. *Ibid.*, p. 15.

91. Missouri General Assembly, *Journal of the House*, 2d General Assembly, 1st Session, 1821, pp. 7–8.

92. Richmond *Enquirer*, July 31, 1821; Folz, *Financial Crisis*, pp. 186 ff.

93. Thomas P. Abernethy, "The Early Development of Commerce and Banking in Tennessee," *Mississippi Valley Historical Review*, XIV (December, 1927), 311–25. Claude A. Campbell, *The Development of Banking in Tennessee* (Nashville: Vanderbilt University Press, 1932); Joseph H. Parks, "Felix Grundy and the Depression of 1819 in Tennessee," *Publications of the East Tennessee Historical Society*, X (1938), 20.

94. William E. Beard, "Joseph McMinn, Tennessee's Fourth Governor," *Tennessee Historical Quarterly*, IV (June, 1945), 162–63; and Philip Hamer, *Tennessee, A History, 1673–1932* (New York: American Historical Society, 1933), pp. 229–40.

95. Parks, Abernethy, Hamer, *passim*.

96. Grundy later became a supporter of Andrew Jackson, a United States Senator, and Attorney-General under Van Buren.

97. Nashville *Clarion*, August 10, 1819. Cited in Parks, "Felix Grundy," p. 21. The *Clarion* was owned by Thomas G. Bradford, a political follower of the wealthy land speculator from rural Bedford County in mid-Tennessee, Andrew Ervin. See Charles G. Sellers, Jr., "Banking and Politics in Jackson's Tennessee, 1817–1827," *Mississippi Valley Historical Review*, LXI (June, 1954), 61–84.

98. Parks, "Felix Grundy," p. 22.

99. For example, the Bank of the State of Tennessee and the Nashville Bank.

100. Tennessee General Assembly, *Journal of the House of Representatives*, 1819, p. 245; *Public Acts of Tennessee*, 1819, p. 44. Sellers' contention that this bill was a weakening of support for relief by Grundy does not seem convincing. Rather it appears to be the first step by the relief forces toward a comprehensive relief program. Sellers, "Banking."

101. Parks, "Felix Grundy," pp. 25 ff.

102. Hamer, *Tennessee*, p. 233.

103. West Tennessee was not a factor in public sentiment, since it was practically unpopulated.

104. Issue of June 20, 1820.

105. Nashville *Whig*, June 7, 1820. Cited in Sellers, "Banking," p. 69.

106. Nashville *Whig*, May 24, 1820; June 14, 1820.

107. Parks, "Felix Grundy," pp. 27 ff. The *Patriot* declared that times were very hard in East Tennessee as well, but that this measure could not improve conditions.

108. Parks, "Felix Grundy," p. 29.

109. Issue of May 23, 1820.

110. Nashville *Gazette*, June 14, 1820. Cited in Parks, "Felix Grundy," p. 29. The Nashville *Gazette*, edited by George Wilson, was established by the dominant Overton faction of Tennessee politics, headed by Nashville land speculator, John Overton, reputed to be the wealthiest man in Tennessee. See Sellers, "Banking."

111. McMinn was an eminent politician of Tennessee, three times elected to the United States Senate, and three times Governor.

112. Tennessee General Assembly, *Journal of the House of Representatives*, 1820 (June 26, 1820), pp. 6–17.

113. *Ibid.*, June 28, 1820, p. 23.

114. Tennessee General Assembly, *Journal of the Senate*, 2d Session, 1820 (July 7, July 14, 1820).

115. *Ibid.*, July 21, 1820.

116. Tennessee General Assembly, *Journal of the House of Representatives*, 1821 (September 17, 1821), pp. 6 ff.

117. *Ibid.*, October 2, 1821, pp. 114–15.

118. Hamer, *Tennessee*, p. 238.

119. This address was praised by the influential Hezekiah Niles, who denounced state relief laws—particularly those of Kentucky and Tennessee—as the work of dishonest debtors seeking special privilege. *Niles' Weekly Register*, XXI (November 3, 1821), 146.

120. Gabriel H. Golden, "William Carroll and His Administration," *Tennessee Historical Magazine*, IX (April, 1925), 19.

121. Thus, see Arndt M. Stickles, *The Critical Court Struggle in Kentucky, 1819–29* (Indiana University, 1929), pp. 20 ff. Also see General Basil W. Duke, *History of the Bank of Kentucky, 1792–1895* (Louisville:

A. C. Morton and Co., 1895), pp. 14–21. For a contemporary account of debt burdens in Kentucky, Philadelphia *Union*, July 3, 1821.

122. Connelley and Coulter, *History*, II, 608 ff.; Samuel M. Wilson, *History of Kentucky* (Chicago: The S. J. Clarke Publishing Co., 1928), II, 121–27; Sumner, *History of Banking*, p. 121.

123. Orval W. Baylor, *John Pope, Kentuckian* (Cynthiana, Ky.: The Hobson Press, 1943), pp. 153–63. Pope, Secretary of State under Governor Slaughter and a director of the Bank of Kentucky, became the leading opponent of the debtors' relief program.

124. Kentucky General Assembly, *Journal of the House of Representatives*, 1819 (December 16, 1819), p. 811.

125. Stickles, *Critical Court Struggles*, p. 23.

126. Kentucky General Assembly, *Journal of the House of Representatives*, 1821–22 (December 19, 1821), p. 475.

127. Kentucky General Assembly, *Journal of the House of Representatives*, 1819, p. 161.

128. "Solon," *Liberty Saved* (Louisville, Ky.: by the Author, no date), p. 8.

129. Thus, Frankfort *Argus*, quoted in Washington (D.C.) *National Intelligencer*, June 9, 1819.

130. Wilson, *History of Kentucky*, p. 133.

131. Frankfort *Argus*, April 27, 1820 and following. See Amos Kendall, *Autobiography* (Boston: P. Smith, 1872), William Stickney, ed., pp. 230–35.

132. Kendall, *Autobiography*, p. 244.

133. Frankfort *Argus*, July 5, 1821; in Kendall, *Autobiography*, p. 245.

III. STATE PROPOSALS AND ACTIONS FOR MONETARY EXPANSION

1. For the economy of Alabama in this period, see Abernethy, *Formative Period*, pp. 25, 50 ff., 86 ff.

2. The Bank of St. Stephens opened in September, 1818, with only $7,700 of paid-in capital. U.S. Congress, *American State Papers: Finance*, III, 637 (February 14, 1822), 767–68.

3. Abernethy, *Formative Period*, pp. 86 ff.

4. Alabama General Assembly, *Journal of the Senate*, 1821, pp. 8–9. By 1823, ex-Governor Bibb had become a director of the Huntsville Bank.

5. Philadelphia *Union*, November 2, 1821.

6. Knox, *A History of Banking*, p. 594.

7. Albert B. Moore, *History of Alabama* (Chicago: American Historical Society, 1927), I, 159–60.

8. Pickens himself was President of the Tombeckbee Bank of St. Stephens. Abernethy, *Formative Period*, pp. 93 ff.

9. Poindexter was one of the leading politicians in the State, and later became a staunch Whig. On the veto of the Runnels Bill, see Robert C. Weems, Jr., *The Bank of the Mississippi; A Pioneer Bank of the Old Southwest, 1809–44* (New York: Columbia University, 1951, microfilm), p. 388.

10. Stephen A. Caldwell, *A Banking History of Louisiana* (Baton Rouge: Louisiana State University Press, 1935).

11. Louisiana General Assembly, *Official Journal of the Proceedings of the House of Representatives*, 1819 (January 18, 1819), p. 16.

12. Issue of May 6, 1820. Quoted in Joseph George Tregle, Jr., "Louisiana and the Tariff, 1816–46," *Louisiana Historical Quarterly*, XXV (January, 1942), 35.

13. Thomas P. Govan, "Banking and the Credit System in Georgia, 1810–60," *Journal of Southern History*, IV (May, 1938), 166 ff.

14. George G. Smith, *The Story of Georgia and the Georgia People, 1732–1860* (Macon: G. and G. Smith, 1900), p. 300.

15. Milton S. Heath, *Constructive Liberalism* (Cambridge: Harvard University Press, 1954), pp. 176–78.

16. Report on the Joint Committee of the Planters' Bank and the Bank of the State of Georgia, June 21, 1820, in U.S. Congress, *American State Papers: Finance*, IV, 1055–56.

17. Govan, "Banking," p. 169.

18. Washington (D.C.) *National Intelligencer*, December 15, 1821; Heath, *Constructive Liberalism*, p. 188.

19. *Ibid.*, p. 182.

20. *Ibid.*, pp. 183 ff.

21. Georgia General Assembly, *Journal of the House of Representatives*, 1820–21 (November 7, 1820), p. 6.

22. For an example of hard money attack on depreciation, see the Washington (Ga.) *News*, reprinted in the Washington (D.C.) *National Intelligencer*, August 4, 1821.

23. Georgia General Assembly, *Journal of the Senate*, 1822 (November 5, 1822), pp. 14–15.

24. Knox, *A History of Banking*, p. 564; Sumner, *History of Banking*, pp. 87, 115.

25. On the report of Stephen Elliott, appointed head of the Bank of the State of South Carolina, criticizing the action of the Bank of the United States, and the allegedly resulting scarcity of money, see Joseph Dorfman, *The Economic Mind in American Civilization* (New York: Viking Press, 1946), I, 370–71.

26. Robert Y. Hayne to Langdon Cheves, February 22, 1819, in Theo-

dore D. Jervey, *Robert Y. Hayne and His Times* (New York: The Macmillan Co., 1909), pp. 85–87. Hayne, wealthy rice planter, was later to become Senator and Governor, and leading proponent of nullification.

27. On Cardozo, see Dorfman, *Economic Mind*, II, 554–55.

28. Editorial in the Charleston *Southern Patriot*, reprinted in the Cleveland *Register*, August 31, 1819.

29. Murphey had been Justice of the State Supreme Court and was to become known as father of the state's public school system. In 1816, Murphey had been a staunch advocate of a branch of the Bank of the United States in Fayetteville, and considered inconvertible paper as "vicious." Now, as a debtor to the Bank, he felt that he was being unjustly compelled to repay. Murphey to Colonel William Polk, July 24, 1821, in William Henry Hoyt, ed., *The Papers of Archibald D. Murphey* (Raleigh: E. M. Uzzell Co., 1914), pp. 216–17. Also Dorfman, *Economic Mind*, I, 376–78.

30. Murphey, *Papers of Archibald D. Murphey*, p. 216.

31. Raleigh *Star and North Carolina State Gazette*, May 14, 1819.

32. Washington (D.C.) *National Intelligencer*, May 26, 1819. Also see the editorial in the Wilmington *Recorder*, June 16, 1819, reprinted in the Washington (D.C.) *National Intelligencer*, July 20, 1819.

33. Raleigh *Star*, December 22, 1820.

34. Knox, *A History of Banking*, p. 549.

35. "Cato," in Washington (D.C.) *National Intelligencer*, June 19, 1819.

36. "Philo-Economicus," in Richmond *Enquirer*, June 15, 1819.

37. New York *Daily Advertiser*, June 12, 1819.

38. "Colbert," in Richmond *Enquirer*, November 6, 1819.

39. Knox, *A History of Banking*, p. 489.

40. *Ibid.* Boston *New England Palladium*, March 2, 1819.

41. New York *American*, March 6, 1819.

42. Dewey, *State Banking*, p. 66.

43. Washington (D.C.) *National Intelligencer*, June 1, 1819.

44. "A Citizen," in the Baltimore *Telegraph*, reprinted in the Richmond *Enquirer*, June 1, 1819.

45. Baltimore *Federal Republican*, July 1, 1819.

46. *Ibid.*, July 13, 1819.

47. For a discussion of Thomas Law and his proposals, see Chapter IV. The charge was inaccurate, since Law primarily advocated a national governmental currency plan, rather than suspension of specie payment by private banks.

48. *Niles' Weekly Register*, XV (September 12, 1818), 33.

49. Maryland General Assembly, *Official Journal of the Proceedings of the House of Representatives*, 1820–21 (February 15, 1821), pp. 109–10.

50. Delaware General Assembly, *Journal of the House of Representatives*, 1819 (January 26, 1819), p. 91.

51. *Ibid.*, 1820 (January 18, 20, 28; February 1, 2, 1820), pp. 58 ff., 73 ff., 128 ff., 132.

52. *Ibid.* (February 8, 11, 1820), pp. 169, 196.

53. New Jersey Legislature, *Votes and Proceedings of the General Assembly*, 1819–20 (June 2, 1820), pp. 202–5.

54. New York *Evening Post*, June 15, 1819.

55. Banks were generally solvent in New Hampshire, Connecticut and Massachusetts, particularly in Boston. *Cf.* Sumner, *History of Banking*, p. 112.

56. Boston *New England Palladium*, July 4, 1820.

57. T. D. Seymour Bassett, "The Rise of Cornelius Peter Van Ness, 1782–1826," *Proceedings of the Vermont Historical Society*, X (March, 1942), 8–16.

58. Van Ness was scheduled to become chairman of the board of the new bank.

59. Vermont General Assembly, *Journal of the House*, 1818–19 (November 3, November 7), pp. 127 ff., 150 ff. The Governor had previously vetoed a less stringent charter for the bank.

60. Vermont General Assembly, *Journal of the House*, 1819–20 (October 15, 1819), pp. 11–12.

61. Raguet Report and documentary appendix.

62. Pennsylvania Legislature, *Journal of the House*, 1819–20 (December 10, 1819), pp. 20–28. Also Philip S. Klein, *Pennsylvania Politics, 1817–32* (Philadelphia: Historical Society of Pennsylvania, 1940), p. 98.

63. Duane was particularly bitter over the leading role played by Findlay, as State Treasurer in 1814, in pushing through a mass chartering of 42 banks over the veto of Governor Simon Snyder.

64. Pennsylvania Legislature, *Journal of the House*, 1819–20 (January 28, 1820), pp. 476–78.

65. Philadelphia *Aurora*, February 4, 1820.

66. Pennsylvania Legislature, *Journal of the House*, 1818–19, p. 450.

67. *Ibid.*, 1819–20 (February 1, 1820), pp. 459–66.

68. Washington (D.C.) *National Intelligencer*, March 25, 1820. See Appendix A on internal improvements as a suggested remedy for the depression.

69. Philadelphia *Union*, August 17, August 24, 1821.

70. For a warning about loan office agitation as late as the end of 1821, see "Adam Lock," in Philadelphia *Union*, December 11, 1821. For early opposition to any government loans, see "A," in the Philadelphia *United States Gazette*, December 22, 1818. The *Gazette* was predecessor of the *Union*.

71. For the Ohio situation, see especially Huntington, *History*, pp. 255–351. Also Sumner, *History of Banking*, p. 152; Greene, "Thoughts on the Present," pp. 121–22; Rowe, "Money and Banks," pp. 74–84; Goss, *Cincinnati*, pp. 139–43.

72. Worthington was a country gentleman and leading political figure in the state, a former Senator and leader of the "Chillicothe Junta." He suffered financial reverses in the depression of 1819. Ohio Legislature, *Journal of the Senate*, 1818–19, p. 222.

73. Brown was a wealthy landowner and former judge. Ohio Legislature, *Journal of the House*, 1819–20 (December 7, 1819), pp. 9–15.

74. Philadelphia *Union*, March 5, 1819; Huntington, *History*, pp. 295–97; R. Carlyle Buley, *The Old Northwest, Pioneer Period, 1815–40* (Indianapolis: Indiana Historical Society, 1950), I, 586.

75. In the Cincinnati *Gazette*, reprinted in Detroit *Gazette*, December 11, 1819.

76. Waldo F. Mitchell, "Indiana's Growth," pp. 384–85; Esarey, *History*, p. 280; Nathan Ewing, President of the Bank of Vincennes, to Secretary Crawford, January 9, 1819, in U.S. Congress, *American State Papers: Finance*, III, 637 (February 14, 1822), 734.

77. Dunn, *Indiana*, pp. 322 ff.

78. Logan Esarey, *State Banking in Indiana* (Indiana University Studies, 1912), pp. 221 ff.; Esarey, "The First Indiana Banks," *Indiana Quarterly Magazine of History*, VI (December, 1910), 144–58.

79. Washington (D.C.) *National Intelligencer*, June 19, 1819.

80. Noble was a member of one of the most eminent families in Indiana. He was a director of the Vincennes Bank and the new state bank. Jennings was President of the Indiana Constitutional Convention, its first Governor, and later Representative in Congress. Hendricks was a Congressman and secretary of the Indiana Constitutional Convention–later to be Governor and Senator. In later years, he followed Jackson, but even so upheld the United States Bank. Esarey, *State Banking*, p. 229.

81. Esarey, "The First Indiana Banks," p. 149.

82. Mitchell, "Indiana's Growth," p. 389; Buley, *Old Northwest*, p. 598.

83. Dunn, *Indiana*, p. 328.

84. Esarey, "The First Indiana Banks," p. 154.

85. Dowrie, *Development*, pp. 9–14, 17–22.

86. Garnett, *State Banks*, pp. 1 ff.

87. Dowrie, *Development*, pp. 23–35; Garnett, *State Banks*, p. 8.

88. On the petition and the introduction of the bill, see Illinois General Assembly, *Journal of the House*, 1820–21 (January 13, 1821), pp. 157–58.

89. *Ibid.* (January 29, 1821), pp. 227–29; Buley, *Old Northwest*, pp. 599 ff.

90. Dowrie, *Development*, p. 24.

91. Bond was a prosperous farmer, and former judge.

92. Illinois General Assembly, *Journal of the House*, 1820–21 (January 30, 1821), p. 236.

93. *Ibid.* (February 2, 1821), pp. 261–71.

94. One of the supporters of the bill in the Senate was immediately appointed a cashier of the bank.

95. Garnett, *State Banks*, pp. 9–12; and Dowrie, *Development*, pp. 26–28.

96. Dowrie, *Development*, p. 35.

97. Davidson and Stuvé, *Complete History*, p. 307; Knox, *History*, p. 716.

98. See Floyd Russell Dain, *Every House a Frontier* (Detroit: Wayne University Press, 1956), p. 103.

99. Anderson, "Frontier Economic Problems, I," pp. 60–62; Cable, *Bank*, pp. 52–70; Cable, "Some Early Missouri Bankers," *Missouri Historical Review*, XXVI (January, 1932), 117–19; Dorsey, "Panic," p. 83.

100. Dorsey, "Panic," p. 84. The letter was published in the St. Louis *Enquirer*, March 17, 1821.

101. Hamilton, "Relief Movement," pp. 58 ff.

102. Franklin *Missouri Intelligencer*, February 26, 1821, quoted in Hamilton, "Relief Movement," p. 56.

103. Missouri General Assembly, *Journal of the House of Representatives*, 1st General Assembly, Special Session, 1821, pp. 74–77, 84–86.

104. Anderson, "Frontier Economic Problems, I," pp. 65, 68.

105. July 14, 1821. Hamilton, "Relief Movement," p. 69.

106. Missouri General Assembly, *Journal of the House of Representatives*, 2d General Assembly, 1821, pp. 152–53.

107. August 14, 1821, September 25, 1821; in Hamilton, "Relief Movement," p. 77.

108. Thus see Primm, *Economic Policy*, pp. 14, 17.

109. Anderson, "Frontier Economic Problems, I," p. 66.

110. *Missouri v. William Carr Lane*. See Cable, *Bank*, p. 79.

111. Tucker came from a very prominent Virginia family. He was a half-brother of John Randolph. He later returned to Virginia to become professor of law at William and Mary College and leading theoretician of the pro-slavery forces.

112. Abernethy, "Early Development," pp. 311–25.

113. Hamer, *Tennessee*, pp. 231–32; Campbell, *Development*, pp. 43 ff.; Beard, "Joseph McMinn," pp. 162 ff.; Parks, "Felix Grundy," p. 29.

114. Hamer, *Tennessee*, pp. 232 ff.

115. Parks, "Felix Grundy." Yeatman, reputed to be the wealthiest merchant in Tennessee, was the son-in-law of Andrew Ervin, and was soon to establish his own private, unchartered bank. Sellers, "Banking."

116. Parks, "Felix Grundy," p. 22; Tennessee General Assembly, *Journal of the House of Representatives*, 1819 (September 20, 1819), p. 22.

117. Tennessee General Assembly, *Journal of the House of Representatives*, 1819, p. 245.

118. From Nashville *Whig*, July 3, 1819. Quoted in Sellers, "Banking," p. 70.

119. Nashville *Clarion*, May 2, 1820; in Parks, "Felix Grundy," p. 27. See above on charges and countercharges by the supporters and opponents of a special session.

120. Hamer, *Tennessee*, p. 233.

121. Tennessee General Assembly, *Journal of the House of Representatives*, 1820 (June 26, 1820), pp. 6–17.

122. *Ibid.* (July 4, 1820), p. 49.

123. *Ibid.* (July 7, 10, 1820), pp. 61, 65.

124. *Ibid.* (July 11, 1820), pp. 68–72.

125. *Ibid.* (July 17, 1820), pp. 99–106.

126. Tennessee General Assembly, *Journal of the Senate*, 1820 (July 5, 1820), p. 45; (July 14, 1820), pp. 77 ff.; (July 15, 1820), pp. 83 ff.

127. *Ibid.* (July 21, 1820), pp. 109 ff.

128. Tennessee General Assembly, *Journal of the House of Representatives*, 1820 (July 19, 1820), p. 123; (July 20, 1820), p. 126; (July 25, 1820), p. 159; (July 27, 1820), pp. 175 ff. Tennessee General Assembly, *Journal of the Senate*, 1820 (July 21, 25, 1820), p. 130; (July 26, 1820), p. 135.

129. Jackson to Major William Berkeley Lewis, July 15, 1820; Lewis to Jackson, July 15, 1820; Jackson to Lewis, July 16, 1820, *New York Public Library Bulletin*, IV (May, 1900), 162; (June, 1900), pp. 188–91; and Parks, "Felix Grundy," p. 32.

130. *Niles' Weekly Register*, XIX (September 2, 1820), 9.

131. *Ibid.* XIX (November 18, 1820), 283.

132. Hamer, *Tennessee*, p. 235.

133. *Ibid.*, pp. 236–37.

134. Tennessee General Assembly, *Journal of the House of Representatives*, 1821 (September 21, 1821), p. 49. Sellers seems to undervalue the extent of Carroll's opposition to the new state bank. Sellers, "Banking."

135. Golden, "William Carroll," p. 19.

136. Sumner, *History of Banking*, p. 150.

137. Duke, *History*, pp. 14 ff. Also see Elmer C. Griffith, "Early Banking in Kentucky," *Proceedings of the Mississippi Valley Historical Association*, II (1908–9), 168–81.

138. See the Report of the Underwood Committee (headed by Representative Joseph R. Underwood) on the causes of the suspension of specie payment by the Bank of Kentucky, Kentucky General Assembly,

Journal of the House of Representatives, 1818–19 (December 11, 1818), pp. 44–49.

139. Cheves to Crawford, June 12, 1819, U.S. Congress, *American State Papers: Finance*, IV, 705 (March 22, 1824), 883.

140. Philadelphia *Union*, June 9, 1819.

141. George M. Bibb was to become one of the main leaders of the relief movement. Bibb, from Lexington, was a distinguished jurist and statesman—a former Chief Justice of the Kentucky Court of Appeals, and former Senator. He later became United States Secretary of Treasury. He was widely known as a "gentleman of the old school." Martin D. Hardin was a famous lawyer from Frankfort, Speaker of the Kentucky House, and former Congressman. He was later to become United States Senator. He had Federalist and later Whig tendencies.

142. John Pope, one of the leading sponsors of the meeting, had represented the Bank of Kentucky at the earlier conference of banks at Frankfort in May.

143. See the Washington (D.C.) *National Intelligencer*, June 9, 19, 23, 26, 1819.

144. New York *Evening Post*, June 15, 1819. Coleman had been installed by Hamilton upon the founding of the New York *Evening Post*. He later became a supporter of Crawford and Jackson.

145. New York *American*, June 9, 1819; New York *Daily Advertiser*, June 10, 1819; Washington (D.C.) *National Intelligencer*, June 5, 1819.

146. Washington (D.C.) *National Intelligencer*, June 9 to 26, 1819.

147. Reprinted in the New York *Evening Post*, June 15, 1819.

148. "Franklin," in the *Kentucky Herald*, reprinted in *ibid.*, and also in the Boston *New England Palladium*, June 25, 1819.

149. *Niles' Weekly Register*, XVI (July 3, 1819), 311.

150. Washington (D.C.) *National Intelligencer*, June 23, 1819.

151. *Ibid.*, June 26, 1819.

152. Connelley and Coulter, *History*, pp. 595 ff.

153. This repeal passed the House by a two-to-one vote, but only narrowly passed the Senate. See *Niles' Weekly Register*, XX (June 9, 1820), 224; Connelley and Coulter, *History*, p. 206; Stickles, *Critical Court Struggle*, p. 22.

154. Stickles, *Critical Court Struggle*, pp. 23 ff.; Connelley and Coulter, *History*, pp. 609–13.

155. Kentucky General Assembly, *Journal of the House of Representatives*, 1820 (November 3, 1820), p. 88; (November 9, 1820), p. 112; (November 10, 1820), p. 117; (November 11, 1820), p. 127; (December 9, 1820), p. 267; (December 12, 1820), p. 276.

156. Kentucky General Assembly, *Journal of the Senate*, 1820 (November 21, 1820), pp. 109–12; (November 22, 1820), pp. 116 ff.

157. Kentucky General Assembly, *Journal of the House of Representatives*, 1821 (October 16, 1821), pp. 9–16.

158. *Ibid.* (October 20, 1821), pp. 61–71. Crittenden was a noted lawyer from Logan County and later from Frankfort, and a close friend of George M. Bibb. He later became Kentucky's leading politician—a Whig, an Adams nominee for the United States Supreme Court, a United States Senator, and Attorney General.

159. *Ibid.* (November 2, 1821), pp. 153–55.

160. *Ibid.* (November 15, 1821), pp. 251–54.

161. Washington (D.C.) *National Intelligencer*, November 27, 1821.

162. Kentucky General Assembly, *Journal of the House of Representatives*, 1822, Part I (May 13, 1822), pp. 6–8.

163. *Niles' Weekly Register*, XX (June 9, 1820), 225.

164. Kentucky General Assembly, *Journal of the House of Representatives*, 1822, Part I (May 15, 1822), pp. 55 ff.; (May 17, 1822), p. 59; (May 21, 1822), pp. 66 ff.

165. *Ibid.* (May 21, 1822), pp. 76–79.

166. *Ibid.* (May 23, 24, 1822), pp. 91–102.

167. B. B. Still to J. C. Breckenridge, August 16, 1821, in Connelley and Coulter, *History*, p. 615.

168. Kentucky *Gazette*, May 9, May 21, in Connelley and Coulter, *History*, p. 617. Also see Baylor, *John Pope*, pp. 163–64.

169. Kentucky General Assembly, *Journal of the House of Representatives*, 1822, Part II (October 22, 1822), pp. 12–14.

170. Wilson, *History*, II, 127.

171. Connelley and Coulter, *History*, p. 618; and Stickles, *Critical Court Struggle*, p. 28.

172. Duke, *History*, p. 21; Wilson, *History*, p. 127.

173. Reuben T. Durrett, *The Centenary of Louisville* (Louisville: J. P. Morton and Co., 1893), pp. 90–92.

IV. PROPOSALS FOR NATIONAL MONETARY EXPANSION

1. "Mercantile Correspondent," Washington (D.C.) *National Intelligencer*, December 30, 1819.

2. Oliver Wolcott, *Remarks on the Present State of Currency, Credit, Commerce, and National Industry* (New York: Wiley Co., 1819).

3. "One of the People—A Farmer," Washington (D.C.) *National Intelligencer*, April 17, 1819. Also see "A Citizen," Baltimore *Telegraph*, reprinted in the Richmond *Enquirer*, June 1, 1819.

4. "Agricola," in Washington (D.C.) *National Intelligencer*, April 21, 1819.

5. "An Anti-Bullionist," *An Enquiry into the Causes of the Present Commercial Embarrassments in the United States with a Plan of Reform of the Circulating Medium* (1819), pp. 45 ff.

6. On Law see Allen C. Clark, *Greenleaf and Law in the Federal City* (Washington, D.C.: W. F. Roberts Co., 1901).

7. Law stated that he had begun recommending his plan in 1812. "Justinian" (T. Law), Washington (D.C.) *National Intelligencer*, November 3, 1821.

8. See the caustic comment of the editors on Law's plan in the Washington (D.C.) *National Intelligencer*, May 19, 1819. Also see the vigorous attack on Law by William Duane in the Philadelphia *Aurora*, October 11, 1820.

9. *Ibid*., May 12, 1819; *City of Washington Gazette*, May 12, 1819.

10. "Justinian" (T. Law), *Remarks on the Report of the Secretary of the Treasury* (Wilmington: R. Porter Co., 1820), pp. 22–23.

11. Law also cited Russia, where the Emperor had wisely established a National Currency Board to provide a new circulating medium for the development of agriculture and manufactures in Russia. "Justinian," *Remarks*, p. 34. Emperor Peter III had established state banks issuing inconvertible paper in 1777, and bank issues expanded and depreciated until 1817. See Michael T. Florinsky, *Russia* (New York: Macmillan Co., 1953), I, 567; II, 708 ff.

12. "Justinian," *Remarks, passim.*

13. *Ibid.*

14. Washington (D.C.) *National Intelligencer*, May 22, May 26, June 1, 1819. Law evoked the authority of Arthur Young and Sir Josiah Child in saying that low interest rates were the soul of commerce.

15. *Ibid*., May 15, 1819.

16. In early 1818, before the economic crisis had arrived, Law answered a critic who had advised that his paper money plan be held in reserve for emergency times, that it would surely succeed better in time of prosperity. *Ibid*., February 10, 1818.

17. *Ibid*., April 24, 1819. Also April 22, May 1, 1819.

18. *Ibid*., October 30, 1819.

19. "Justinian," *Remarks*, p. 30. This does not imply that Law was hostile to tariffs. Far from it. Indeed, Law fulminated against the competition of cheap Asian labor in the form of cotton goods and urged exclusion of these goods from the country. Washington (D.C.) *National Intelligencer*, June 1, 1819; *City of Washington Gazette*, May 12, 1818.

20. "Justinian," *Remarks*, p. 37.

21. *Ibid*. The main evil of the banks was their requirement of specie payments for their notes. *City of Washington Gazette*, May 12, 1818.

22. Washington (D.C.) *National Intelligencer*, May 19, 1819.

23. *Ibid.*, April 1, 1820.

24. *Ibid.*, November 28, 1820.

25. *Ibid.*, October 31, 1821.

26. *Ibid.*, November 3, 1821.

27. *Ibid.*, July 21, 1819. The writer was vague on whether 100 percent specie backing was necessary for legitimacy, or whether redeemability would suffice.

28. (Anonymous), "The Circulating Medium," *Niles' Weekly Register*, XV (November 21, 1818), 220.

29. "Agricola," in Washington (D.C.) *National Intelligencer*, January 25, 1820.

30. "An Independent Citizen of North Carolina," in *ibid.*, January 13, 1820. Also see "Hominus Amicus" from Baltimore, *ibid.*, May 15, 1819.

31. Swan was an adventurer and land speculator, who had participated in the Boston Tea Party, and later became an agent of the French Republic; he had lived in Boston, but the last two decades of his life he made headquarters in a French debtor's prison from which he wrote this pamphlet. His plan was presented in his pamphlet, James Swan, *An Address to the President, Senate, and House of Representatives of the United States* (Boston: W. W. Clapp, 1819), pp. 1–24; Dorfman, *Economic Mind*, II, 243–46, 310–12.

32. "A Reader from North Carolina," Washington (D.C.) *National Intelligencer*, August 11, 1819. Also *ibid.*, February 11, 1819, and Wolcott, *passim.*

33. New York *American*, December 15, 1819. Also see the criticism in the New York *Daily Advertiser*, January 17, 1820.

34. New York *Daily Advertiser*, July 30, 1819.

35. Philadelphia *Aurora*, August 19, 1819. Duane, by the way, was certainly an outstanding exception to the general "era of good feeling" and support of President Monroe. He fought Monroe's re-election with great bitterness.

36. *Niles' Weekly Register*, XVI, July 31, 1819.

37. On February 24, 1820. *Reports of the Secretary of the Treasury of the United States* (Washington, 1837), II, 481–525. Also reprinted in U.S. Congress, *American State Papers: Finance*, III, 582 (February 24, 1820), 494–515.

38. Law, in fact, maintained that Crawford privately agreed with his monetary views. Clark, *Greenleaf and Law*, p. 320.

39. On the necessity of continued diminution of circulation see Philadelphia *Aurora*, October 2, 1821.

40. Philadelphia *Aurora*, October 11, 1820.

41. "On Crawford's Currency Report," Richmond *Enquirer*, March 21, 1820, March 28, 1820, April 7, 1820.

42. "Justinian," *Remarks*, p. 40.

43. Madison to C. D. Williams, February, 1820. James Madison (Gaillard Hunt, ed.) *Writings* (New York: G. P. Putnam Sons, 1910), IX, 26–27.

44. *Niles' Weekly Register*, XV (January 9, 1819), 364.

45. *Ibid.*, XVII (December 11, 1819), 227.

46. *Ibid.*, XVI (July 31, 1819), 320.

47. "Seventy-Six," *Cause of and Cure for Hard Times* (New York, 1819).

48. Washington (D.C.) *National Intelligencer*, May 19, 1819. Also the Norfolk *Herald*, May 29, 1819.

49. New York *National Advocate*, September 7, 1818. Also see "Solon," Philadelphia *United States Gazette*, December 24, 1818. "Solon" attacked the East India trade on the familiar ground of imbalance and absence of possible reciprocity. Also see "Franklin," Baltimore *Federal Republican*, July 23, 1819, "Hominius Amicus," Washington (D.C.) *National Intelligencer*, May 15, 1819; *Niles' Weekly Register*, XV (December 5, 1818), 241.

50. "Solon," New York *Gazette*, December 9, 1818.

51. "H" in New York *Gazette*, December 10, 1818.

52. These arguments were reminiscent of the ones used by the defenders of the East India trade in Britain in the seventeenth and eighteenth centuries.

53. "A Virginian," Washington (D.C.) *National Intelligencer*, January 16, 1819.

54. "Piano E Sano," *City of Washington Gazette*, reprinted in the Boston *New England Palladium*, January 18, 1820.

55. "Hamilton," Philadelphia *United States Gazette*, December 9, 1818.

56. Adam Smith, *An Inquiry into the Nature and Causes of the Wealth of Nations* (New York: Random House, 1937), p. 406.

57. "Anti-Bullionist," *Enquiry*, p. 41.

58. "N.O." in New York *Evening Post*, February 6, 1819.

59. U.S. Congress, *American State Papers: Finance*, III, 549 (January 25, 1819), 3939 ff.

60. Crawford to Representative Eppes. Finance Committee, December 29, 1818. *Annals of Congress*, 15th Congress, 2d Session, pp. 181–84.

61. Report of House Committee, U.S. Congress, *American State Papers: Finance*, III, 614 (February 2, 1821), 660.

62. U.S. Congress, *American State Papers: Finance*, III, 591 (April 17, 1820), 530. Also see A. Barton Hepburn, *A History of Currency in the United States* (New York: Macmillan Co., 1915), pp. 46 ff.

63. "Senex," New York *Daily Advertiser*, March 19, 1819.

V. RESTRICTING BANK CREDIT: PROPOSALS AND ACTIONS

1. Crawford, *Report*, p. 15.

2. Also see "Agricola," in Washington (D.C.) *National Intelligencer*, April 21, 1819, December 31, 1819, and *ibid.*, January 11, 1820; "A Farmer," *ibid.*, March 25, 1819.

3. Georgia General Assembly, *Journal of the House of Representatives*, 1818–19 (December 1, 1818), p. 56; (December 10, 1818), pp. 76 ff. For an attack on excessive bank paper, see Washington (Ga.) *News* editorial reprinted in the Washington (D.C.) *National Intelligencer*, August 4, 1821.

4. Heath, *Constructive Liberalism*, p. 188.

5. *Niles' Weekly Register*, XV (September 19, 1819), 59.

6. Georgia General Assembly, *Journal of the House of Representatives*, 1818 (November 18–20, December 1, 1818), pp. 31–40 ff.

7. Also see Ambler, *Thomas Ritchie*, p. 76.

8. Reprinted in Philadelphia *Union*, June 4, 1819. Also see the Richmond *Enquirer*, July 16, 1819.

9. "On Crawford's Currency Report," in Richmond *Enquirer*, March 21, 1820.

10. Washington (D.C.) *National Intelligencer*, March 2, 1819.

11. "A Virginian," *City of Washington Gazette*, December 22, 1818. "Philo-Economicus" cited Adam Smith in support of the abolition of corporate banking. The reference was erroneous, since Smith had expressly asserted the advantages of the corporate form for the banking business. "Philo-Economicus," Richmond *Enquirer*, June 1, 1819; Adam Smith, *Wealth of Nations*, pp. 714–15.

12. "Quaesitor," Richmond *Enquirer*, June 1, 1819; "Colbert," *ibid.*, November 16, 1819.

13. "Amphictyon" (Roane), "Hints in Relation to a General Reform of our Banking System," Richmond *Enquirer*, April 18, 1820. Roane's article is omitted from the collection of his writings in the *Enquirer* published in the *John P. Branch Historical Papers*, Randolph Macon College, Vols. I, II (1904–5).

14. Ritchie on Crawford's Currency Report, Richmond *Enquirer*.

15. Jefferson to John Adams, November 7, 1819, in his *Writings* (T. E. Bergh, ed.) (Washington, D.C.: Jefferson Memorial Association of the United States, 1904), XV, 224.

16. Jefferson to William C. Rives, November 28, 1819, *ibid.*, XV, 229–32.

17. Jefferson to Charles C. Pinckney, September 23, 1820, in *ibid.*, XV, 279. Also see Jefferson to Hugh Nelson, March 12, 1820, *ibid.*, p. 258;

Jefferson to A. Gallatin, November 24, 1818; December 26, 1820. Also see Washington (D.C.) *National Intelligencer*, March 2, 1819.

18. Virginia General Assembly, *Journal of the House of Delegates*, 1820–21 (December 4, 1820), pp. 11–12.

19. Delaware General Assembly, *Journal of the House of Representatives*, 1819 (February 3, 1819). Only one of the legislators voted for both compulsory resumption and the relief proposals.

20. *Ibid.*, 1820 (January 29, 1820), pp. 109–14. Apparently, it was the general practice in the state for a bank simply not to appear in answer to a summons against it, and the court would thereupon dismiss the case. Brinckle's bill provided that in such cases judgment against the bank be recovered by default.

21. *Niles' Weekly Register*, XV (September 12, 1818), 33.

22. For commendations of Niles for his anti-bank paper stand, from citizens of Tennessee, Maryland, and Virginia, see *Niles' Weekly Register*, XV (September 5, 1818), 36.

23. The *Federal Gazette*, in fact, took the lead in calling for a general suspension of specie payments. See the criticism in the New York *Daily Advertiser*, March 23, 1819.

24. For example see *Niles' Weekly Register*, XIV (August 1, 1818), 377; XV (September 19, 1818), 58, 245; XX (March 7, 1821), 36.

25. Daniel Raymond, *Thoughts on Political Economy* (Baltimore: F. Lucas, Jr. and E. J. Coale, 1820). Second, more widely known edition was *Elements of Political Economy*, 2 vols. (Baltimore: F. Lucas, Jr. and E. J. Coale, 1823). On Raymond, especially his pro-tariff views, see Dorfman, *Economic Mind*, II, 566–74.

26. On this question, see also "A Virginian," "Reflections Excited by the Present State of Banking Operation in the United States," *City of Washington Gazette* (December 22, 1818); "A Merchant," Boston *New England Palladium*, June 8, 1819; "Colbert," Richmond *Enquirer*, November 16, 1819.

27. Raymond, *Elements*, II, 132 ff. Also see *ibid.*, I, 248–53.

28. Washington (D.C.) *National Intelligencer*, March 22, 1819.

29. "A Stockholder," Baltimore *Federal Republican*, May 27, 1819, reprinted in Washington (D.C.) *National Intelligencer*, June 21, 1819. Also see "Cato," *ibid.*, June 19, 1819; Philadelphia *Union*, June 4, 1819; "Piano E Sano," Boston *New England Palladium*, January 18, 1820.

30. "Nicholas Dumbfish," Washington (D.C.) *National Intelligencer*, January 11, 1820.

31. The report was signed on October 4, 1819. The Tammany Society had appointed a committee on August 30 to report on the state of the National Economy.

32. John Woodward, *Address of the Society of Tammany to Its Absent Members* (New York, 1819), p. 40.

33. James Madison to Clarkson Crolius, December, 1819, in Washington (D.C.) *National Intelligencer*, January 22, 1820.

34. "Aristides" (William Peter Van Ness), *A Letter to the Secretary of the Treasury on the Commerce and the Currency of the United States* (New York: C. S. Van Winckle, 1819).

35. Also see "A Richmond Correspondent" in Boston *New England Palladium*, May 28, 1819.

36. New York *American*, March 6, 1819.

37. "Seventy-Six," *Cause of and Cure for Hard Times* (New York: by the author, c. 1819).

38. New York Legislature, *Journal of the Assembly*, 1820 (February 21, 1820), pp. 466–69.

39. New York Legislature, *Journal of the Senate*, 1819 (January 6, 1819), pp. 4–14.

40. *Ibid.* (January 26, 1819), pp. 66–70.

41. For proposals to eliminate rural banks outside of New York City and Albany, see Albany *Argus*, June 29, 1819, reprinted in the New York *Evening Post*, July 2, 1819.

42. "Senex," New York *Daily Advertiser*, March 24, 1819. On "Senex," see Murray N. Rothbard, "Contemporary Opinion of the Depression of 1819–21" (Unpublished master's essay, Columbia University, 1946), pp. 20 ff.

43. New York Legislature, *Journal of the Senate*, 1818 (February 28, 1818), p. 98.

44. Jacob Barker, (*Appeal*) *to the Public* (New York, 1819).

45. "Plain Sense," *An Examination of Jacob Barker's Appeal to the Public* (New York, 1819).

46. "A Merchant," in New York *Daily Advertiser*, January 16, 1822.

47. Pennsylvania Legislature, *Journal of the House*, 1818–19 (December 29, 1818, January 30, 1819), pp. 334–39; *ibid.*, 1819–20 (January 4, 1820), pp. 160–62.

48. *Niles' Weekly Register*, XV (September 19, 1818), 58–59.

49. Pennsylvania Legislature, *Journal of the House*, 1818–19 (January 5, 1819), p. 138; *ibid.* (February 1, 1819), p. 345.

50. Pennsylvania Legislature, *Journal of the Senate*, 1819–20 (February 14, 1820), pp. 311–37.

51. *Ibid.*, 1819–20 (January 29, 1820), pp. 221–26.

52. In Raguet's terminology, banks going beyond 100 percent reserves were, in this respect, "banks of circulation." In their capacity of storing money, they were "banks of deposit," and in their capacity of lending

their own money or the borrowed funds of others, they were "banks of discount." Raguet's report on bank charters, *ibid.*, 1820–21 (January 15, 1821), pp. 252–68.

53. Reprinted in Philadelphia *United States Gazette*, January 30, 1819.

54. "A Pennsylvanian," in Philadelphia *Union*, February 11, 1820.

55. *Niles' Weekly Register*, XV (January 2, 1819), 350.

56. *Ibid.*, XVI (April 17, 1819), 132.

57. Washington (D.C.) *National Intelligencer*, April 15, 1819.

58. Brigham, "The Period," p. 292.

59. Vermont General Assembly, *Journal of the House*, 1820 (November 10, 1820), pp. 198 ff., also (November 13, 1820), pp. 212 ff. For an example of New Hampshire anti-bank opinion, see "C.S." in Washington (D.C.) *National Intelligencer*, November 11, 1819.

60. *Ibid.*, November 28, 1820.

61. "O." in Boston *New England Palladium*, July 4, 1820.

62. John Adams to John Taylor, March 12, 1819, in John Adams, *Works* (Boston: Little, Brown & Co., 1856), X, 375.

63. John Quincy Adams to Peter Paul Francis De Grand, November 16, 1818. De Grand proposed that the government issue paper and lend it at 3 percent to the Bank of the United States, which would in turn lend it at 6 percent to private borrowers. Adams (Worthington C. Ford, ed.), *Writings* (New York: The Macmillan Co., 1916), VI, 472–73.

64. Esarey, "The First Indiana Banks," p. 152.

65. On May 16, 1819. See Washington (D.C.) *National Intelligencer*, June 19, 1819.

66. Anderson, "Frontier Economic Problems, I," p. 63.

67. Ohio General Assembly, *Journal of the House*, 1819–20 (December 7, 1819), pp. 9–15.

68. Washington (D.C.) *National Intelligencer*, February 8, 1819.

69. *Niles' Weekly Register*, XVII (October 30, 1819), 139.

70. Hammond was the recognized leader of the Ohio bar, leader of the Federalist Party in Ohio, and was later to decline a United States Supreme Court nomination tendered him by John Quincy Adams. See Charles Galbreath, *History of Ohio* (Chicago: American Historical Society, 1925), II, 468.

71. Maryland and Kentucky had also levied a tax on the Bank before the depression. Kentucky accepted the decision of the Maryland case.

72. The meeting took place on January 30, 1819. See Detroit *Gazette*, February 5, 1819.

73. Secretary of the meeting was J. P. Sheldon, publisher of the Detroit *Gazette*, and also designated printer of the U.S. Laws for the Michigan Territory. Chairman of the Committee was James Abbott, a dry

goods merchant. The committee periodically reported its findings in the *Gazette.*

74. Dain, *Every House a Frontier*, pp. 102–3.

75. Nashville *Gazette*, September 15, 1819, cited in Parks, "Felix Grundy"; Tennessee General Assembly, *Journal of the House of Representatives*, 1820 (June 28, 1820), p. 925.

76. *Ibid.*, 1819, pp. 75 ff., 132 ff., 182 ff. Of the 20 votes in favor, 17 came from East Tennessee, while only 3 came from mid-Tennessee. Similarly, of the 14 votes opposed, 12 came from mid-Tennessee. Yet, as seen previously, there was a great deal of anti-expansionist opinion in mid-Tennessee. Also see Parks, "Felix Grundy," pp. 19–43.

77. Joseph H. Parks, *Felix Grundy* (Baton Rouge: Louisiana State University Press, 1940), p. 109.

78. Tennessee *House Journal*, 1820, pp. 39–40; Tennessee General Assembly, *House Journal*, 1821 (September 21, 1821), p. 49.

79. Nashville *Whig*, October 13, 1823; quoted in Charles G. Sellers, Jr., *James Polk, Jacksonian, 1795–1843* (Princeton: Princeton University Press, 1957), pp. 79 ff.

80. Jesse Bledsoe, *The Speech of Jesse Bledsoe, Esq. . . . Concerning Banks* (Lexington, Ky.: Norvell, 1819).

81. Kendall, *Autobiography*, *passim.*

82. Kentucky General Assembly, *House Journal*, 1818–19 (December 2, 1818), pp. 9–19.

83. Connelley and Coulter, *History*, p. 605.

84. Baylor, *John Pope*, p. 150.

85. Kentucky General Assembly, *House Journal*, 1818–19 (December 19, 1818), pp. 87–91.

86. Connelley and Coulter, *History*, p. 605. See also Bray Hammond, *Banks and Politics in America* (Princeton: Princeton University Press, 1957), p. 608.

87. The charters were repealed at the end of 1820 to take effect in May, 1821. See Stickles, *Critical Court Struggle*, p. 22.

88. *Niles' Weekly Register*, XX (June 17, 1820), 296.

89. Spencer came from a leading New York family. He was a leading Clintonian, later a Whig and Secretary of War under Tyler, and a rejected Tyler appointee to the United States Supreme Court.

90. *Annals of Congress*, 15th Congress, 2d Session (February 18, 1819), p. 1254; (February 24, 1819), pp. 1404–9; also see M. St. Clair Clarke and D. A. Hall, *Legislative and Documentary History of the Bank of the United States* (Washington, D.C., 1831), pp. 682 ff.

91. Representative Kent to House of Representatives, *American State Papers: Finance*, III, 575 (February 2, 1820), p. 470. Kent was a leading

politician and farmer who later became a leading Whig, a senator and three times governor.

92. "One of the People" (Churchill C. Cambreleng), *An Examination of the New Tariff* (New York: Gould and Banks Co., 1821), pp. 189–202.

93. Professor Schur, in a recent article, seriously underweights both the inflationary role of the bank in 1817–18, and the extent to which the reaction against the bank stemmed from hard money views. Leon M. Schur, "The Second Bank of the United States and the Inflation after the War of 1812," *The Journal of Political Economy*, LXVIII (April, 1960), 118–34.

VI. THE MOVEMENT FOR A PROTECTIVE TARIFF

1. U.S. Congress, *American State Papers: Finance*, III, 455 (December 13, 1815), p. 32; 458 (December 22, 1815), p. 52; 460 (January 5, 1816), p. 56; 533 (April 7, 1818), p. 265; 476 (March 6, 1816), p. 103; 501 (February 4, 1817), p. 168. Also see *Niles' Weekly Register*, X (March 23, 1816), 49; X (April 13, 1816), 99; XI (November 9, 1816), 424; XI (May 10, 1817), 166–67.

2. Most of them cited a statement advocating deliberate dumping made by the influential Lord Brougham before a Parliamentary Committee. *Niles' Weekly Register*, XI (December 28, 1816), 284.

3. The minimum duty of 25 cents per square yard was equivalent to an over 6 cents per yard rise in price. Clark, *History of Manufactures*, II, 275.

4. Bishop, *History*, pp. 230 ff. Also see *Niles' Weekly Register*, XII (March 29, 1817), 75; New York *Evening Post*, June 14, 1817.

5. The report of the Corresponding Committee to the American Society for Encouragement of Manufactures, in the New York *Evening Post*, February 28, 1819.

6. In the summer of 1821, the citizens of ardently protectionist Wilmington, Delaware, presented Carey with a plaque commemorating his services to the cause. *Niles' Weekly Register*, XX (July 28, 1821), 345.

7. For examples, see Carey, *Essays*, pp. 141, 198 ff., 230, 318 ff., 416. Also see Washington (D.C.) *National Intelligencer*, May 26, 1819.

8. Of the 36 delegates, there were 12 from New York, 7 from Pennsylvania, 5 from New Jersey, and 5 from Connecticut. For the personnel of the three-day convention, see *Niles' Weekly Register*, XVII (December 11, 1819), 229.

9. For the petition, see U.S. Congress, *American State Papers: Finance*, III, 560 (December 20, 1819), p. 440. Also see the very similar petition of the American Society of New York City for the Encouragement of Domestic Manufactures, *ibid.*, 561 (December 27, 1819), p. 443; and, their

later petition, *ibid.*, 593 (April 24, 1820), p. 532. Leaders were William Few, Peter Schenck, and John E. Hyde. Few, a leading lawyer and banker, had had in former days a distinguished career in Georgia. Few had been United States Senator from Georgia, a delegate to the Constitutional Convention, and Federal Judge. Also see *Petition of A Convention of Friends of National Industry in New Jersey* (Washington: Gales and Seaton Co., 1820). The American Society of New York, in particular, stressed recovery from the depression as the reason for advocating protection.

10. Most of Carey's numerous writings in this period are collected in his *Essays*. See particularly his widely distributed Addresses of the Philadelphia Society for the Promotion of National Industry, in *ibid.*, pp. 18 ff., 36–38. Also see Philadelphia *Union*, September 17, 1819.

11. Carey, *Essays*, pp. 67, 362 ff. Also see New York *Patron of Industry*, July 9, 1820.

12. Carey, *Essays*, pp. 13 ff. An almost identical argument was offered by Niles. *Niles' Weekly Register*, XVII (October 23, 1819), 117. Niles also printed Carey's Philadelphia as well as other material, and arguments of his own. *Ibid.*, XVI (April 17, August 28, 1819). For Niles as a protectionist leader see Norval N. Luxon, *Niles' Weekly Register* (Baton Rouge: Louisiana State University Press, 1947), p. 110.

13. For Jackson's writings, see Carey, *Essays*, pp. 175–87.

14. See the petition for protection of cottons and woolens by Peter S. Du Ponceau and other citizens of Pennsylvania, in U.S. Congress, *American State Papers: Finance*, III, 569 (January 17, 1820), pp. 454 ff. Also the petition of the Society of Paper Makers of Pennsylvania and Delaware, *ibid.*, III, 571 (January 18, 1820).

15. Carey, *Essays*, pp. 36–38.

16. *Ibid.*, pp. 68 ff. Also see Edith Abbott, *Women in Industry* (New York: D. Appleton & Co., 1915), pp. 51 ff.

17. New York *Patron of Industry*, July 1, 1820.

18. "Plain Truth," in Pittsburgh *Gazette*, reprinted in New York *Patron of Industry*, August 10, 1820.

19. Lyman Beecher, *The Means of National Prosperity* (New York: J. Sayre Co., 1820). Thanksgiving Sermon, December 2, 1819.

20. "A Manufacturer," in Philadelphia *Union*, May 29, 1819. Also see "A Friend of His Country," in Washington (D.C.) *National Intelligencer*, January 21, 1819, and report of the Joint Committee on Domestic Manufacture of the Ohio Legislature; Ohio Legislature, *Journal of the House of Representatives*, 1819–20 (January 24), pp. 252–53.

21. Frank W. Stonecipher, "Pittsburgh and the Nineteenth Century Tariffs," *Western Pennsylvania Historical Magazine*, XXXI (September–December, 1948), 87 ff. Also see Russell J. Ferguson, *Early Western*

Pennsylvania Politics (Pittsburgh: University of Pittsburgh Press, 1938), pp. 236–44.

22. M. Flavia Taylor, "The Political and Civic Career of Henry Baldwin, 1799–1830," *Western Pennsylvania Historical Magazine*, XXIV (March, 1941), 37–50. Dorfman, *Economic Mind*, I, 386.

23. *Annals of Congress*, 16th Congress, 1st Session (April 21, 1820), p. 1944, speech of Representative Baldwin.

24. First President of the Association was prominent glass manufacturer, George Sutton. See William Bining, "The Glass Industry of Western Pennsylvania, 1797–1857," *Western Pennsylvania Historical Magazine*, XIX (December, 1936), 263; *History of Pittsburgh and Its Environs* (American Historical Society: New York, 1922), p. 60; Bishop, *History*, pp. 250 ff.

25. Arthur C. Bining, "The Rise of Iron Manufacture in Western Pennsylvania," *Western Pennsylvania Historical Magazine*, XVI (November, 1933), 242; Eiselen, *The Rise*, pp. 46 ff.

26. Kehl, *Ill Feeling*, pp. 79, 189.

27. Pennsylvania Legislature, *Journal of the House*, 1819–20 (January 28, 1820), p. 413; *Journal of the Senate*, 1819–20 (January 28, 1820), pp. 219–20.

28. *Duane Report;* for Governor Findlay's support of protection see Pennsylvania Legislature, *Journal of the Senate*, 1820–21 (December 7, 1820), p. 30.

29. Philadelphia *Union*, April 10, 1821.

30. Alfred B. Sears, "Thomas Worthington, Pioneer Businessman of the Old Northwest," *Ohio State Archeological and Historical Quarterly*, LVIII (1949), 76; "Source Illustrations of Ohio's Relations to National History, 1816–40," *Ohio Archeological and Historical Publications*, XXV (1916), 143.

31. Ohio General Assembly, *Journal of the Senate*, 1819–20 (January 25, 1820), pp. 219–29.

32. New York *Columbian*, November 10, 1819.

33. Boston *New England Palladium*, January 7, 1820.

34. Gronert, "Trade," pp. 313–23.

35. Anderson, "Frontier Economic Problems, II," p. 199.

36. Delaware General Assembly, *Journal of the House of Representatives*, 1819 (February 2, 1819), p. 138.

37. Du Pont was a delegate to the protectionist Convention of December, 1819. *Niles' Weekly Register*, XVIII (December 11, 1819), 229.

38. Delaware General Assembly, *Journal of the House of Representatives*, 1820 (January 29, 1820), pp. 109–11.

39. *Ibid.*, 1820 (February 10, 1820), p. 191. Governor John Clarke heartily endorsed protection and the subsidy measures. See Clarke's mes-

sage, *ibid.* (January 5, 1820), pp. 8–11. New Hampshire rejected a similar proposal by a three-to-two majority. See New Hampshire General Court, *Journal of the House*, 1819 (June 28, 1819), pp. 300 ff.

40. Delaware General Assembly, *Journal of the House of Representatives*, 1820 (February 4, 1820), pp. 141 ff.

41. North Carolina General Assembly, *Acts*, 1821, p. 3; also see C. S. Sydnor, *Development of Southern Nationalism, 1819–48* (Baton Rouge: Louisiana State University Press, 1948), p. 118.

42. The subject here deals only with arguments over protection which had the depression as their base. Thus, the New York *American*, a pro-Tammany, neo-Federalist publication, supported protection on the grounds of retaliation against British restrictions. See New York *American*, September 22, 1819. Also see "Zeno" in Washington (D.C.) *National Intelligencer*, November 13, 1819.

43. "A New York Gentleman to a Friend in Boston," New York *Columbian*, August 11, 1819. Also see *ibid.*, June 10 and June 12, 1819.

44. "H.B." in *ibid.*, February 19, 1819. For emphasis on the protection for cotton and woolens also see the petition of the citizens of Middletown, Connecticut, U.S. Congress, *American State Papers: Finance*, III, 568 (January 10, 1820), p. 45 and the New York *Columbian*, August 11, 1819.

45. For an example of the *Patron*'s use of poetry as a weapon, see New York *Patron of Industry*, July 22, 1820.

46. For an example of protectionist opinion upstate, see Albany *Argus*, September 17, 1819.

47. Woodward, *Tammany Address*, p. 18.

48. The following states—Vermont, Maryland, Kentucky, Tennessee, Indiana, Illinois—were also alleged to be overwhelmingly protectionist, *Annals of Congress* (May 4, 1820), p. 655.

49. Pennsylvania Legislature, *Journal of the House*, 1819–20 (January 28, 1820), pp. 410 ff. New York *Evening Post*, January 30, 1818.

50. U.S. Congress, *American State Papers: Finance*, III, 571 (January 18, 1820), p. 460. Leaders were Mark Willcox, president, and Thomas Gilpin, secretary.

51. *Ibid.*, III, 572 (January 26, 1820), pp. 462 ff.

52. "An Agriculturist," in Philadelphia *Union*, October 19, 1821. Also see speech by Gideon Granger, president of the Ontario, New York Agricultural Society, New York *Patron of Industry*, December 13, 1820, and *ibid.*, December 23, 1820; "Agricola of Ontario, N.Y.," in Washington (D.C.) *National Intelligencer*, January 25, 1820.

53. *Niles' Weekly Register*, XVII (October 23, 1810), 117.

54. U.S. Congress, *American State Papers: Finance*, III, 568 (January

10, 1820). Leaders of the petition were Jonathan Lawrence Lewis, chairman, and Arthur W. Magill, secretary.

55. *Annals of Congress*, 16th Congress, 1st Session (April 21, 1820), p. 1944.

56. *Ibid.* (May 4, 1820), pp. 655 ff. Also see *Niles' Weekly Register*, XVIII (May 6, 1820), 169.

57. Stonecipher, "Pittsburgh."

58. The Lexington *Kentucky Reporter*, in which the suggestion appeared, lamented that such a step would probably be unconstitutional. See Washington (D.C.) *National Intelligencer*, September 22, 1819.

59. "Plain Truth," in New York *Patron of Industry*, August 10, 1820.

60. Detroit *Gazette*, April 23, 1819.

61. Eiselen, *The Rise*, p. 53.

62. "A Pennsylvanian," in Philadelphia *Union*, February 11, 1820.

63. Thus, see U.S. Congress, *American State Papers: Finance*, III, 596 (November 27, 1820), p. 540, petition of citizens of Petersburg, Virginia, Major Thomas Wallace, chairman, John F. May, secretary; *ibid.*, III, 603 (December 18, 1820), p. 577, petition of United Agricultural Society of Virginia, Richard Field, president, Edward Ruffin, secretary; *ibid.*, III, 604 (December 22, 1820), p. 578, petition of Roanoke Agricultural Society, Thomas M. Nelson, president, Charles L. Wangfield, secretary; *ibid.*, III, 564 (January 3, 1820), p. 447, petition of Virginia Agricultural Society of Fredericksburg, Va., James M. Garnett, president, William G. Gray, secretary. These men were leading planters of Virginia and the South. Garnett was a friend of Madison, Taylor, and Randolph, and a leader in the anti-tariff struggle. He later became first president of the United States Agricultural Society. Ruffin was a famous agricultural experimenter, later publisher of the *Farmers' Register*.

Also see *ibid.*, III, 573 (January 31, 1820), p. 463, petition of Merchants of Salem and towns in vicinity; *ibid.*, III, 594 (April 28, 1820), p. 533, petition of Chamber of Commerce of Philadelphia; president was Robert Ralston.

64. Thus, see Report of House Committee on Agriculture, *ibid.*, III, 613 (February 2, 1821), pp. 65 ff. Also see memorial of the United Agriculture Societies of Virginia, written by John Taylor, *ibid.*, III, 570 (January 17, 1820), pp. 458 ff. Secretary of the societies was Edward Ruffin, and the president was John Pegram. Also see "Public Good," in Boston *New England Palladium*, September 28, October 1, 1819.

65. Dorfman, *Economic Mind*, I, 306.

66. Raguet *Report*, 1820.

67. From the Portland *Gazette*, reprinted in the Philadelphia *Union* (August 6, 1820). Leaders were Arthur McClellan, chairman, and Henry Clarke, secretary. Also see the report of the Convention of Merchants of

Portsmouth, New Hampshire, in Washington (D.C.) *National Intelligencer*, October 25, 1820. See "Nob," a Virginia correspondent, *ibid.*, May 8, 1819.

68. U.S. Congress, *American State Papers: Finance*, III, 573 (January 31, 1820), p. 463. The same position was taken by the Chamber of Commerce of Philadelphia, *ibid.*, III, 594 (April 28, 1820), pp. 533 ff., which pointed to the plight of commerce and surplus agriculture *until* domestic manufactures would be established.

69. Thus, see "Cato," in Washington (D.C.) *National Intelligencer*, April 18, 1820.

70. "Public Good," in Boston *New England Palladium*, September 28, 1819.

71. In Boston *Daily Advertiser*, reprinted in the New York *Evening Post*, September 13–14, 1820.

72. U.S. Congress, *American State Papers: Finance*, III, 558 (April 13, 1820), p. 522. For other attacks on protection as a depressing force in the economy, see Memorial of a Convention of Merchants of Philadelphia by William Bayard, president, *ibid.*, III, 597 (November 27, 1820), p. 543; and Philadelphia *Union*, December 5, 1820.

73. U.S. Congress, *American State Papers: Finance*, III, 600 (December 8, 1820), p. 563. On Elliott, see Dorfman, *Economic Mind*, I, 370–71.

74. See the statement by the influential Representative William Lowndes, a planter from South Carolina, in *Niles' Weekly Register*, XVIII (June 10, 1820), 259, and a brief statement by a committee of citizens of Boston made after an address to them by Representative Daniel Webster, in Washington (D.C.) *National Intelligencer*, October 14, 1820.

75. Philadelphia *Union*, August 29, 1820.

76. *Ibid.*

77. U.S. Congress, *American State Papers: Finance*, III, 613 (February 2, 1821), pp. 650 ff.

78. Washington (D.C.) *National Intelligencer*, May 29, 1819.

79. Cambreleng, *An Examination*, *passim*; Dorfman, *Economic Mind*, I, 371–72.

80. Memorial of United Agricultural Societies of Virginia, U.S. Congress, *American State Papers: Finance*, III, 580 (January 17, 1820), p. 457.

81. New Orleans *Louisiana Gazette*, May 6, 1820; Tregle, "Louisiana and the Tariff."

82. Washington (D.C.) *National Intelligencer*, August 25, 1821. The "Friends of Natural Rights" also attacked "Professor Daniel Raymond" for presuming to correct Adam Smith, and faring no better than Lord Lauderdale.

83. Tyler came from an aristocratic family. Later Governor and Senator, as well as President, he was a Jacksonian until the removal of de-

posits and sub-treasury issues arose. Silsbee was a leading Salem merchant and shipowner. Formerly noted as a Jeffersonian, Silsbee was a director of the Boston branch of the Bank of the United States and later U.S. Senator.

84. *Annals of Congress*, 16th Congress, 1st Session, pp. 1952 ff.

85. *Ibid.*, pp. 1987 ff.

86. Petition of Merchants and Citizens of Baltimore, U.S. Congress, *American State Papers: Finance*, III, 565 (January 5, 1820), p. 448. The Baltimore merchants were led by William Patterson. Also see the petition of the New York City Merchants, in New York *Daily Advertiser*, December 14, 1819; Convention of Friends of National Industry, *Petition;* "No Inflation," New York *Commercial Advertiser*, December 21, 1819; "C.W." in New York *American*, February 9, 1820; New York *Evening Post*, December 20, 1819.

87. U.S. Congress, *American State Papers: Finance*, III, 560, pp. 440 ff. Also see petition of William Few's American Society of New York City for Employment of Domestic Manufactures, *ibid.*, 561, p. 443; Bishop, *History of Manufactures*, pp. 256 ff.

88. New York *Daily Advertiser*, December 17, 1819, February 11, 1820; "Galeani," in New York *Evening Post*, April 25, 1820; Cambreleng, *An Examination*, pp. 151–54. (James De P. Ogden) "Publeus," in New York *Commercial Advertiser*, December 15, 1819; John Pintard, New York *Daily Advertiser*, January 6, 1820; "R.L." in Washington (D.C.) *National Intelligencer*, December 30, 1819.

89. U.S. Congress, *American State Papers: Finance*, III, 567 (January 6, 1820), p. 451.

90. *Ibid.*, III, 579 (February 8, 1820), pp. 484 ff. Also see Petition of Chamber of Commerce of Philadelphia, Robert Ralston, president, *ibid.*, III, 586 (March 11, 1820), p. 518.

91. From the Baltimore *Telegraph*, reprinted in the Richmond *Enquirer*, January 1, 1819.

92. On the rise of the auction system in this period, see Westerfield, "Early History," pp. 200 ff.

93. Philadelphia *Union*, February 8, 1820; "H.B." in New York *Columbian*, February 19, 1819.

94. "A Pennsylvanian," Philadelphia *Union*, February 11, 1820; "C.W." in New York *American*, February 9, 1820; New York *Evening Post*, December 20, 1819.

95. New York *Evening Post*, January 11, 1817.

96. Bishop, *History*, II, 258. U.S. Congress, *American State Papers: Finance*, III, 567 (January 6, 1820), p. 51. Petition of Chamber of Commerce of New York City, William Bayard, president, John Pintard, secretary.

97. *Ibid.*, III, 560 (December 20, 1819), 440 ff. Also petition of citizens of Middleton, Connecticut, *ibid.*, III, 568 (January 10, 1820), p. 452. Also see Convention of Friends of National Industry in New Jersey, *Petition, passim.*

98. *Annals of Congress*, 16th Congress, 1st Session, pp. 2174–75. Actually the 10 percent tax was to apply only to important items such as woolens, cottons, etc. Minor items were to pay 1 to 2 percent. See *Niles' Weekly Register*, XVIII (May 5, 1820), 182 ff.

99. New York *Patron of Industry*, June 6, 1821.

100. *Niles' Weekly Register*, XX (July 21, 1821), 322.

101. New York *Patron of Industry*, June 16, 17, 20, 1821.

102. *Niles' Weekly Register*, XXI (October 13, 1821), 103. The report was presented on September 24 and signed by Stephen Lockwood, chairman.

103. Maryland Legislature, *House Journal*, 1820–21.

VII. CONCLUSION

1. Here free traders joined forces with protectionists, who constantly inveighed against the use of imported luxuries.

2. Neither can this study endorse the opposite ideal-type of Bray Hammond, whose recent work tends to the contrary extreme of identifying agrarians with hard money, and merchants and businessmen with inflation. Hammond, *Banks and Politics in America, passim.*

3. On the great extent to which English and French economists were reprinted, translated, and sold in America during this period, see Esther Lowenthal, "American Reprints of Economic Writings, 1776–1848," *American Economic Review*, XLII (December, 1952), 876–80, and "Additional American Reprints, 1776–1848," *ibid.*, XLIII (December, 1953), 884–85; and David McCord Wright, *The Economic Library of the President of the Bank of the United States, 1819–23* (Charlottesville: University of Virginia Press, 1950).

4. See Michael J. L. O'Connor, *Origins of Academic Economics in the United States* (New York: Columbia University Press, 1944), pp. 29, 73, 102.

APPENDIX A

1. Taylor, *Transportation Revolution*, p. 21.

2. Philadelphia *Union*, March 14, 1820. Also see Lehman's Committee Report, *ibid.*, March 10, 1820, and the debate, *ibid.*, March 21, 1820.

3. See "Appias," in the Philadelphia *Union*, December 15, 1820.

4. Pennsylvania, *House Journal*, 1821 (December 5, 1821).

5. Philadelphia *Union*, August 24, 1821.

6. H. Jerome Cranmer, *The New Jersey Canals: State Policy and Private Enterprise, 1820–32* (New York, Columbia University, microfilmed, 1955), pp. 32–38.

7. Murphey, *Papers*, II, 107, 216–17.

8. Boston *New England Palladium*, January 7, 1820. On Missouri moves for internal improvements, see Anderson, "Frontier Economic Problems, II," p. 190.

9. Parks, *Felix Grundy*, p. 137.

10. New Jersey Legislature, *Votes and Proceedings of the General Assembly*, 1820 (January 24, 1820), p. 132.

11. *Ibid.* (November 10, 1820), pp. 67–68.

12. Parks, *Felix Grundy*, pp. 111–12.

13. "Polonius," in the *Kentucky Commentator*, reprinted in the Boston *New England Palladium*, January 15, 1819.

14. "Mercator," in Richmond *Enquirer*, January 14, 1819.

15. "A Citizen," in Philadelphia *Union*, January 14, 1819.

16. Vermont General Assembly, *House Journal*, 1820–21 (November 2, 1820), pp. 147 ff., and (November 9, 1820), pp. 187 ff.

17. Frank T. Cole, "Thomas Worthington," *Ohio Archaeological and Historical Publications*, XII (1903), 366.

18. New York *American*, October 2, 1819. On the other hand, the *American* endorsed emergency food relief for paupers, *ibid.*, October 13, 1819.

19. Woodward, *Tammany Address*, pp. 9–10.

20. "Amicus Patriae Suae," in Philadelphia *Union*, December 4, 1820; Delaware General Assembly, *Journal of the House of Representatives*, 1821 (January 3, 1821), pp. 16–24, and (January 12, 1821), p. 67.

21. Virginia General Assembly, *Journal of the House of Delegates*, 1820–21 (December 14, 1820), p. 41.

22. Boston, *The Christian Disciple and Theological Review* (1822), p. 157.

23. Reprinted in the Boston *New England Palladium*, September 1, 1820.

24. William A. Sullivan, "A Decade of Labor Strife," *Pennsylvania History*, XVII (January, 1950), 24.

25. Sullivan, *Industrial Worker*, pp. 79 ff., 128 ff.

26. Pintard, *Letters* (June 2, 1819), p. 197. A cartel of domestic salt manufactures in Kanawha County (West Virginia) also failed to maintain a high price of salt ($2 a bushel) during the depression. The pressure of deflation and heavy imports of cheap salt plummeted the price down to sixty cents in 1821.

BIBLIOGRAPHY

GOVERNMENT PUBLICATIONS

Annals of Cleveland. Vol. I. 1818–20. WPA in Ohio. Cleveland, 1938.

Cincinnati Directory. 1819. Cincinnati, 1819.

Clarke, M. St. Clair, and D. A. Hall. *Legislative and Documentary History of the Bank of the United States.* Washington, D.C., Gales & Seaton, 1831.

Common Council of the City of New York. *Minutes.* Vol. IX. New York, 1820.

Delaware General Assembly. *Journal of the House of Representatives.* 1818–21.

—— *Journal of the Senate.* 1823.

Holmes, George K. *Cotton Crop of the United States, 1790–1911.* U.S. Department of Agriculture, Bureau of Statistics, Circular 32. Washington, D.C., 1912.

—— *Rice Crop of the United States, 1712–1911.* U.S. Department of Agriculture, Bureau of Statistics, Circular 34. Washington, D.C., 1912.

Illinois General Assembly. *House Journal.* 1820–21.

Indiana General Assembly. *Laws.* 1819–20.

Kentucky General Assembly. *Journal of the House of Representatives.* 1818–22.

Louisiana General Assembly. *Official Journal of the Proceedings of the House of Representatives.* 1819.

Maryland General Assembly. *Votes and Proceedings of the House of Delegates.* 1820–21.

Massachusetts, Department of Labor. "Historical Review of Wages and Prices, 1782–1860," *Sixteenth Annual Report,* Vol. III. Boston, 1885.

Missouri General Assembly. *Journal of the House of Representatives.* 1821.

New Hampshire General Court. *House Journal.* 1819.

New Jersey Legislature. *Votes and Proceedings of the General Assembly.* 1819–20.

New York Legislature. *Assembly Journal.* 1820.

—— *Senate Journal.* 1818–21.

—— *Assembly Documents.* No. 10. 1843.

North Carolina, Historical Records Survey Project. *A Calendar of the Bartlett Yancey Papers.* Raleigh, 1940.

Pennsylvania Archives. Fourth Series. Edited by George E. Reed. Vol. V. Harrisburg, 1900.

Pennsylvania Legislature. *Journal of the House.* 1818–20.

—— *Laws.* 1819–20.

—— *Journal of the Senate.* 1819–21.

Richardson, James D., ed. *A Compilation of the Messages and Papers of the Presidents.* Vol. II. New York, Bureau of National Literature, 1897.

Tennessee General Assembly. *Journal of the House of Representatives.* 1818–21.

—— *Journal of the Senate.* 1820.

United States, Comptroller of the Currency. *Annual Report, 1876.* Washington, D.C., 1876.

United States Congress. *American State Papers: Finance.* Vols. III and IV. Washington, D.C., Gales & Seaton, 1834.

—— *Annals of Congress of the United States.* 15th Congress, 2d Session to 17th Congress, 1st Session.

—— *Public Statutes at Large.* Vol. II. Boston, Wells & Lilly, 1827.

United States Department of Commerce. *Historical Statistics of the United States, 1789–1945.* Washington, D.C., 1949.

United States, House of Representatives. *Annual Report of the Commissioner of Navigation, 1901.* Document No. 14. 57th Congress, 1st Session.

United States Treasury Department, Bureau of Statistics. *Monthly Summary of Imports and Exports for the Fiscal Year 1896.* Washington, D.C., 1896.

United States Treasury Department. *Reports of the Secretary of the Treasury of the United States.* Vol. II. Washington, D.C., Blair & Rives, 1837.

Vermont General Assembly. *House Journal.* 1818–21.

Virginia General Assembly. *Journal of the House of Delegates.* 1818–21.

PRIMARY SOURCES

Adams, John. *Works.* Vol. X. Boston, Little, Brown & Co., 1856.

Adams, John Quincy. *Writings.* Vol. VI. Edited by W. C. Ford. New York, The Macmillan Co., 1916.

"An Anti-Bullionist." *An Enquiry into the Causes of the Present Commercial Embarrassments in the United States with a Plan of Reform of the Circulating Medium.* 1819.

Annapolis *Maryland Gazette.*

Baltimore *Federal Republican.*

Barker, Jacob. (*Appeal*) *to the Public.* New York, 1819.

Beecher, Lyman. *The Means of National Prosperity*. New York, J. Sayre, 1820.

Bledsoe, Jesse. *The Speech of Jesse Bledsoe, Esq. . . . Concerning Banks.* Lexington, Ky., Norvell, 1819.

Boston *New England Palladium.*

Cambreleng, Churchill C. (signed "One of the People"). *An Examination of the New Tariff*. New York, Gould & Banks, 1821.

Carey, Matthew. *Essays in Political Economy*. Philadelphia, H. C. Carey & I. Lea, 1822.

Charleston *Southern Patriot.*

Cleveland *Herald.*

Cleveland *Register.*

Corbin, Francis, to James Madison, October 10, 1819, in *Massachusetts Historical Society Proceedings*, XLII (January, 1910), 261.

Detroit *Gazette.*

Greene, William. "Thoughts on the Present Situation and Prospect of the Western Country, April 21, 1820," in Rosamund R. Wulsin, ed., "A New Englander's Impression of Cincinnati in 1820—Letters by William Greene," *Bulletin of the Historical and Philosophical Society of Ohio*, VII (April, 1949), 116–22.

Jackson, Andrew, to Major William Berkeley Lewis, July 15, 1820; Lewis to Jackson, July 15, 1820, in *New York Public Library Bulletin*, IV (May, 1900), 162; and (June, 1900), 188–91.

Jefferson, Thomas. *Writings*. Vol. XV. Edited by T. E. Bergh. Washington, D.C., Thomas Jefferson Memorial Association of the U.S., 1904.

Kendall, Amos. *Autobiography*. Edited by William Stickney. Boston, P. Smith, 1872.

Law, Thomas (signed "Justinian"). *Remarks on the Report of the Secretary of the Treasury*. Wilmington, R. Porter, 1820.

Madison, James. *Writings*. Vol. IX. Edited by Gaillard Hunt. New York, Putnam's Sons, 1910.

Murphey, Archibald D. *Papers*. Vol. I. Edited by William Henry Hoyt. Raleigh, N.C., E. M. Uzzell and Co., 1914.

New York *American.*

New York *Columbian.*

New York *Commercial Advertiser.*

New York *Daily Advertiser.*

New York *Evening Post.*

New York *Gazette.*

New York *National Advocate.*

New York *Patron of Industry.*

Niles' Weekly Register.

"Observer." *Review of Trade and Commerce of New York, 1815-to-Present.* New York, 1820.

Petition of a Convention of Friends of National Industry in New Jersey. Washington, D.C., Gales & Seaton, 1820.

Philadelphia *Aurora.*

Philadelphia *Poulson's American Daily Advertiser.*

Philadelphia *Union.*

Philadelphia *United States Gazette.*

[Phillips, Willard.] "Seybert's Statistical Annals," *North American Review,* IX (September, 1819), 207–39.

Pintard, John. *Letters to His Daughter.* Vol. I. 1816–20. New York, N. Y. Historical Society, 1940.

Pittsburgh *Gazette.*

"Plain Sense." *An Examination of Jacob Barker's Appeal to the Public.* New York, 1819.

Presbyterian Church of the U.S.A. *Extracts of the Minutes of the General Assembly, 1819.* Philadelphia, 1819.

Raleigh *Star and North Carolina State Gazette.*

Raymond, Daniel. *Elements of Political Economy.* Baltimore, F. Lucas, Jr., & E. J. Coale, 1823.

Ricardo, David. *Minor Papers on the Currency Question, 1809–23.* Edited by Jacob Hollander. Baltimore, The Johns Hopkins Press, 1932.

Richmond *Enquirer.*

"Seventy-Six." *Cause of and Cure for Hard Times.* New York, 1819.

Smith, Adam. *An Inquiry into the Nature and Causes of the Wealth of Nations.* New York, Modern Library, 1937.

"Solon." *Liberty Saved.* Louisville [n.d.].

Swan, James. *An Address to the President, Senate, and House of Representatives of the United States.* Boston, W. W. Clapp, 1819.

Van Ness, William Peter (signed "Aristides"). *A Letter to the Secretary of the Treasury on the Commerce and Currency of the United States.* New York, C. S. Van Winkle, 1819.

Washington (D.C.) *National Intelligencer.*

Wolcott, Oliver. *Remarks on the Present State of Currency, Credit, Commerce, and National Industry.* New York, Wiley, 1820.

[Woodward, John.] *Address of the Society of Tammany to Its Absent Members.* New York, 1819.

SECONDARY SOURCES

Abbott, Edith. *Women in Industry.* New York, D. Appleton and Co., 1915.

Abernethy, Thomas P. "The Early Development of Commerce and Banking in Tennessee," *Mississippi Valley Historical Review,* XIV (December, 1927), 311–25.

—— *The Formative Period in Alabama, 1815–28.* Montgomery, The Brown Printing Co., 1922.

Albion, Robert G. *The Rise of New York Port.* New York, C. Scribner's Sons, 1939.

Ambler, Charles H. *Thomas Ritchie, A Study in Virginia Politics.* Richmond, Bell Book and Stationery Co., 1913.

Anderson, Hattie M. "Frontier Economic Problems in Missouri, 1815–28," *Missouri Historical Review,* XXXIV (Oct., 1939), 38–70; XXXIV (Jan., 1940), 189.

Andrews, Matthew P. *Tercentenary History of Maryland.* Vol. I. Chicago, S. J. Clarke Co., 1925.

Bassett, T. D. Seymour. "The Rise of Cornelius Peter Van Ness, 1782–1826," *Proceedings of the Vermont Historical Society,* X (March, 1942), 8–16.

Baylor, Orval W. *John Pope, Kentuckian.* Cynthiana, Ky., The Hobson Press, 1943.

Beard, William E. "Joseph McMinn, Tennessee's Fourth Governor," *Tennessee Historical Quarterly,* IV (June, 1945), 162–63.

Berry, Thomas S. "Wholesale Commodity Prices in the Ohio Valley, 1816–60," *Review of Economic Statistics,* XVII (August, 1935), 92.

—— *Western Prices Before 1861.* Cambridge, Harvard University Press, 1943.

Bezanson, Anne, Robert D. Gray, and Miriam Hussey. *Wholesale Prices in Philadelphia, 1784–1861.* Vol. II. Philadelphia, University of Pennsylvania Press, 1936.

Bining, Arthur C. "The Rise of Iron Manufacture in Western Pennsylvania," *Western Pennsylvania Historical Magazine,* XVI (November, 1933), 242.

Bining, William. "The Glass Industry of Western Pennsylvania, 1797–1857," *Western Pennsylvania Historical Magazine,* XIX (December, 1936), 255–68.

Bishop, J. Leander. *A History of American Manufactures, 1608–1866.* Vol. II. Philadelphia, E. Young and Co., 1864.

Brigham, Clarence S. "The Period from 1820 to 1830," in *State of Rhode Island and Providence Plantations at the End of the Century: A History.* Vol. I. Edited by Edward Field. Boston, The Mason Publishing Co., 1902.

Bruce, Kathleen. *Virginia Iron Manufacture in the Slave Era.* New York, The Century Co., 1931.

Buck, Norman S. *Development and Organization of Anglo-American Trade, 1800–50.* New Haven, Yale University Press, 1925.

Buley, R. Carlyle. *The Old Northwest, Pioneer Period, 1815–40.* Vol. I. Indianapolis, Indiana Historical Society, 1950.

Burns, Arthur F., and Wesley C. Mitchell. *Measuring Business Cycles.* New York, National Bureau of Economic Research, 1946.

Cable, J. Ray. *The Bank of the State of Missouri.* New York, Columbia University Press, 1923.

—— "Some Early Missouri Bankers," *Missouri Historical Review,* XXVI (January, 1932), 117–19.

Caldwell, Stephen A. *A Banking History of Louisiana.* Baton Rouge, Louisiana State University Press, 1935.

Campbell, Claude A. *The Development of Banking in Tennessee.* Nashville, Vanderbilt University Press, 1932.

Catterall, R. C. H. *The Second Bank of the United States.* Chicago, University of Chicago Press, 1903.

Chambers, William Nisbet. *Old Bullion Benton.* Boston, Little, Brown & Co., 1956.

Clark, Allen C. *Greenleaf and Law in the Federal City.* Washington, D.C., W. F. Roberts, 1901.

Clark, Victor S. *History of Manufactures in the United States, 1607–1860.* Vol. II. Washington, D.C., Carnegie Institute, 1916.

Cole, Arthur H. *The American Wool Manufacture.* Vol. I. Cambridge, Harvard University Press, 1926.

—— "Cyclical and Seasonal Variations in the Sale of Public Lands, 1816–60," *Review of Economic Statistics,* IX (January, 1927), 42 ff.

—— *Wholesale Commodity Prices in the United States, 1700–1861.* Vol. I and Supp. Cambridge, Harvard University Press, 1938.

Cole, Frank T. "Thomas Worthington," *Ohio Archaeological and Historical Publications,* XII (1903), 366.

Conger, John L. "South Carolina and Early Tariffs," *Mississippi Valley Historical Review,* V (March, 1919), 415–25.

Connelley, William E., and E. M. Coulter. *History of Kentucky.* Vol. II. Chicago, American Historical Society, 1922.

Cranmer, H. Jerome. *The New Jersey Canals: State Policy and Private Enterprise, 1820–32.* New York, Columbia University, 1955. Microfilmed.

Crockett, Walter Hill. *Vermont, the Green Mountain State.* Vol. III. New York, The Century Co., 1921.

Cushing, Thomas, ed. *History of Allegheny County, Pennsylvania.* Chicago, A. Warner & Co., 1889.

Dain, Floyd Russell. *Every House a Frontier.* Detroit, Wayne University Press, 1956.

Davidson, Alexander, and Bernard B. Stuvé. *A Complete History of Illinois.* Springfield, Rokker Co., 1881.

Davis, Harold E. "Economic Basis of Ohio Politics, 1820–40," *Ohio*

Archaeological and Historical Quarterly, XLVII (October, 1938), 290–309.

Day, Clive. "The Early Development of the American Cotton Manufacture," *Quarterly Journal of Economics*, XXXIX (May, 1925), 452.

Dewey, Davis R. *State Banking Before the Civil War*. Washington, Government Printing Office, 1910.

Dorfman, Joseph. *The Economic Mind in American Civilization, 1606–1865*. 2 vols. New York, Viking Press, 1946.

Dorsey, Dorothy B. "The Panic of 1819 in Missouri," *Missouri Historical Review*, XXIX (January, 1935), 79–91.

Dowrie, George W. *The Development of Banking in Illinois, 1817–63*. Urbana, University of Illinois Press, 1913.

Duke, General Basil W. *History of the Bank of Kentucky, 1792–1895*. Louisville, J. P. Morton & Co., 1895.

Dunn, Jacob Piatt. *Indiana and Indianans*. Chicago, American Historical Society, 1919.

Durrett, Reuben T. *The Centenary of Louisville*. Louisville, J. P. Morton & Co., 1893.

Eiselen, Malcolm R. *The Rise of Pennsylvania Protectionism*. Philadelphia, privately printed, 1932.

Emerick, C. F. *The Credit System and the Public Domain*. Vanderbilt, Tenn., Southern History Society, No. 3, 1898.

Esarey, Logan. "The First Indiana Banks," *Indiana Quarterly Magazine of History*, VI (December, 1910), 144–58.

—— *History of Indiana*. Vol. I. Indianapolis, B. F. Bowen & Co., 1918.

—— *State Banking in Indiana*. Bloomington, Indiana University Press, 1912.

Evans, George Heberton, Jr. *Business Incorporations in the United States*. New York, National Bureau of Economic Research, 1948.

Ferguson, Russell J. *Early Western Pennsylvania Politics*. Pittsburgh, University of Pittsburgh Press, 1938.

Fleming, George T. *The History of Pittsburgh and Its Environs*. Vol. II. New York, American Historical Society, 1922.

Flint, James. *Letters from America*. Vol. IX of *Early Western Travels, 1748–1846*. Edited by Reuben G. Thwaites. Cleveland, The A. H. Clark Co., 1904–07.

Florinsky, Michael T. *Russia*. 2 vols. New York, The Macmillan Co., 1953.

Folz, William E. "The Financial Crisis of 1819—A Study in Post War Economic Readjustment." Ph.D. dissertation, University of Illinois, 1935.

Galbreath, Charles B. *History of Ohio*. Vol. II. Chicago, American Historical Society, 1925.

Gallatin, Albert. *Considerations on the Currency and Banking Systems in the United States*. Philadelphia, Carey and Lea, 1831.

Garnett, Charles H. *State Banks of Issue in Illinois*. Urbana, University of Illinois Press, 1898.

Golden, Gabriel H. "William Carroll and His Administration," *Tennessee Historical Magazine*, IX (April, 1925), 19.

Goss, Charles F. *Cincinnati, the Queen City, 1788–1912*. Vol. I. Chicago, The S. J. Clarke Publishing Co., 1912.

Gouge, William M. *Journal of Banking*. Philadelphia, J. Van Court, 1842.

—— *Short History of Paper Money and Banking*. New York, B. & S. Collins, 1835.

Govan, Thomas P. "Banking and the Credit System in Georgia, 1816–60," *Journal of Southern History*, IV (May, 1938), 160 ff.

Gras, N. S. B. *The Massachusetts First National Bank of Boston, 1784–1934*. Cambridge, Harvard University Press, 1937.

Greer, Thomas H. "Economic and Social Effects of the Depression of 1819 in the Old Northwest," *Indiana Magazine of History*, XLIX (September, 1948), 227–43.

Griffith, Elmer C. "Early Banking in Kentucky," *Proceedings of the Mississippi Valley Historical Association*, II (1908–9), 168–81.

Gronert, Theodore G. "Trade in the Blue Grass Region, 1810–1820," *Mississippi Valley Historical Review*, V (1918), 313–23.

Gruchy, Allen G. *Supervision and Control of Virginia State Banks*. New York, D. Appleton-Century & Co., 1937.

Hamer, Philip. *Tennessee, A History, 1673–1932*. Vol. I. New York, American Historical Society, 1933.

Hamilton, W. J. "The Relief Movement in Missouri, 1820–22," *Missouri Historical Review*, XXII (October, 1927), 51–92.

Hammond, Bray. *Banks and Politics in America*. Princeton, Princeton University Press, 1957.

Harlan, Louis R. "Public Career of William Berkeley Lewis," *Tennessee Historical Quarterly*, VII (March, 1948), 13.

Heath, Milton S. *Constructive Liberalism*. Cambridge, Harvard University Press, 1954.

Hedges, Joseph E. *Commercial Banking and the Stock Market Before 1863*. Baltimore, The Johns Hopkins Press, 1938.

Hepburn, A. Barton. *A History of Currency in the United States*. New York, The Macmillan Co., 1915.

Huntington, Charles C. *A History of Banking and Currency in Ohio Before the Civil War*. Columbus, Ohio Archaeological and Historical Society, 1915.

Jervey, Theodore. *Robert Y. Hayne and His Times*. New York, The Macmillan Co., 1909.

Johnson, Emory R., and Others. *History of Domestic and Foreign Commerce of the United States*. Vol. II. Washington, D.C., Carnegie Institute of Washington, 1915.

Kehl, James A. *Ill-Feeling in the Era of Good Feeling; Western Pennsylvania Political Battles, 1815–1825*. Pittsburgh, University of Pittsburgh Press, 1956.

Klebaner, Benjamin J. *Public Poor Relief in America, 1790–1860*. New York, Columbia University, 1952. Microfilmed.

Klein, Philip S. *Pennsylvania Politics, 1817–32*. Philadelphia, Historical Society of Pennsylvania, 1940.

Knox, John Jay. *History of Banking in the United States*. New York, B. Rhodes and Co., 1900.

Lee, Alfred E. *History of the City of Columbus*. Vol. I. New York: Numsell and Co., 1892.

Livingood, James W. *The Philadelphia-Baltimore Trade Rivalry, 1780–1860*. Harrisburg, Pennsylvania Historical Commission, 1947.

Lowenthal, Esther. "American Reprints of Economic Writings, 1776–1848," *American Economic Review*, XLII (December, 1952), 876–80; XLIII (December, 1953), 884–85.

Luxon, Norval N. *Niles' Weekly Register*. Baton Rouge, Louisiana State University Press, 1947.

Madeleine, Sister M. Grace. *Monetary and Banking Theories of Jacksonian Democracy*. Philadelphia, The Dolphin Press, 1943.

Miller, Harry E. *Banking Theories in the United States Before 1860*. Cambridge, Harvard University Press, 1927.

Mints, Lloyd W. *A History of Banking Theory*. Chicago, University of Chicago Press, 1945.

Mitchell, Waldo F. "Indiana's Growth, 1812–20," *Indiana Magazine of History*, X (December, 1914), 385.

Mitchell, Wesley C. *Business Cycles, Vol. I, The Problem and Its Setting*. New York, National Bureau of Economic Research, 1927.

Moore, Albert B. *History of Alabama*. Vol. I. Chicago, American Historical Society, 1927.

Moore, Frederick W. "Fluctuations in Agricultural Prices and Wages in the South," in *The South in the Building of the Nation*. Vol. V. Richmond, Southern Historical Publication Society, 1909.

O'Connor, Michael J. L. *Origins of Academic Economics in the United States*. New York, Columbia University Press, 1944.

Parks, Joseph Howard. *Felix Grundy*. Baton Rouge, Louisiana State University Press, 1940.

—— "Felix Grundy and the Depression of 1819 in Tennessee," *Publications of the East Tennessee Historical Society*, X (1938), 20–32.

Pitkin, Timothy. *Statistical View of the Commerce of the United States of America.* 3d ed. New Haven, Durrie and Peck, 1835.

Primm, James Neal. *Economic Policy in the Development of a Western State, Missouri, 1820–60.* Cambridge, Harvard University Press, 1954.

Rezneck, Samuel. "The Depression of 1819–22, A Social History," *American Historical Review,* XXXIX (October, 1933), 28–47.

Rich, Wesley E. *The History of the United States Post Office to the Year 1829.* Cambridge, Harvard University Press, 1924.

Rothbard, Murray N. "Contemporary Opinion of the Depression of 1819–21." Unpublished Master's essay, Columbia University, 1946.

Rowe, John J. "Money and Banks in Cincinnati Before the Civil War," *Bulletin of the Historical and Philosophical Society of Ohio,* VI (July, 1948), 74–84.

Scharf, J. T. *History of Delaware.* Vol. II. Philadelphia, L. J. Richards and Co., 1888.

—— and T. Westcott. *History of Philadelphia, 1669–1884.* Vol. I. Philadelphia, L. H. Everts and Co., 1884.

Schur, Leon M. "The Second Bank of the United States and the Inflation After the War of 1812," *The Journal of Political Economy,* LXVIII (April, 1960), 118–34.

Scott, W. R. *The Constitutions of English, Scottish and Irish Joint-Stock Companies to 1720.* Vol. I. Cambridge, England, The University Press, 1912.

Sears, Alfred B. "Thomas Worthington, Pioneer Businessman of the Old Northwest," *Ohio State Archaeological and Historical Quarterly,* XVIII (January, 1949), 76.

Secrist, Horace. "The Anti-Auction Movement and the New York Workingmen's Party of 1829," *Wisconsin Academy of Sciences, Arts and Letters, Transactions,* Vol. XVII, Part 1 (1914), p. 166.

Sellers, Charles G., Jr. "Banking and Politics in Jackson's Tennessee, 1817–1827," *Mississippi Valley Historical Review,* XLI (June, 1954), 61–84.

—— *James K. Polk, Jacksonian, 1795–1843.* Princeton, Princeton University Press, 1957.

Smith, George G. *The Story of Georgia and the Georgia People, 1732–1860.* Macon, G. G. Smith, 1900.

Smith, Walter Buckingham. *Economic Aspects of the Second Bank of the United States.* Cambridge, Harvard University Press, 1953.

—— "Wholesale Commodity Prices in the United States, 1795–1824," *Review of Economic Statistics,* IX (October, 1927), 181–83.

—— and Arthur H. Cole. *Fluctuations in American Business, 1790–1860.* Cambridge, Harvard University Press, 1935.

"Source Illustrations of Ohio's Relations to National History, 1816–40," *Ohio Archaeological and Historical Publications*, XXV (1916), 143.

Sterns, Worthy P. "The Beginning of American Financial Independence," *Journal of Political Economy*, VI (1897–98), 191.

Stickles, Arndt M. *The Critical Court Struggle in Kentucky, 1819–29.* Bloomington, University of Indiana Press, 1929.

Stonecipher, Frank W. "Pittsburgh and the Nineteenth Century Tariffs," *Western Pennsylvania Historical Magazine*, XXXI (September–December, 1948), 87 ff.

Sullivan, William A. "A Decade of Labor Strife," *Pennsylvania History*, XVII (January, 1950), 24.

—— *The Industrial Worker in Pennsylvania, 1800–1840.* Harrisburg, Pennsylvania Historical and Museum Commission, 1955.

Sumner, William Graham. *History of Banking in the United States.* New York, H. Holt and Co., 1896.

Swartzlow, Ruby J. "The Early History of Lead Mining in Missouri," *Missouri Historical Review*, XXIX (January, 1935), 114.

Sydnor, C. S. *Development of Southern Nationalism, 1819–48.* Baton Rouge, Louisiana State University Press, 1948.

Taylor, George Rogers. *The Transportation Revolution, 1815–60.* New York, Rinehart and Co., 1951.

—— "Wholesale Commodity Prices at Charleston, S.C., 1796–1861," *Journal of Economic and Business History*, IV (August, 1932), 856–70.

Taylor, M. Flavia. "The Political and Civic Career of Henry Baldwin, 1799–1830," *Western Pennsylvania Historical Magazine*, XXIV (March, 1941), 37–50.

Tregle, Joseph George, Jr. "Louisiana and the Tariff, 1816–46," *Louisiana Historical Quarterly*, XXV (January, 1942), 35.

Tucker, Rufus S. "Gold and the General Price Level," *Review of Economic Statistics*, XVI (February, 1934), 24.

—— "Real Wages Under Laissez-Faire," *Barron's*, XIII (October 23, 1933), 7.

Walsh, John J. *Early Banks in the District of Columbia, 1792–1818.* Washington, Catholic University of America Press, 1940.

Ware, Caroline F. *The Early New England Cotton Manufacture.* Boston, Houghton Mifflin Co., 1931.

Westerfield, Ray B. "Early History of American Auctions—A Chapter in Commercial History," *Connecticut Academy of Arts and Sciences, Transactions*, XXIII (May, 1920), 164–70.

Weems, Robert C., Jr. *The Bank of the Mississippi; A Pioneer Bank of the Old Southwest, 1809–44.* New York, Columbia University, 1951. Microfilmed.

Wilson, Samuel M. *History of Kentucky*, Vol. II. Chicago, The S. J. Clarke Publishing Co., 1928.

Wismer, D. C. *New York Descriptive List of Obsolete Paper Money.* Fredericksburg, Md., J. W. Stovell Printing Co., 1931.

—— *Pennsylvania Descriptive List of Obsolete State Bank Notes, 1782–1866.* Fredericksburg, Md., J. W. Stovell Printing Co., 1933.

Wright, David McCord. *The Economic Library of the President of the Bank of the United States, 1819–23.* Charlottesville, University of Virginia, 1950.

—— "Langdon Cheves and Nicholas Biddle: New Data for a New Interpretation," *Journal of Economic History*, XIII (Summer, 1953), 310 ff.

INDEX

Bei Fragen zur Produktsicherheit wenden Sie sich bitte an:
If you have any questions regarding product safety,
please contact:

Walter de Gruyter GmbH
Genthiner Straße 13
10785 Berlin
productsafety@degruyterbrill.com